The Best of Russian Cooking

DATE DUE

Hippocrene is NUMBER ONE in
International Cookbooks

Africa and Oceania
Best of Regional African Cooking
Egyptian Cooking
Good Food from Australia
Traditional South African Cookery
Taste of Eritrea

Asia and Near East
The Best of Taiwanese Cuisine
Imperial Mongolian Cooking
The Joy of Chinese Cooking
The Best of Regional Thai Cuisine
Japanese Home Cooking
Healthy South Indian Cooking
The Indian Spice Kitchen
Best of Goan Cooking
Best of Kashmiri Cooking
Afghan Food & Cookery
The Art of Persian Cooking
The Art of Turkish Cooking
The Art of Uzbek Cooking

Mediterranean
Best of Greek Cuisine
Taste of Malta
A Spanish Family Cookbook
Tastes of North Africa

Western Europe
Art of Dutch Cooking
Best of Austrian Cuisine
A Belgian Cookbook
Cooking in the French Fashion (bilingual)
Celtic Cookbook
Cuisines of Portuguese Encounters
English Royal Cookbook
The Swiss Cookbook
Traditional Recipes from Old England
The Art of Irish Cooking
Feasting Galore Irish-Style
Traditional Food from Scotland
Traditional Food from Wales
The Scottish-Irish Pub and Hearth Cookbook
A Treasury of Italian Cuisine (bilingual)

Scandinavia
Best of Scandinavian Cooking
The Best of Finnish Cooking
The Best of Smorgasbord Cooking
Good Food from Sweden
Tastes and Tales of Norway
Icelandic Food & Cookery

Central Europe
All Along the Danube
All Along the Rhine
Best of Albanian Cooking
Best of Croatian Cooking
Bavarian Cooking
Traditional Bulgarian Cooking
The Best of Czech Cooking
The Best of Slovak Cooking
The Art of Hungarian Cooking
Hungarian Cookbook
Art of Lithuanian Cooking
Polish Heritage Cookery
The Best of Polish Cooking
Old Warsaw Cookbook
Old Polish Traditions
Treasury of Polish Cuisine (bilingual)
Poland's Gourmet Cuisine
The Polish Country Kitchen Cookbook
Taste of Romania
Taste of Latvia

Eastern Europe
The Best of Russian Cooking
Traditional Russian Cuisine (bilingual)
The Best of Ukrainian Cuisine

Americas
A Taste of Quebec
Argentina Cooks
Cooking the Caribbean Way
Mayan Cooking
The Honey Cookbook
The Art of Brazilian Cookery
The Art of South American Cookery
Old Havana Cookbook (bilingual)

The Best of Russian Cooking

Alexandra Kropotkin

HIPPOCRENE BOOKS
New York

Originally published by Charles Scribner's Sons, New York.
Hippocrene Books, Inc. paperback edition, 1993.
Hippocrene Books, Inc. Expanded Edition, 1997.
Third printing of Expanded Edition, 2007.

For information, address:
Hippocrene Books, Inc.
171 Madison Avenue
New York, NY 10016

ISBN-13: 978-0-7818-0131-7
ISBN-10: 0-7818-0131-1

Printed in the United States of America.

FOREWORD

In this day and age of shifting moods on an international scale it might be wise if the people of the world were to institute a chef-to-chef or a cook-to-cook exchange. Princess Alexandra Kropotkin in this volume has put it another way. When eating is concerned politics don't count.

Whatever the state of the Russian kitchen today—and according to most accounts its scope is from first rank caviar and commendable soups to rather sobering fare of pedestrian rank —it is a point of international interest. There is no question, of course, that the food served in that vast land is only a relic of a former glory. And yet Russia has a decided culinary heritage. This book reflects that heritage better than any volume I know. I first discovered it in a secondhand store on New York's Fourth Avenue ten years ago. It is a book to which I have made frequent reference when writing about Russian dishes, of which several have made a permanent mark in many American homes. One of the most popular dishes served in the United States today is in fact actually of Russian origin. It is Beef Stroganoff, a chafing dish specialty that is as popular at a church social in the mid-West as it is in a Manhattan penthouse. There is also borsch and to a lesser degree blini and piroshki and that most delectable creation, breast of chicken Kiev style.

Princess Kropotkin's work is more than a collection of recipes from her native land. It is a book that makes interesting reading as well. One learns, for example, that the sauces used in Russian cooking are the classic sauces of France, imported 200 years ago during the reign of Catherine the Great and that Beef Stroganoff was created by or for Count Paul Stroganoff who flourished in the Gay Nineties of the last century. This is a work that should appeal to all cook book fanciers whatever their political affiliations.

CRAIG CLAIBORNE

PREFACE

Russians love to eat—all Russians, rich, poor or middling. Wherever they are, in their homeland or where the erratic waves of history may have stranded them, from the Orient to Labrador, from South Africa to the Argentine, they stay Russian in their table preferences. If they can't get their Russian-type groceries, their *smetana* (sour cream), their cabbage, their beets, their own kind of Russian bread, they grouse and grumble. Moscow officials arriving in Cairo were met by a plaintive query from the Soviet *chargé d'affaires*: "Did anyone bring some black bread?"

Also Russians are very hospitable folk. Whatever they have to eat, they love to share it with guests. There is only one *must*. Even of the simplest fare, there must be lots and lots of it. That is a mania with all of us. I was recently subjected to unmerciful ribbing by my American husband because I had only *just enough* curried chicken at a special *rijsstafel* dinner we put on for a friend. My husband says it's the first time, in the 36 years we've been married, that there wasn't far too much on the table!

Nowadays, as always in the past, any mention of Russia brings on a red-hot political argument. All my life I have listened to such controversies. The Tsar and his government provided the issue when I was a girl—with all of us talking violently against the old regime, or stubbornly defending it. The Tsar has become a faded memory, but the political debates continue, perhaps even more heated and bitter against the

Soviet Government, Marxist ideology, power politics, etc., etc.

In the noise and clash of theories, the Russian people are all too often forgotten. Of course I deplore this, feeling as I do that Russians are pretty nice people. Though in certain parts of Russia the admixture of Oriental blood may lend a definite touch of deviousness to their thought and behavior, fundamentally they are friendly, patient people, alive with curiosities, tirelessly energetic, sometimes incredibly lazy. Their very strong artistic talents cannot be denied, as America enjoys increasing chances to observe from the various imported Russian shows now so popular.

Politicians and diplomats are another matter. They rarely reflect what is best in any country.

If you want to know the *people* of a nation, to judge for yourself what sort they really are, I am sure you can learn a great deal more about them from their home life—their cooking and eating traditions—than you can from the words and actions of their government officials.

I hope you will like what I am going to tell you about the table and kitchen customs of the Russian home, and how to prepare the native dishes that Russia loves. I hope this book will win American friends for Makar and Marfa—which is the Russian way of saying "Mr. and Mrs. Russia."

In selecting recipes to give you, I have included all the most characteristic Russian specialties, discarding only those that seem impractical here. For example, Russia's yeast-raised rolls and breads are prepared in an old-fashioned way which entails much work. There are newer, easier methods for the housewife bent on baking her own. Bakeries, chain stores, delicatessens and specialty shops offer an infinite variety of pastries, including the sweet rolls adored by all Russians—except me.

During the years that have passed since 1947, when this

book was first published, great changes have taken place both in the eating habits of this country, and in the increased facilities of obtaining ingredients for the preparation of dishes which are somewhat unusual.

Sour cream is obtainable now in any grocery, chain store or delicatessen. It wasn't so easy to find, years ago. And I remember very well that I was quite a pioneer when I mentioned sour cream as an ingredient of one of the recipes in my *To the Ladies* page which appeared every week in Liberty Magazine, for so many years. Each week I gave an unusual recipe as one of the features of the page. I've always wished that sour cream could be more widely known as *smetana*. That word, "sour," still puts many people off.

Plain yoghourt is not only popular today; it is also easy to get; and it substitutes admirably for our Russian *prostokvasha* (curds or clabbered milk), as a perfect dressing for sliced tomatoes, cucumbers or finely shredded lettuce (Simpson preferred). Dill, too, has become an everyday commodity. Even conservative groceries now have fresh dill on sale.

Sable—lightly smoked fish, known as the poor-man's sturgeon, is to be found at most delicatessens and makes a wonderful replacement for sturgeon in the Champagne-and-Sturgeon soup you'll find farther on, in my chapter on soups. Sable is also excellent as a cocktail snack, served on bits of black bread with a dash of freshly ground pepper. (Don't forget the pepper!)

There is one flaw in this country's supply picture, as far as Russians are concerned: NOT ENOUGH DIFFERENT KINDS OF MUSHROOMS!

So here I go on a new crusade.

All kinds of edible mushrooms grow happily here. I am not speaking of the commercial "field mushrooms"—which no longer grow in fields. Plenty of these are on hand, and more power to them. At certain times of the year they are inexpensive and should be used more generally, since they furnish a splendid protein proxy for high-priced meat. Try using them as a main dish, not merely as a garnish.

But where are our native American *cèpes* and delightful orange-colored *chanterelles*? They grow as well here as in Europe, yet they never grace our domestic markets. Those magnificent species of mushroom are available only when flown in from France, for affluent gourmets to eat, at $2.80 per pound. Silly!

Some of my Russian friends in New England and New York State gather wild mushrooms—about six different varieties. This I do not advocate. It is deadly dangerous for anyone who isn't expert at spotting the true, good mushroom from the poisonous mushroom which often resembles the edible mushroom very closely in looks.

I am indebted to my friend, Albert Stockli, Chef Director of Restaurant Associates, for a great deal of my mushroom information. Mr. Stockli is an expert from way back—a Swiss born in Zurich, and the son of a father who was a mushroom *fiend*.

In Massachusetts there lives a gentleman who grows and sells the super-tasty *morilles*, known here as morel. It is a curious, wrinkled-up brown mushroom with an exquisite flavor. Beats the truffle, in my opinion. And out in Oregon, a genuine benefactor of mankind has been trying to develop a market for the *cèpes* he grows. He grows them on rocks. They are the meatiest of all the mushrooms. But they languish here because of no demand, no market. No dice!

What's the matter with all you so-called gourmets!

I must add that I am not in the mushroom business. I am not

acquainted with the two mushroom growers I've mentioned. But I surely would like to be able to shop around, once in a while, for as many delicious varieties of mushroom as one can buy abroad—as many as one used to feast upon in Russia.

ALEXANDRA KROPOTKIN

CONTENTS

*All recipes in this book, unless otherwise indicated,
are intended to serve six persons.*

THE BEST OF
RUSSIAN COOKING

INTRODUCTION

1. On Russian Eating and Russian People.—Russians love to eat. We love to eat in company, for in company we have plenty of talk with our meals, and Russians are just as fond of talking as they are of eating. The more at table, the merrier the Russian. The Russian spirit is a community spirit. It has always been so, from the very beginning of our history when Russians were nomads.

In times when food is easy to get, if a Russian household is at all well off the meal will consist of many different dishes, a large generous spread. When supplies are scarce or the family is poor, guests will still be invited to share the soup and the pot of baked buckwheat *kasha*—and everyone will be glad to make the best of it.

It is a Russian convention that lots of food must be left over after any party. Enough isn't enough in Russia. Unless there's a big surplus, people suspect the host and hostess of being stingy, and stinginess is an unforgivable sin among Russians. Call a Russian a liar, call him a so-and-so, even call him a thief—sooner or later he will forgive and forget. But don't call him a *skriaga*, a penny pincher. He'll hold it against you as long as he lives.

Like nearly all other people who dwell in sparsely populated places where diversions are few and far between, Russians enjoy being generous hosts whenever they have the chance.

The most casual visitor at a Russian home will be urged to stay for dinner. Though I was born and raised in England, my Russian blood runs true to type as soon as I have a caller at my house. I feel uncomfortable if I don't ask the caller to remain and break bread with me. Our attitude toward hospitality is an ingrained Russian trait.

The first time I went to see Constantin Stanislavsky, director of the Moscow Art Theater and one of the greatest of Russian aestheticians, he was deeply shocked when I got up to leave his apartment after our interview was over. "You can't—you *can't* leave without eating with us. It is nearly lunchtime. You must stay and share our meal. Madame Stanislavsky and I would never feel at home with you again if we permitted you to be so English as to go away without eating."

All Russians adore banquets. They did before the Revolution, and they do today. Russian banquets go on for hours and hours; they go on interminably as Eric Johnston attests in his book about his trip to the land of the Soviets. Also they start and finish at the strangest times.

Russia's traditional dinnertime has always been between three o'clock and five o'clock in the afternoon. In the old days the only Russians who dined later than five were those who imitated foreign customs and habits. At present there are so many dining rooms attached to factories and government offices that many Russians now eat their dinner at noon, but those who dine at home continue to eat about five o'clock.

As to Russia's most popular national dishes, these have not changed at all from the old days to the new. Tsarists or Communists, if they are really Russian, they all like the same things to eat. However violently they may disagree in politics, they all join their voices in celebrating the unparalleled virtues of Russian black bread. Far from home they all long for Russian cabbage soup, for our cabbage pies, our pots of baked buck-wheat, our game-bird croquettes, the fish broth we call *ooha,* and our foamy little *pastilla* candies which taste like fresh fruit.

Everywhere we go we forage for local ingredients with which to satisfy our yearning for Russian dishes. Here in America we have very little difficulty. The markets here are stocked with close approximations of nearly everything we look for, and many of the products are identical with those in Russia.

Russians are always delighted to show the people of other nations what Russian food is like, and to convert them to it if possible. As a steady diet some of it might be a little too snug for American ribs, yet there are a great many Russian specialties that suit American home cooking. I am presenting the most adaptable of Russian recipes in this book, and I hope they will please your taste and become 100-per-cent American favorites. In my own home here my New England husband now asks for Russian meat pie more frequently than for corned-beef hash.

Russians eat hearty. No Russian would dream of dieting if he wasn't flat on his back, sick in bed. Russians would rather be robustly fat than fashionably lean. I imagine this trait may have developed as a psychological reaction to the terrible famines which have starved Russia so many times in ages past. As I said before, in Russia enough isn't enough, and stories of capacity eating are always popular. One classic saying quotes the Russian who complained that a goose is a silly bird, "Too much for one, not enough for two."

An interesting characteristic of the Russian cuisine derives from the large number of native dishes we have borrowed from other countries and other races of men. Our cooks have been as international-minded as our politicians. It isn't language facility alone that helps Russians make themselves at home in foreign places; our easy acceptance of alien food is a great help too.

Through the centuries Russian cooking has incorporated the pilafs and skewered meat broils of Persia and Turkey; the French cuisine introduced by Parisian chefs at the court of Catherine; the ice creams and fancy pastries brought by the Italian architects and workmen whom Ivan the Terrible imported to build parts of the Kremlin; and the many vegetable dishes and spiced honey cakes attributable to Peter the Great, who lived surrounded by Dutchmen.

From the old wars, the alliances, the Napoleonic period, German and Polish and English cooking have implanted permanent traces of their influence in the Russian cuisine.

To this day, the national beverage of Russia retains its original Chinese name. Tea in Chinese is *ch'ai;* in Russian it is *tchai.*

2. Russian Mealtimes.—We like to eat four meals a day: breakfast, lunch, and dinner, then a late evening snack around the samovar. I have devoted a whole chapter to the samovar snacktime because it is the coziest repast of them all, enjoyed at the hour when Russians really expand, talking straight from their hearts about their religion, their politics, and their love life. Meanwhile they eat their way through cold cuts of meat, cheeses, layer cakes, fruit, candies, and homemade jams. They drink tea *ad infinitum.*

Russians believe that a good appetite assists the struggles of the soul. They drink their tea very weak.

Curious to relate, the term for "breakfast" in the Russian language is "morning coffee"—although most Russians take tea with milk as their breakfast beverage. Soft-boiled eggs are quite usual, but the breadbasket is the real center of breakfast interest. The basket displays a variegated layout of black bread slices, white bread slices, plain rolls, and fancy sweet rolls. Unsalted butter is preferred. We put it on the table in a large communal slab—not in individual portions.

Lunch is called *zavtrak*. Usually the luncheon hour is from twelve to one. Russians rarely eat more than two dishes, unless working conditions make this the principal meal of the day. Even in the old pre-Revolution Russia, lunch wasn't much.

If you lunched with a Russian family, you might be served a moderate helping of chops or kidneys dressed with a sauce of Madeira wine. Or perhaps a *pirog*, a crusty pie, envelope-shaped, filled with either meat and eggs, braised cabbage, rice and mushrooms, or rice and fish. The *pirog* recipes are exhaustingly numerous. I have given some of the best of them in chapter IV. For a simple family luncheon, the main dish might be fish, or pot-cheese cakes, with the pot of baked buckwheat *kasha* invariably in attendance, and a big pitcher of milk would appear on the table. You would be expected to fill up on milk and *kasha*. Then you might get a dish of stewed fruit, or an infantile milk pudding.

Russian lunches are *not* sophisticated, but the dinners are. Our Russian word for dinner looks strange in English. The word is *obed*.

Obed is very seldom served on time unless the Russian family has undergone foreign influence. Your real Russian takes household delays as a matter of course, and nobody thinks it extraordinary if dinner happens to be a few hours late. Official Soviet banquets, scheduled to begin at eight o'clock, with distinguished foreign guests seated at the speakers' table, have been known to mark time until ten or eleven.

In a private Russian home, a good excuse is always relied upon to explain the hitch. We couldn't wake Papa up from his before-dinner nap....Aunt Olga's train didn't arrive on schedule....Or the menage may be upset because a housemaid hasn't returned from sojourning among her country relatives.

The girl isn't worried. She knows you will understand. "There was so much news in our village," she says, "I didn't realize how the time flew. Now, Madame, please don't scold me. Everything will be ready in a little half-hour."

That little half-hour is a fantastically elastic measure of time, the way Russians calculate it. It may be forty-five minutes, an hour, an hour and a half, or two hours. This you can be sure of: it will never be thirty minutes.

Russian dinners allow for such time-slips by expanding the hors d'œuvres, which we call *zakooska*. We take so much time over our *zakooska* that nobody can be late for dinner. It has been said that my Rurik ancestor brought the *zakooska* idea to Russia from his native Scandinavia in the year A.D. 862, when the Russians invited him to come to their country and "rule and legislate." Thereafter the Ruriks were enthroned in Russia for six hundred years—long enough to establish their taste for *zakooska* as well as for pomp and power.

Translated freely, *zakooska* means "the little bite." At a plain family dinner the *zakooska* course is usually limited to three or four uncomplicated items—slices of sausage, dill pickles, herrings, and cheese. The herring is the most important article. With it you drink vodka, which should be poured out of a small carafe, ice cold. At family dinners all this goes on at the dining-room table, but when there are guests a special *zakooska* table is set up. In chapter II you will find *zakooska* customs and recipes.

Now the soup. And with the soup come the *piroshki*— piecrust fingers about four inches long, filled with meat or fish, eggs, or vegetables. If it is meat soup, we give you little meat or cabbage *piroshki* to eat with it. If it is a fish soup, we give you little *piroshki* filled with fish.

At a family dinner in Russia you probably would get meat or fish after your soup, but not both, or perhaps you'd eat a game bird. At a party dinner you would have fish, then a roast of meat, then game after that, with a vegetable to follow.

Russians like to present elaborate desserts whenever they can be contrived. Party dinners always feature a magnificent ice-cream dessert.

The setting of the table for a Russian dinner is specialized only by the fact that flowers are rarely used as a centerpiece. Fruit, arranged with artistic care in a cut-glass bowl, is the approved décor. Russians admire cut glass. They say the sparkle of it is suitably gay and lively at dinner.

3. Russian Table Traditions.—When honored guests arrive at a Russian home, the host and hostess go out to meet them at the door, carrying a platter with a loaf of bread and a little mound of salt. Bread and salt, *hleb ee sol*, are symbolic words of hospitality in Russia. There is wisdom and charm, it seems to me, in the age-old ceremony. It means that, although the house may be able to offer nothing more than bread and salt, the guests are welcome to share whatever there is to eat.

The platter with the offering of bread on it is presented with a snow-white cloth under the bread. The salt is on the family's very best dish of silver, glass, or china. The host and hostess bow low, from the waist. They say, *"Dobro pojalovat,"* "Welcome, with good will." The guest then cuts a slice from the loaf, dips it in the salt, and eats it.

Newlyweds are installed in their first housekeeping establishment with the same ritual of the bread and the salt, offered in this case by the parents or elderly relatives of the bride and groom. When a newly married couple goes visiting, at the threshold of each home they visit they are greeted with the *hleb ee sol* salutation. It is a heart-warming experience.

The Russian protocol for seating guests at the table differs considerably from that of other countries. A Russian hostess sits at the head of the table, and the *oldest* of the guests—male or female—is given the place of honor at the right of the hostess. Only at official functions is the right-hand place reserved for the guest of highest official rank.

The host doesn't sit at the foot of the table. That would be too suggestive of formality. After the right-hand place beside the hostess is taken, the host invites the rest to seat themselves at random. Among them the host then sits down anywhere he pleases. This scheme is not as careless as it looks. It gives the man of the house a chance to pick his table neighbors.

The Easter season is the most important Russian festival. At that time we have certain things to eat that are not only dictated by sentimental tradition—they are imperative to any Russian with a sound feeling for religious or aesthetic precepts.

Easter wouldn't be Easter without the special supper we serve after midnight, when Orthodox Russians break the Lenten fast, and when all Russians of old or new doctrinal teaching still say, "Christ is risen," then follow with the response, "Truly risen." They also exchange three kisses on the cheek.

Upon every Easter table in Russia stands the *paskha*—a confection of pot cheese and sugar, pyramid-shaped, decorated with bright paper flowers and marked on the sides with a cross, an angel, and a lily.

Along with the *paskha* we partake of the Easter *kulitch*. Our *kulitch* is a high, cylindrical yeast cake with raisins in it.

You must always cut it across, horizontally, never vertically. I don't know why. We eat a slice of *kulitch* together on the same plate with a slice of *paskha*. That is the rule.

Easter eggs, dyed gaudy colors, are heaped in bowls on the supper table, and Russians in fortunate circumstances serve a variety of cold dishes such as boiled ham, *pâté* of game, several salads, and all sorts of smoked fish. Candy is put out in the finest of crystal or silver epergnes. Our Easter supper table is supposed to look as gala as we can make it look.

For dinner on Easter Sunday we have a suckling pig, boiled whole and served cold, with a sauce of horse-radish and sour cream.

A roast goose for Christmas dinner, garnished with roast apples. In our traditional holiday eating, that's as far as we Russians go—except for a very few old-school religious purists.

To break their pre-Christmas fast, after the first star has risen on the evening of December 24, they eat sauerkraut with a millet soup, and rice boiled in sweetened water with a few raisins. The rice-and-raisin is also Orthodox fare at a funeral wake.

During the weeks before Lent, Russians go in for a veritable orgy of buttered pancakes. This is our famous *Maslyanitsa*, the "butter festival," when everyone eats all the little *blini* pancakes that can be stuffed down, slathered with butter.

Real Russian *blini* are small pancakes of buckwheat flour raised with yeast. They are much easier to make with one of the prepared pancake mixes we have here in America, and almost as good.

To eat your *blini* the Russian way, spread them with melted butter, then put on a slice or two of smoked salmon, or sturgeon, or salt herring—or good fresh caviar, which is the best of all, if you can get it.

The standard *blini* pancake is about 3 inches in diameter. Eat at least 10 of them, or you are a sissy in the eyes of any rugged Russian.

4. Russian Table Service.—Your well-trained Russian cook is an expert at carving up a whole roast of meat or game or poultry, and then putting all the pieces back in place so that the bird or the joint appears to be completely intact, and you never would think any knife had touched it. The carving is done in the kitchen, or sometimes at a side table called a *servante,* this word quite obviously being a corruption of French.

Soup always comes to the table in a big family tureen. The lady of the house ladles the soup into the plates, and the plates are passed by the maid. At a partified dinner the maid brings in the tureen, uncovers it and shows the soup to the lady of the house for her approval, then puts the tureen on a side table, where she ladles and passes the soup, one plate at a time. The same procedure is followed with the roast or game unless the maid takes round a large platter, offering it to the guests, who help themselves.

Soup must be piping hot or Russians won't eat it. They like it best when it's scalding hot. Blowing on your first spoonfuls of soup is considered perfectly good manners—in fact, to blow is to compliment your hostess for having the soup brought to the table properly hot.

Russian manners also permit the host and hostess to tease and cajole the guests into eating more. A guest who takes a modest helping is even urged by the serving maid to take more; and at a sign from the hostess, or at her own impulse, the girl will point to some especially nice bit on the platter, telling you to take that one.

Guests are always expected to praise the food. Not to do so

is to commit a serious breach of good manners. After you have told your hostess how much you are enjoying the meal, her regulation answer is, "*Yeshte na zdorovie*," which means, "Please eat and have good health."

At the end of a dinner, each and every guest approaches the hostess before the company leaves the dining room and thanks her for the meal. The men kiss her hand—at least they used to—but hand-kissing is now rather old hat. The ceremony of saying thank you to the hostess for the dinner is still an absolute must, however, in all polite Russian homes. At family dinners where correctness is observed the lady of the house is thanked by children and grownups alike.

The Russian host and hostess take their duties with equal earnestness. As soon as you sit down at their table both will coax you, "Try this, try that. A little food never hurts anyone." So if Russian friends invite you to a meal, don't think for a moment that you can get away with any excuse for eating moderately. You can't. Moderation is bad manners at the table of a Russian!

5. The Russian Kitchen.—The kitchen stove in Russia is a remarkable institution. By day it cooks the meals, then at night it becomes a bed. Our Russian word for this kind of a stove is *pleeta*.

In a house of average size the *pleeta* is about 6 feet long, 4 feet wide, 3½ feet high. The stove in a very large Russian house may be all of 18 feet in length, 10 feet in width. The *pleeta* is built of bricks and has an iron top. The bricks are faced on the outside with a covering of cement, or, in fine apartments, with glazed white tiles. The stove has no feet, being built up solid from the floor, always against a wall. The room next to the kitchen, on the side where the *pleeta* stands, is always cozy and warm in winter, though of course much too hot in summer, but that is a trifling inconvenience compared to the blessing of the stove's heat in cold Russian weather.

Wood is the fuel we burn in the *pleeta*. After the flat iron top of the stove has cooled off enough so that it won't scorch you, it is transformed into a bed by the simple expedient of putting a mattress on it. In present-day Russia the more modern dwellings have a small room for the housemaid, but in older apartments the help had only a windowless alcove adjoining the kitchen, and often not even that. The maid's room in many a house was merely the *pleeta*. At any event, whether or not there was a maid's room, friends or relatives of the maid would come visiting, or the laundress would want to stay overnight, so you would nearly always find someone sleeping on the stove. Two mattresses must always be provided on the bed in the maid's room—the extra mattress ready at all times to be laid on the top of the stove for a kitchen guest.

When I first started housekeeping in Russia, it took me a while to accustom myself to this double-duty function of the *pleeta*, my English upbringing having left me unprepared for such a casual arrangement of bed accommodations. I learned quite soon, however, that my seamstress or laundress really meant it when she said very sweetly, "Going home tonight isn't worth the trouble. I'd rather spend the night here." If I had company, if there were parties going on, the girl would often stay night after night, and she expected no extra pay. All she wanted was the fun of hearing what went on at the party, a little candy perhaps, and a mattress on the stove.

Peasant cottages have a bed-sized shelf built out from the wall so that the shelf is directly over the *pleeta*, and this shelf is the most desirable of beds, usually reserved for the master of the house, or for some ailing old grandparent.

The construction of the *pleeta* is extremely practical. A tank lined with tin is set into one end of the kitchen stove, and this supplies the household with hot water, for rare indeed is the Russian home that has a furnace or hot-water boiler, except possibly a water heater in the bathroom. This heater burns wood, as do the tile stoves in the living rooms. The tank in the kitchen stove is an absolute necessity.

The *pleeta* has two ovens, one for quick baking and one for slow baking. In Russian an oven is called a *douhovka*. The slow *douhovka* bakes beautiful loaves of yeast bread and raised cakes, and it does a splendid baking job with beans or with the earthenware pots containing *kasha*—the baked cereals we eat so much of in Russia. You leave your *kasha* pot all day in the *douhovka*, and it comes out perfect.

Under the grate of the stove, where the embers of the wood fire glow, we have an ingenious device for broiling our *shash-lik*. It consists of a narrow-spaced grill with a movable carriage on which you put long skewers of meat for broiling. The *shash-lik* method of broiling comes from the Caucasus, where mutton prevails, so a genuine *shashlik* should be made with pieces of mutton and fat speared alternately on each skewer. Steaks are never broiled in this manner. We don't eat broiled steak in Russia—only pan-fried.

Just above the *pleeta,* or at one side of it—wherever the chimney may be—there is a round hole with an iron cover that can be taken off. The round hole fits the stovepipe that carries away the charcoal fumes from the samovar.

Samo-var means "self-cooker." That's the actual translation of the word. Russians use the samovar exclusively to heat the water for their tea—they never make the tea itself in the samo-var. The tea is made in a small china pot into which you pour boiling water from the samovar. To get your samovar hot you begin by placing charcoal in its fire pan, then some thin slivers of wood to kindle the charcoal, then you drop in a couple of red embers from the fire in your *pleeta*. Next you clamp the elbow angle of the stovepipe over the samovar and fit the other end of the pipe into the hole in the stove. Thus a draft is created, and the fumes of the burning charcoal go up the chimney. Unless you follow these rules with care you are likely to be stricken with a splitting headache. As soon as the charcoal burns red, there are no more fumes, the water is boiling, and the samovar is ready to be detached from its pipe and carried from the kitchen to the dining room, where it is deposited in state on a small marble-topped table of its own, close beside the big dining-room table. The samovar table is always placed at the right hand of the lady of the house.

6. Russian Cooking Utensils.—Pots and pans in the Russian kitchen are nearly all made of cast iron, for the purposes of slow cooking. Our type of stove demands this cooking method. Someday when gas and electric ranges take the place of our old *pleeta* stoves, then perhaps our heavy iron pots and pans will be discarded along with the slow cooking we have practiced for centuries, and Russia may turn then to the modern quick-style preparation of meals. But at present the old ways prevail.

In every Russian kitchen, from the finest to the poorest, you will see an outsized pot for soup and a large earthenware pot —very much like an American beanpot—for the *kasha*. Any grain baked for hours in a slow oven is called *kasha*. It can be buckwheat groats, or barley, or corn, or millet. The *kasha* is brought to the table in its hot baking pot at the same time with the soup. For a vast majority of Russians, soup and *kasha* form the staple diet throughout the year, the only variety being a slight seasonal difference between one month's soup and the next.

14

Every kitchen also has a *jarovna* for oven-roasting and for pot-roasting on top of the stove. Our *jarovna* is deeper than the covered roasting pan used in America. Made of cast iron lined with white enamel, the *jarovna* is about 24 inches long, 10 or 12 inches wide, 8 inches high. The ends are round and the lid fits tight. A chicken roasted in a *jarovna* comes out succulent and golden brown, and it hasn't shrunk. This is something of a miracle, because Russian chickens are on the stringy side—they aren't very good chickens. We roast them in a closed *jarovna* until the last 15 minutes, when we take off the lid to brown the bird.

A Russian device of happy ingenuity is our special griddle for frying *blini* pancakes. It is really a nest of 6 or 8 pancake griddles, all in one piece. Five or 7 small round pans are joined together in a circle with another pan in the center. Each pan is about 3 inches across, and the whole business is made of heavy cast iron. With this dandy kitchen helper you can fry 6 or 8 *blini* pancakes at the same time, a worth-while saving of labor when you realize that any *moderate* Russian *blini* fan will tuck away at least 15 of them at a sitting.

The up-to-date Russian kitchen may be equipped with a couple of aluminum pans, though these are strictly a luxury. Aluminum has always been expensive in Russia. Usually the pride of the Russian housewife is her big flat copper pan for preserving jams and jellies, and her collection of smaller copper pans for sauces. Molds for desserts and for jellied meat and jellied fish are of heavy white metal or earthenware. Cake pans, earthenware ordinarily, are always very large.

You won't find any dainty little individual molds or individual casseroles in any Russian kitchen. I don't believe they will ever catch on in Russia. The idea of individual servings runs contrary to Russian psychology. Russians don't like to

15

see food served in individual dishes. It strikes them as a restriction on the amount of food each person is supposed to be served with, and to the depths of their souls they resent such an implication.

The kitchen table in Russia is of plain wood, well scoured. The big bowls for mixing dough are also made of wood. Oblong in shape, the mixing bowls are hollowed out by hand from wood of a smooth, fine texture. Other wooden bowls are of peasant design in lacquered colors. You've seen them sold here in America where people put them on the table filled with fruit, nuts, or pretzels. In Russia they are used for many household functions in lieu of chinaware. Peasants eat soup out of them, with bright-lacquered wooden spoons to match.

In examining these lacquered bowls and spoons of Russian peasant handicraft, you may have been surprised to see the lotus flower employed as a frequently occurring motif in their decoration. Nowhere in Russia does there grow a single species of the lotus, which is of Hindu and Egyptian origin, yet Russian peasants have long made the lotus flower a standard element of their applied design—and thereon hangs a tale.

The story of how the lotus pattern came to Russia was told me years ago by the famous Russian explorer, Colonel Peter Kozloff, the scientist who discovered the lost city of Khara-Khoto in the Gobi Desert.

Khara-Khoto was a great commercial center at a crossroads on the Eastern trade routes of the ancient world. Merchant caravans traveled to this flourishing town from China and Persia, from Turkestan and India. Merchants also came trading to Khara-Khoto from Europe and the Scandinavian North, and from Russia. Merchandise from all these far-flung countries changed hands in Khara-Khoto, and it was from there that Russia received examples of handiwork from India.

The city of Khara-Khoto perished hundreds of years in the past, buried under the Gobi sands, a victim, perhaps, of the widespread desiccation of Asia. Or the rich merchants of Khara-Khoto may have brought about their own ruin, may have deforested the surrounding land until a dust-bowl desert resulted, the sand drifting in to choke the streams and wells, killing every growing thing, finally driving away the last inhabitants.

Deep in the Gobi, Colonel Kosloff unearthed the remains of the once prosperous and celebrated city. He found treasures from distant lands, thousands of books, and fabrics as bright as when they were woven—all preserved in the dry desert sand.

Colonel Kozloff brought one of his Khara-Khoto treasures to my father's house. On our dining-room table he exhibited a Hindu statue with a lotus flower carved at the base. On the table, beside the statue, stood a Russian peasant bowl of contemporary make. Colonel Kozloff pointed to the lotus flowers on the bowl. He said:

"Probably the Russian peasant who painted those flowers has never heard of India, never heard of old Khara-Khoto. It's likely that that Russian peasant never has seen or heard of a lotus flower—yet the lotus on the bowl is the same as the lotus on the Hindu statuette. Centuries ago this lotus pattern must have reached peasant Russia through Khara-Khoto on fabrics or carvings from India, and the lotus has been admired and copied in Russia ever since."

A large set of scales, with a long balance rod and big iron weights, occupies a place of honor in every self-respecting Russian kitchen. There is also a smaller set of scales and weights, since cups marked for measuring are unknown. An ordinary unmarked water glass serves as the measure for flour and for the liquid ingredients that go into our cooking recipes. Anything less than a full glass is pure guesswork!

Wooden spoons are always used for mixing ingredients and for turning over a roast. Every good kitchen has a large soupspoon of solid silver, usually an heirloom handed down from mother to daughter. This spoon belongs in the kitchen and is never allowed out of the kitchen. It is for stirring sauces, for skimming jams and jellies. All Russian cooks will tell you solemnly that this silver spoon won't ever be the same, that it will spoil the sauce, the jam, the jelly, if it is used for anything else. They believe it, too.

Villainous-looking kitchen knives are kept murderously sharp for chopping up meat. Meat grinders are never used. Russians claim they grind all the juice out. A cleaver, a hatchet, a pastry board are included invariably in the kitchen equipment, and there are always a number of sieves made of horsehair. These are used for straining purées, which Russians adore. Eggs and cream are beaten with whisks of metal or wicker. There are no revolving egg beaters. Two dippers always hang on the kitchen wall and they are essential. One is for dipping hot water out of the tank in the stove; the other is to drink water from.

Tucked away somewhere on a shelf are the special pans for the traditional Easter cake, the *kulitch*. Kept with the *kulitch* pans are the 4 triangular pieces of wood used to form the pyramid shape of the Easter *paskha*.

The Russian kitchen is bare of electrical equipment, has no laborsaving mixers, toasters, juicers, percolators. Someone will make a fortune, someday, selling kitchen gadgets to Russian housewives, for they like them as much as American women do. Russia merely hasn't got around to them yet.

CHAPTER 1

RUSSIAN EATING MATERIALS

A good deal of our Russian food is rich and substantial. In normal times the Russian markets have plenty of eggs, milk, cream, and butter for sale at moderate prices, and our sour cream, which we call *smetana,* is so much in use that it constitutes a distinctive feature of Russian cooking. Butter is used with a very lavish hand. When I lived in Russia I had a hard time persuading my cook that I really preferred not to have every dish swimming in butter. No Russian cook would believe me. Nothing could convince her that I didn't like my food so rich. In her opinion I was trying to economize on butter.

Nearly all Russian soups are made with a basis of strong meat bouillon, except during Lent. Meat and vegetables are generally served in hearty quantities, and the fish course is almost always accompanied by an enriched sauce.

Desserts are very sweet and filling as a rule, apart from the rather childish dessert known as *kissel*—the juice of stewed fruit thickened with cornstarch, eaten cold with milk poured over it. Everybody in Russia eats *kissel.*

Light repasts such as the American salad luncheon are practically unknown in Russia, and Russians who come to this country are inclined at first to be derisive about them. The average Russian would think it better to stay hungry until he could get a square meal, since the only time he wants to eat lightly is when he's sick.

On the other hand, Russian food is easily adaptable to American taste, for most of the ingredients used in Russian dishes can be bought at American grocery stores or at delicatessens. For some of the ingredients you may need to shop around among grocers catering to a Russian or Jewish or Hungarian clientele, but on the whole there aren't many specialties of our Russian pantry that cannot be tracked down here with a little perseverance.

Along this line mushrooms are of prime importance. Lots of good Russian recipes demand mushrooms. Ordinarily the American mushroom fills the bill. Most of the Russian varieties are unobtainable, one of these being the *gruzdi* mushroom, which we Russians preserve in salt. The white mushroom of Russia, known in France as the *cèpe*, is also missing from the American scene. The dried mushrooms we use in many Russian sauces and soups are largely imported to this country from Europe, and while the best of them are to be found in stores of Hungarian or Russian character, the kind sold in Italian stores are often easier to obtain. Moreover, there is a steadily increasing supply of dried mushrooms from California. All dried mushrooms are somewhat high-priced, but we use them in small quantities, so their cost isn't as prohibitive as it may seem.

Your true Russian, I must warn you, entertains a violent passion for dill—and dill is an herb that can permeate your life if you don't watch it. Fresh green dill is usually carried in stock by Scandinavian, German, Hungarian, or Russian stores, as is the Russian type of parsley, which is frequently termed "Jewish parsley," an excellent herb for soups. Russian parsley and dill are both very cheap—five cents will buy enough to be used on four successive occasions. Before putting dill away in your refrigerator, wrap it in at least two thicknesses of greaseproof paper—otherwise your milk, your butter, your orange juice, your Jello, and even your eggs will be flavored with dill. Dill imposes its personality on everything that comes near it. My American husband declares that in Russia his breakfast cereal tasted of dill!

The wide range of sea food available on the American market makes it a fairly simple matter to adapt any Russian fish recipe, despite the fact that several species of Russian fish are completely alien to American waters. In each case there is an American fish that serves as a suitable substitute. The game situation isn't as good, unfortunately. The Russian market is abundantly supplied with game at modest prices, whereas the American housewife seldom has a chance to serve game unless she is wealthy, or unless she lives in a neighborhood sufficiently rural for her menfolk to go hunting.

It may surprise you, however, to learn that the number of Americans who never have tasted caviar is probably smaller than the number of native Russians in Russia who never have tasted it. In Russia, no less than here, caviar has always been a gourmet's luxury.

We wouldn't get far in our introduction to Russian cooking and eating if sour cream were not a constant commodity at nearly all stores in America where dairy products are sold. The dark Russian pumpernickel, which is served almost invariably with a genuine Russian meal, has become so popular in recent years that it can now be found without much difficulty in most American cities.

In their original form the classic old Russian recipes for pastry and cake leave out all reference to baking powder, for there was no baking powder on the shelves of the corner store in Russia. But any Russian cook was only too glad to throw out her hit-or-miss mixtures of soda and cream of tartar the very first time she made the acquaintance of a baking-powder can, for American baking powder made better Russian pastry than she could make in the primitive old Russian way. The same is true of many other standard American products. They give us up-to-date short cuts for preparing Russian dishes, yet our Russian dishes remain as Russian as ever.

1. Meat, Poultry, Game.—The word *miaso* in the Russian language applies to meat in general, but when Russians use the word they usually have beef in mind. *Miaso*—beef—comes first in the Russian category of popular meats; then comes veal in second place; then pork and mutton. Russian mutton is powerful stuff, coarse-textured and strong with the flavor of the animal. The best Russian mutton and lamb come from the Caucasus, homeland of Joseph Stalin.

Russian butchers carve out their cuts of meat according to a system entirely different from the American way. Steaks in Russia are thinner than we like them to be in America, but a good juicy fillet of beef isn't as scarce a cut in Russia as it is in this country. Russians roast a whole fillet in one piece, very quickly in a very hot oven so that it chars outside and remains rare inside. The fillet is sliced at table.

Because refrigerating techniques are in their infancy in Russia, the consumption of pork is limited to the cold-weather months. You can't talk any Russian into eating pork except in the wintertime. In southern Russia, where most of the pigs are raised, side meat is a regular stand-by. Any American from south of the Mason-Dixon line could sit down and feel entirely at home in the Ukraine, for the meal would closely resemble his own home combination of potlikker and salt side meat.

Ham is a universal Russian favorite. Usually we serve it boiled, or freshly denuded from the covering of dough in

22

which we have baked it. Westphalian ham is also popular as a *zakooska* snack with the vodka before dinner.

Chickens in Russia are lean and muscular. They run all over the place, foraging for themselves. But the Russian poultry farmers have long known how to cultivate capons, and they raise spring chickens by the thousands. These young spring chickens are called *tsiplyata*. They are smaller than the American broiler, and are considered to be a very special Russian delicacy. With a green-gooseberry sauce they are indeed a treat. In a deep-dish pie, with a Russian crust that melts on your tongue, they are something to rave about!

Geese and ducks are quite customary Russian fare. We stuff our Russian goose with buckwheat groats and roast apples in the pan along with it.

No buffet supper is complete in Russia without a turkey. The turkeys come from the Ukraine. The climate there is just right for raising turkeys of fine quality in large numbers.

After living a while in Russia, foreigners who are fond of game cannot bear to go home. No other country in the world today compares with Russia as a hunting ground. There are limitless flocks of wild duck, partridge and grouse and woodcock in profusion, and any amount of *glouhar*, called capercaillie in English.

The most numerous of all the Russian game birds is the *riabchick*, a small bird, sweet-fleshed, with a broad plump breast of white meat. The English variety is called hazel hen, but this bird does not appear in America.

Deer are plentiful in certain parts of Russia, though they are nowhere as common as the wild hares, which provide the meat for a famous Russian specialty—the *pashtet*. A *pashtet* is a loaf of wild hare, chopped up, well spiced, and baked.

23

2. Fish—Fresh, Pickled, and Smoked.—Russians turn up their noses at any town or village that doesn't have a river flowing near it, if not through it. A lake in the immediate vicinity of the town is welcomed as a luxury, but a river is a necessity, though a very small stream will do at a pinch. All other Russians pity those who live in the riverless villages of the Steppes region. Out of the rivers come many of the kinds of fish that Russians love best to eat; and in the rivers in the summertime all Russians love to go swimming.

Since Russia has big and little rivers galore, and lots of lakes, and inland seas as well as ocean seaboard, the fish supply is varied and plentiful. And fish is not a makeshift substitute for meat in Russia. People eat fish there with gusto at any time, not merely on fast days. Most Russians are also ardent fans for the sport of fishing.

The fish from the Russian rivers and lakes make very good eating, but I won't describe them in detail, for in many instances you can't buy exactly that same kind of fish in American markets. Our Russian methods of cooking fish are another matter. They can usually be adapted for American fish—butterfish or porgies cooked in sour cream, for example, being nearly identical in taste to the *karace* that is eaten popularly all over Russia.

Salmon, pike, smelts, sturgeon, trout, are some of the varieties shared in common by America and Russia. We are enormously fond of our Russian pastries made with fresh salmon, and of the smelts that we fry first, then pickle. They're delicious. We serve perch with an especially good sauce of horse-radish and apple.

Of all river creatures, the dearest to the Russian is the crayfish. Russians haven't yet set aside a national holiday for the eating of crayfish, as the Scandinavians have, but the consumption of crayfish is no less vigorous in Russia.

When, as a young girl, I visited Russia for the first time, I was taken in hand by a prominent Russian author, an equally well-known painter, and a Moscow industrialist—all bent on Russianizing me without delay because they were horrified to see that I didn't know how to eat crayfish. They organized a banquet lunch to which I was invited with my cousin chaperoning me. The tying of the voluminous napkin around my neck inaugurated me with the dignity of ritual, whereafter I was painstakingly taught how to crack the back of a crayfish with my fingers, how to pull out the meat, how to dip it in drawn butter, and finally to pop the exquisite morsel, all adrip, into my mouth. After luncheon the empty shells were counted, and I was disgraced by my low score. I had only 12 shells to show, while everyone else had at least 25. A Russian crayfish is about 3 times the size of an American jumbo shrimp. Crayfish are superb—but 25 of them at a time will always be too many for me!

The Russian market abounds in smoked fish, and I believe some of it is the best smoked fish in the world. Finest of all is the *seeg*, a fish caught in Lake Ladoga and in the upper waters of the Neva River, which flows through Leningrad. *Seeg* is a long narrow fish with very few bones. Its golden skin comes off easily when smoked, and the flesh underneath is tender and pink. The Russian embassy in Paris used to boast, in former times, that the knottiest problem in Franco-Russian diplomacy could be solved with no trouble at all if the couriers brought smoked *seeg* from Russia to be fed to the French statesmen in Paris. It is said that no French politician ever was known to refuse an invitation to partake of this magnificent fish.

A wide range of smoked and salted fish furnishes an important part of the *zakooska* course that you start off with at any real Russian dinner. Herrings are the cheapest kind of *zakooska* fish, but the best of the salted ones are still known, to this day, as the King's Herring, and they come from Scotland.

To be truly Russian, any meal should always begin with salt herring. The Russian word for it is *selodka*. You drink vodka with it, in small glasses, and you must toss each glass of vodka down, bottoms up.

Herrings, both salt and smoked, are used also in many cooked dishes, often combined with scalloped potatoes or made into small pasties which we serve with fish broth. We have a very popular Russian dish called *forshmak*, in which herring and meat and potato are used together with a light egg mixture to form a semi-soufflé.

I must mention caviar here, since it is a fish product, but I will tell you a good deal more about caviar in my *zakooska* chapter. The most expensive caviar is grayish and is salted very slightly. It is the roe of the sturgeon.

There is historical evidence that ancient epicures of the Golden Age of Greece were acquainted with caviar through their trade with what is now the Kuban district of Russia, and that Russian caviar was considered a choice Greek delicacy.

Pressed caviar was used as a military ration by the warriors in olden times, because it is a concentrated food and can be kept in good condition for long periods. Just as colonial Amercans rode with jerked beef in their saddlebags, so the Kuban Cossacks pack a slab of the dark pressed caviar when they go on hunting expeditions.

But the fresh variety of caviar remains a luxury in Russia. The pressed kind, made from an inferior grade of roe, is less expensive. Cheapest of all is the red caviar made from salmon roe. Nevertheless, the red salmon caviar sold in Russia has an excellent flavor, and is not to be compared with some of the red caviar produced in other countries from the roe of various unidentified fishes.

3. Dairy Products.—We have a milk complex in Russia. Russians drink all the milk they can get, and they want it good and rich, with the cream left on. When they talk about the joys of country life, the first thing they mention is the creamy fresh milk of which you drink your fill if you live on a farm.

In addition to cow's milk, Russians are fond of mare's milk. This is a taste derived from the Tartar tribes, who not only drink milk fresh from the mares, but also brew a powerful fermented beverage with it. Mare's milk is said, in Russia, to be very strengthening for tuberculosis patients. It is called *kumiss*. On the middle Volga, in the Kuybisheff district, several sanitariums make a practice of prescribing *kumiss*. Russians are so convinced of the beneficial properties of mare's milk that they would no doubt emulate the father of the French artist Toulouse-Lautrec if they knew about him. Old Lautrec was a retired cavalry officer, a habitual drinker of mare's milk and something of a scoffer at polite society. Riding on Sunday afternoons amid the elegant Parisian carriages of the ladies and gentlemen airing themselves in the Bois de Boulogne, he used to dismount at a conspicuous place in the park, milk his mare into a tin cup, drink the milk, wipe his mustache with a flourish, then mount his mare again and ride nonchalantly away!

One of our Russian dairy tastes goes generally unshared by foreigners. We love our sour milk, whereas other people are seldom very partial to it. But all Russians swear by the healthful and refreshing nature of sour milk, and throughout the summer

27

we take large quantities of it as a principal item of food. Actually it is what used to be known in old-fashioned English as a "dish of curds." A bowl of milk, after being allowed to ferment in a warm place, is put on ice for a few hours. We call it *prosto-kvasha,* which means "plain soured." Sometimes we add a teaspoon of sour cream to the warm milk to hasten the process. We eat our *prosto-kvasha* just as it is, or perhaps with a little sugar. A very fancy person may sprinkle it with a dash of cinnamon.

Sour cream is used lavishly in cooking, and is often served at table to put in the soup. Potatoes, mushrooms, green vegetables, and the smaller fishes are sautéed in sour cream, and we use it in a number of special pastry recipes.

Pot cheese is a staple and universal dairy favorite in Russia. Migrating in recent years to lands abroad, the Russian pot-cheese eaters have lately spread its popularity far and wide. We eat it plain or with sour cream and a garnish of chopped dill. We also bake it in small open tarts to serve with our beet soup, and we have a tasty sort of pot-cheese cakes called *sirniki* which we eat at lunchtime.

For our coffee we have an unusual preparation known as "baked milk." Very fresh raw milk—unpasteurized or homogenized—is baked for hours in shallow pans in a slow oven till it changes color to a pale shade of pink with a brown skin on top. The pieces of brown skin are prized as special treats by many Russian families, and some members of the household get up extra early in order to grab the choicest baked-milk skins for their morning coffee cup.

Russians prefer unsalted butter for table use. For cooking we use a type of butter rendered down for the purpose, called *toplenoye maslo.* The Russian word for butter is *maslo.*

Vast quantities of eggs are featured on the national menu.

At breakfast we like them soft-boiled. At lunch or supper we like them fried, and any Russian will relish an omelet at any hour of the day or night. No one in Russia would ever think of eating fewer than 3 fried eggs at a time, nor would anyone make an omelet with less than 4 eggs. A handsomely free use of eggs is the rule in the making of cakes, desserts, pastries, meat loaves, and salads.

Dairy products and eggs were almost unbelievably cheap in Russia in times of peace, and the use of them was unstinted.

As to cheese, Russians are such constant fanciers of it that no well-furnished supper table is complete without a generous cheese display. Swiss cheese is most in favor. Excellent cheeses of this type are made at Russian dairies in the Caucasus, and in certain parts of northern Russia. The Siberian cheese industry, already very well organized, is expected some day to rival the production of cheese industries as great as those of Canada.

4. Vegetables.—George Bernard Shaw complained to me about the endless array of fresh and pickled cucumbers he was urged to eat when he visited Russia. He said, "You Russians appear to *live* on cucumbers. What I can't understand is how you seem to keep on loving them devotedly no matter how many you eat. Now, after my Russian trip, I hate the sight of cucumbers."

It is certainly true, as G.B.S. observed, that Russians eat cucumbers morning, noon, and night, and never get tired of them. There are several good Russian reasons for this. To begin with, the cucumbers grow luxuriantly all over Russia, and they grow without any laborious cultivating, which endears them to every Russian heart because Russians are passionately prejudiced in favor of any edible plant that doesn't make them work to grow it.

In the second place, cucumbers provide us with dill pickles, and dill pickles and sauerkraut are often the only vitamin foods we can get for months at a time in vast sections of Russia where no green vegetables are to be had through the long, severe winters. I think perhaps our national fondness for cucumbers may derive most of all from the fact that they start growing very early in the summer. With our lilacs, they come as the year's first gift from Heaven, heralding our deliverance from cold and snow, signaling the approach of summer days.

Even the poorest of Russians will scrape together a few kopecks to buy a bunch of the first lilacs. Lilac toilet water is the perfume preferred by all Russians because of its springtime scent—and I have no doubt we would joyfully splash ourselves with cucumber perfume if such a preparation existed. Lilacs and cucumbers are virtually symbolic to any Russian, symbols of the bounty of the earth; and in Russia our spiritual gratitude for Nature's benefactions is so profound an instinct that no political or economic doctrine can ever dim it.

Russian cucumbers are grown here by a few of our gardeners, I know, for I find them occasionally on sale at American markets. As a rule they are labeled "Jewish cucumbers." They aren't as large as the native American cucumber. They have a rougher skin, smaller seeds, and are much more aromatic.

Actually there isn't any kind of vegetable that doesn't flourish somewhere in Russia's huge expanse of territory, which includes every sort of climate and soil. With the eventual organizing of transport and refrigeration, fresh vegetables in profuse variety can be brought to market all the year round in every part of Russia, as they are in this country. But such is not yet the case, and at present the use of greenstuffs is still limited in some localities, though very widely developed in others. That's why the vegetable recipes, from one Russian district to another, are so often entirely different.

Corn on the cob has always been a favorite dish in the Ukraine region of southern Russia. Ukrainians eat corn on the cob precisely as Americans do—buttery noses and all—and they tear into it with the same gusto. Outside of the Ukraine, nearly all Russian corn is used as corn meal or for cattle fodder.

Tomatoes, green peppers, eggplants—all these are everyday commodities in the Ukraine, and farther south the vegetables of Crimea and the Caucasus make truck gardening an essential industry, with a high premium on the earliest spring products sent north to Moscow or Leningrad, where they are welcomed as de luxe delicacies. The Moscow thermometer may be lurking below zero when you carry home your first purchase of Crimean carrots or green peas wrapped in thick layers of paper and cotton to protect them from the frost.

Commonest of Russian vegetables are: cabbage—the large, firm, white variety—potatoes, onions, carrots, turnips, beets, and a black-skinned radish with white flesh and a very strong odor. This radish is called *rediska*. You take your raw *rediska*, shred it fine, moisten it with salad oil, and munch it with black bread. Celery, lettuce, spinach, red cabbage, kohlrabi, cauliflower, peas, and green beans are found less frequently on the Russian table, but they are in fairly common use and are neither prohibitive in price nor unfamiliar.

One distinct novelty to foreign vegetarians in Russia is the small round *karotelle* carrot. We also have a delicious little Russian turnip, as yellow as butter and very tender. I can't imagine why our *karotelle* and our special little Russian turnip are completely unknown in America. Both are so supremely good and should grow well here.

Squash grows abundantly in Russia. I'm sure you'll like the

picturesque Russian name we have for squash. We call it *kabachok,* which means "little tavern." This nice descriptive name was inspired by the fact that the inside of the squash is crowded with seeds, just the way a Russian tavern is always crowded with people.

5. Preserved Food.—Russians consume enormous quantities of sauerkraut. Most of it is the same as sauerkraut in other countries—shredded cabbage put up in wooden tubs; but we also have a number of interesting variations. To our keg of sauerkraut we add a few sliced carrots and some bright-red lingonberries. The berries and carrot slices make our sauerkraut look much more attractive, and we think they improve its taste. The children always like it better this way.

Sometimes instead of shredding the cabbage we put it up in large hunks, cutting the cabbage in quarters or eighths, then with our meat course at dinner we serve these big, appetizing pieces just as they come from the tub. And there is another kind of Russian sauerkraut that foreigners invariably exclaim over when they first discover it. In the tub with the cabbage we put a few whole apples, apples straight from the tree, unpeeled and uncored. Even after several months they retain their firmness, but the apples become transparent through and through, and the slight fermentation of the cabbage gives them an unusual flavor that is extremely pleasant.

Mocheniya yabloki are apples preserved by themselves in the identical sauerkraut manner, but without the cabbage. Literally translated, *mocheniya yabloki* means "soaked apples." The art of making them has never been widely known outside the kitchens of country estates, so they are rather hard to find. Eaten with game or roast meat, they are greatly enjoyed not alone by Russians but equally by any foreign travelers in Russia who are lucky enough to encounter them. I can't say as much for the pears we preserve by this same *mocheniya* method. Though some Russians like them, they aren't very popular.

Every day in the week, on every Russian table, at every meal except breakfast, dill pickles appear. For our dill pickles we use cucumbers of medium proportions—not the jumbo size—and we pickle them in earthenware crocks or in wooden tubs as capacious as our sauerkraut tubs. No garlic in our Russian dill pickles. We put in oak leaves to keep them firm, black-currant leaves for a nice zestful aroma, and plenty of dill, you may be sure.

Salt herring, along with other smoked or salted fishes of many sorts, are among the principal items on Russia's list of preserved foods. We eat tons and tons of salt and smoked fish.

Smoked goose is a favorite article of preserved food in the Ukraine, where it is quite a common commodity. Siberia supplies cured and smoked haunches of bear meat, but this is considered to be a special and delicate treat. I don't know why. A bear haunch is always tough and can't be compared in any way whatever with a good ham. The wild-boar hams from southern Russia are an entirely different story. Fed on Indian corn and acorns, the wild boars get fat and their flesh is sweet. These hams are excellent.

Russian canned goods, formerly scarce and expensive, are now being produced on a rapidly growing scale at efficient new canneries organized by the Soviet Government, generally under the direction of American experts. This is an important step in the development of Russian eating habits, since it now affords nation-wide distribution to certain native foodstuffs that in previous generations have been limited to one locality.

For example, we have a large type of game bird resembling the woodcock—the *tetereva,* we call it—which migrates annually from northern Russia to the southern shores of the Caucasus. Thousands of the *tetereva* were bagged by sporting gentlemen in times past, yet the ordinary people seldom had an opportunity to taste this succulent bird. Now the Soviet hunters deliver their game bags at the new Caucasian canneries, and the *tetereva* migrate—in cans—all over the Soviet Union.

In the Ukraine, the Caucasus, in Crimea and in Tashkent, industrial canning of fruits and vegetables is extensive. There are smaller canneries near Moscow, Leningrad, and Rostov. Dairy products are canned near Vologda, in northern Russia. Meat is canned in Siberia, while most of the fish canneries are situated on the shores of the Black Sea and the Caspian.

The progress made during recent years in these canning industries has broadened the Russian diet to a considerable degree. Moreover, all Russians are enthusiastically convinced that Russian canned goods are the best canned goods in the world. They are inclined, in fact, to be fanatically emphatic about the superior taste of their Russian canned goods. Every Muscovite of my acquaintance shares this opinion, and I must say I agree when it comes to canned poultry or game. Owing perhaps to the processing or the flavoring, Russian brands of canned chicken, canned partridge, canned venison, etc., are unquestionably miles ahead of any I have sampled elsewhere.

Fruit and berries canned in Russia aren't as handsome in appearance, however, as American canned fruit. Tomatoes canned whole, or peaches canned in perfect halves, are still to be achieved by Russian canners. No doubt they will accomplish this at some not-too-distant date, for the standards there, like the canning standards here, are set by the fastidious housewife. If she has a good stove and enough sugar to spare, every Russian housewife makes her own jams, puts up her own preserved and pickled fruit. So she knows what's what.

In the department of Russia's preserved foodstuffs, the dried mushroom is one more item requiring particular mention. It plays an essential part in Russian cooking. Soups made with dried mushrooms instead of meat furnish the main·dish of the meal through the Lenten season and on other meatless days of religious fasting. Dried mushrooms, well soaked, are stewed to enrich many sauces, and are often chopped up in the stuffing of a Russian meat or vegetable pie.

6. Fruit.—Scratch a Russian and you will find a fruit patriot. You find a nationalist who will stoutly declare that Russian fruit in general, and Russian berries in particular, are the finest that grow anywhere on earth. I have spent only part of my life in Russia, yet my blood promptly asserts its heritage when I talk about fruit, for I too become rapturous at the memory of fruit in Russia. The flavor and the perfume of our Russian fruit is what we love—not so much the pretty looks and the size.

The aroma of Russian strawberries is unforgettable. Strawberries are *kloobnika* in Russian, and are the darling of all fruits to most of us. We also love watermelon. Russian watermelons are plentiful, and very sweet, with brightest of bright red flesh inside, and the blackest of seeds. We dry these watermelon seeds and nibble on them all year round.

Russia grows many varieties of apples, quite a number of which have been crossed advantageously here with American and Canadian apples. But some of our most succulent apples, the *Anton* for one, thrive only in Russia. The *Antons* are large yellow apples that ripen late in the year, usually after the first light frost has touched them.

In New York a very progressive Soviet official revealed him-

35

self as being Russian to the marrow of his bones by declaring the *Anton* apple to be the champion of the world. He enthused to me. Keep two *Anton* apples, he said, in your room for two or three days, then eat them. Their delicate aroma will perfume your room for a week.

This Soviet representative also reminded me of the purely Russian custom of dropping a slice of raw apple, instead of lemon, into a cup of tea. "Then you drink the essence of autumn!" he exclaimed.

Siberia produces many of the finest Russian apples, though apple trees grow well all over the country. Wild apples are hunted for use in *sour schtee,* special kind of cabbage soup.

Except in the far-northern regions, Russia has widely distributed crops of plums, pears, melons, cherries, and peaches. Peaches are superlative in the Caucasus, where chestnuts are another local product *par excellence.* Other kinds of nuts are grown extensively in Siberia and the South.

Central Russia, primarily the Vladimir province, is the home of the great cherry orchards. The cherries there are purple-red and so juicy they splash in your face when you bite one. And there's no other word for it—their flavor is simply divine. Russians living outside of Russia are forever seeking some foreign cousin to their beloved Vladimir cherry.

Raspberries, both wild and cultivated, are very popular in Russia. You can please all your Russian friends by offering them weak tea with good raspberry jam on the side. Watch them stir a spoonful of the jam into each cup of tea, and you'll behold smiling, happy Russians.

The wild raspberries are gathered chiefly in Siberia. When I was a little girl my mother used to thrill me with a story of her own girlhood at Tomsk, in Siberia. She was picking wild raspberries at the edge of the forest when all of a sudden she came face to face with a big wild Russian bear. He was standing up like a man, picking berries from the other side of the bush, and he was just as frightened of Mother as she was of him. They both ran as fast as they could go, in opposite directions.

Blackberries, huckleberries, gooseberries are all eaten fresh during the Russian summer, and are made into large stocks of preserves. We have red currants, white currants, and plenty of black currants. Black-currant syrup is always given in hot tea to cure a cold, to grownups as well as to children—and no true Russian will ever forsake the idea that dried huckleberries, called *chernika,* aren't the very best medicine there is for stomach ailments in summer.

Frost-nipped berries from the mountain ash tree are made into jelly, and an extraordinarily good liqueur-cordial is concocted with them. This is *riabinovaya vodka,* which we serve as an *apéritif* before meals. It's a fine drink, when you can get it, which isn't often enough. It has a slightly bitter tang, a lovely red color, a good zestful taste. A little of it used to be imported here from the Baltic provinces. It should be better known.

The berry that you see most of in Russia is the small red lingonberry type of cranberry. In America you call it the partridge berry, or mountain cranberry. It is also a popular berry in Scandinavian countries, and is sold here at Swedish and Danish delicatessen stores. Lingonberries are made into a not-too-sweet jam to eat with meat and game, but are more favored when they are preserved in wooden tubs like sauerkraut. This way, they serve as a favorite relish with meat balls, goose or duck, turkey or game. The larger American type of cranberry is put up in the same way in Russia, and is extensively used. I should add, however, that our Russian cranberry isn't quite the same as the American, being thinner skinned, darker red, and somewhat smaller. We use the preserved cranberries, cooked and strained, in many desserts, and we candy the berries whole, an inexpensive form of confectionary.

Foreign visitors often comment on the lack of citrus fruits in Russia. Oranges, even lemons, have been a luxury, it is true, but only because of limited facilities of transportation. The Crimea and the Caucasus are potentially as good for the growing of citrus fruit as California and Florida. The planting of citrus-fruit orchards in these districts and the organization of citrus-fruit transport have already made great advances in recent years. New citrus-fruit groves are prospering now in the country of the Kuban Cossacks, and with the peacetime return of normal freight service, Russia should soon have plenty of oranges, grapefruit, lemons, and tangerines. In the past Russian housewives have always hoarded every scrap of lemon and orange peel to flavor their desserts and cakes.

Everyone in the Crimea and in the Caucasus eats all sorts of fruits, eats fruit all the time. Even in the cities of the Caucasus, every house has a pomegranate tree in the yard. Southern Russians use the pomegranate juice in cooking. First a whole pomegranate is left in the sunshine until its skin becomes as dry as a nutshell, and as hard. The pomegranate is then cracked open and the juice pressed from the fruit. The pieces of mutton that go on the skewers for the famous *shashlik* are marinated beforehand in this pomegranate juice, and a good Caucasian cook will insist that marinating your *shashlik* in wine and vinegar is a poor substitute, no matter how fashionable the chef who does it that way.

You will be pleasantly surprised, I think, by the delicate and different flavor that pomegranate juice imparts to a salad.

Try it instead of vinegar. I believe you will find it a valuable addition to your list of salad fixings.

7. Smetana.—I very much wish sour cream had another name in the English language. I think the word "sour" puts some Americans off. Without ever tasting it they make up their minds that they won't like it. *Smetana,* our Russian word for sour cream, sounds much more appetizing.

It is impossible to give Russian recipes without frequent mention of this ingredient, so I had better explain at once what *smetana* really is.

Sour cream of good quality is not actually very sour. It is thick and rich and should be absolutely fresh. A good dairy or delicatessen store will verify the freshness of their sour cream if you ask them to take a look at it and tell you, before you buy it. Always insist on getting sour cream that is fresh.

Elsewhere in this book I have suggested it may be wiser not to bring up the subject of sour cream at the family table when you have used it as an ingredient in one of these Russian recipes. If the dish meets with approval, and if you *must* reveal your cooking secrets, speak of *smetana,* or call it Russian cream. Just forget that word "sour." The chances are ten to one nobody will know you have used it unless you tell.

Russians use a lot of *smetana,* but *good* Russian cooks add no more than a few tablespoons of it in most cases. There are certain recipes that call for a greater quantity. They are the exception. For sauces, the cook with an overlavish *smetana* hand is not the best cook.

CHAPTER 2

ZAKOOSKAS

One of the times of day that Russians enjoy the most is the hour before dinner, when we whet our appetites with vodka and zakooska, accompanied of course by the greatest possible amount of talk. This gay, informal interlude is known as the zakooska hour, and the zakooskas are the various titbits you eat between drinks. Lasting somewhat longer than the period for cocktails and canapés that precedes an American dinner, the zakooska hour takes a full 60 minutes. New acquaintances have ample opportunity to break the conversational ice so that everyone is at ease when you go on to the dining room. The host and hostess need not fear those deadly silences which can devastate a dinner party. After a zakooska hour everybody talks to everybody.

There is a great advantage, I think, in our Russian custom of having the zakooskas arrayed on a table of their own, with all the guests congregating at the zakooska table, helping themselves, exchanging remarks about special delicacies, then going back from time to time for another snack. It keeps us on the move, keeps the party from congealing in small groups as occurs so often during the more static cocktail assemblage, where trays are passed to the guests.

The zakooska table may be set up in the living room, or a side table in the dining room may be used. Wherever it is, all the guests go there to get their drinks and make their own selections, carrying their plate and vodka glass around with them as they mingle and talk. Everything is set out on the zakooska table. Small plates, forks, and napkins are arranged in neat stacks or rows. Carafes of vodka, and the glasses from which to drink it, are placed on trays. The vodka glasses are very small—the size of American cordial glasses.

The correct Russian serving of zakooskas calls for narrow oval dishes about 8 inches long, 4 inches wide, 1 inch deep. Each different kind of zakooska is served in a separate dish. If you haven't enough matching dishes of this sort, buy a dozen of the coarsest plain white quality, individual platter size, from a restaurant supply house. They will look much nicer than a patchy layout of elegant but unmatched china. The hot zakooskas should be served from a casserole.

Lay your slices of smoked fish carefully along the center of their individual platter, each slice neatly overlapping the next. On their own dishes do the same with your sliced sausage and your slices of Swiss cheese.

Do not decorate with parsley or any other green stuff. Real Russian zakooskas are never ornamented!

Two kinds of bread, light and dark, are served in bread-baskets of silver or wickerwork. The dark bread is essential —preferably a heavy Russian pumpernickel. For hand-to-mouth comfort as zakooska conveyors, the slices of bread should be cut about 2 inches square, or 3 inches by 2 inches. Serve the butter in a dish of its own. Have the butter scalloped in little curls or shaped in small pats. If you are serving more than 6 people, provide 2 butter dishes.

At the end of this chapter you will find a number of sample menus for the zakooska table. Each menu includes 5 cold zakooskas and 1 hot dish. According to Russian practice this is adequate but not lavish for a small informal party. Even for a party of only 6 people, we feel truer to our traditions of Slavic hospitality when we serve 6 or 7 cold zakooskas, perhaps including caviar, and 1 hot zakooska. Many Russians would say the zakooska table isn't complete with less than 10 dishes to choose from, but the new generation seems inclined to be more moderate. Before the Revolution every good restaurant in Russia used to throw out shameful quantities of untouched zakooskas every day in the week, for the entire assortment had to be made all new and fresh every day, while only a fraction of it ever got eaten.

It was of prime importance that the zakooska table should be tempting to the eye, and that its great variety of dishes should present every guest with some irresistible bite. Actually the zakooskas were free lunch. You weren't charged for them on your bill; you merely paid for the glasses of vodka you drank with them. But restaurant patrons in general were Russian men who took an astonishing number of glasses, and the profit from vodka was so enormous it more than covered the cost of all the wasted zakooskas.

What Zakooskas Are.—Any of the following items can be used as zakooska snacks:

Fresh gray caviar
Pressed black caviar
Red caviar

Pickled herring
Herring marinated in wine
Herring with mustard sauce
Herring in sour cream
Chopped herring with eggs
Herring salad with beets or other vegetable

Smoked boeckling
Smoked salmon
Kippered salmon
Smoked flounder
Smoked whitefish
Smoked whiting
Smoked eels
Smoked sturgeon
Jellied eels
Anchovies
Kilki (Norwegian anchovies)
Sardines (all kinds)
Pickled smelts
Pickled mackerel in tomato sauce
Raw oysters
Shrimps in mayonnaise
Lobster in mayonnaise

All meats should be served in small slices:

Spicy sausage (all kinds)
Ham, baked or boiled
Prosciutto ham
Smoked reindeer meat
Smoked tongue
Head cheese
Liver loaf
Liver or meat pâté
Smoked turkey

Radishes in sour cream
Cucumbers in sour cream
Pickled mushrooms

43

Pickled globe artichokes
Pickled beets
Pickled red cabbage
Small pickled onions
Eggplant caviar

Salad Olivier
Potato-and-smoked-salmon salad
Salad of calves' brains in mayonnaise
Salad of any cooked vegetables
Salad of cold duck and vegetable
Salad of fish and vegetable

Zakooska Salads.—Almost any combination of cooked and raw vegetables, mixed together with cold fish, smoked fish, cold game, or cold meat, can be made into a good zakooska salad, provided the dressing is spicy, the ingredients cut small, and the salad not watery or thin. The dressings for zakooska salads usually are mixtures of mayonnaise and sour cream, about half and half. We also use a number of vinaigrette salads in which the ingredients are dressed simply with oil and vinegar. The vinaigrette salads are made with the same kind of ingredients used for the mayonnaise salads. No fruit is ever used in any zakooska salad.

Hot Zakooskas.—Hot zakooska dishes are:
Dragomir Forshmak
Mushrooms in sour cream sauce
Chicken livers in Madeira
Frankfurters in tomato sauce.

Besides these 4 hot zakooskas, for which I give the recipes, other hot zakooskas sometimes served are:

Meat balls, well spiced and walnut-sized, in tomato
    sauce
Piroshki (piecrust rolls stuffed with meat).

Swiss cheese or any well-matured cheese of the Cheddar
type is suitable as a zakooska.

VODKA

There's no reason why you shouldn't serve a milder drink
with your zakooskas if the notorious violence of vodka scares
you, although I must admit that to my taste there is no really
competent substitute. Eat enough zakooskas with it, and the
vodka won't hit you too hard. But do not hesitate to serve
cocktails at your zakooska table in case you can't get over
feeling terrified of vodka. Teetotalers can have a zakooska
hour with tomato juice. Why not?

I vote for vodka, however, and I believe our Russian manner of taking it is the best way.

Translated literally from Russian, the word vodka is an
affectionate diminutive meaning "dear little water." White
vodka should be as clear and colorless as water, and the
100-proof vodka that all true Russians prefer ought to go down
your throat like liquid fire. Strong stuff, comrades! Always
serve it *ice cold*. It should came to table in a small carafe
that has been thoroughly chilled in the refrigerator. Often
we have two carafes of vodka, one at each end of the zakooska table. Because it is so strong, we drink our vodka out
of extremely small glasses, and the special glasses made for
vodka drinking have no stems. Some of them have handles.
They are like little glass cups, but since they appear to be

almost unobtainable in this country, ordinary cordial glasses will probably have to do.

American vodka is sold in two different degrees of potency, an 86-proof kind as well as the 100-proof. Imported vodka is scarce.

Zubrovka is a popular Russian variation of vodka. Zubrovka is yellowish in color, flavored with herbs. You can buy it in America now at some of the liquor stores that stock foreign specialties.

In New York before the war I was able occasionally to find *riabinovka*, the ruby-red vodka made in Russia's Baltic provinces from berries of the mountain ash. Slightly bitter in tang, *riabinovka* is an excellent appetizer, somewhat less alcoholic than white vodka. No doubt it will again be imported here eventually.

Among Russians in prosperous times, a well-set zakooska table would offer all three kinds of vodka—white, yellow, and red. Also a bottle of Swedish aquavit, which is very strong, slightly flavored with aniseed. And for timid ladies there would be an innocent bottle of some sweeter drink such as peach brandy.

As to the physical act of drinking vodka, please let me say emphatically that vodka is *never supposed to be sipped!* Take my advice—don't sip it. Sipping it is your peril. That is the way it gets you much too tight, much too quick.

Filled to the brim, your tiny glass of vodka should always be tossed off at one swallow—bottoms up. Immediately after you drink it, take a bite of some zakooska. This will prevent you from choking, and will keep you in a decently unbefuddled state. A bite of Swiss cheese, all by itself without bread or butter, is the most efficient sobriety-preserver after a glass of vodka. Nevertheless you should be warned that Swiss cheese won't save you—*nothing* will save you—unless you're careful to watch out how many glasses of vodka you take.

Most Russians can get away with at least 6 little glasses without turning a hair, but Americans who are unaccustomed to vodka will be smart to stay within the 3-glass limit. Otherwise you may wake up feeling as though you'd been handed a *Misha* Finn.

My statement on this subject is verified by heart-rending stories from sturdy American war correspondents who have tried drinking vodka with the Russian Army in Europe. I have heard many accounts from the lips of American newspapermen, and they all tell the same harrowing tale. They say, "Every Russian wants to drink your health. He's insulted if you don't drink it with him. Pretty soon there's a terrific explosion inside your head. That's all you remember."

The ceremonial drinking of toasts with vodka, which all Russians practice, is indeed a pitfall. Russians consider it impolite not to say, "*Vasheh Zdorovyeh*," meaning, "Your health," when they gulp down a glass of vodka, and they expect you to do the same, repeating the toast and downing glass after glass with every one of them. The only escape is to draw the line smilingly but firmly at a reasonable point.

In Russia many accomplished vodka drinkers care for no zakooska other than a bite of herring, or even a plain crust of dark bread with salt on it. They like anything salty, which gives them a sustained thirst for more drinks.

To Americans who either distrust vodka or who dislike the taste of it, I recommend a dry cocktail for the zakooska hour. The drink must be dry. Sweet cocktails don't go at all well with zakooska dishes. Personally I consider short drinks better than long ones, though highballs can be served.

Here in America when I set up a zakooska table, I usually

47

have a small carafe of vodka for those who like it, and dry martini cocktails for those who don't.

CAVIAR

Some kind of caviar usually has a place on the zakooska table. It may be the fresh gray variety that was always expensive even in the old days in Russia, or it may be the more proletarian red caviar. Be it plutocratic gray or democratic red, it should be served in a bowl surrounded with ice, and should have no trimmings of any sort. No chopped egg or onion is seen with any kind of caviar on a real Russian table. When caviar appears among the zakooskas, only a small amount of it is put out, since it is accompanied by an assortment of other snacks. For the pressed black caviar you can omit the bowl and the ice. Well chilled before serving, the pressed caviar is cut in slices and thus arranged on a zakooska dish.

Beluga caviar is the very top grade, the highest priced. It has large pale gray grains. Sevruga caviar, the next highest grade, has pale gray grains of a slightly smaller size. Ossetrina caviar, the next grade, has small eggs of a darker gray. Beluga, Sevruga, and Ossetrina caviar are always sold fresh, usually in 1-pound cans. The top price is about $24 per pound.

Pressed caviar is black, costing about $18 per pound. It can be bought in quantities of less than 1 pound.

Red caviar is made from salmon roe instead of sturgeon roe. The grains of the red caviar are quite large, but the flavor is not valued as highly. It can be bought cheaply in small glass containers. For its own flavor, red caviar has a considerable number of devotees, myself among them.

Fastidious gourmets prefer caviar as a first course at dinner rather than as a zakooska. When dinner begins with caviar, the caviar is of the finest fresh variety, served in a bowl of generous proportions, and with it comes one of the world's most delicious kinds of bread. This is a special Russian bread ring called a *kalatch,* something like an English muffin in texture, but smoother and well baked through, not doughy inside. You spread a little unsalted butter on your *kalatch.* Some Russians put a squeeze of lemon juice on their caviar, but loftier connoisseurs call them vandals for doing so.

I have heard it said by caviar fanatics that there is no such thing as enough caviar. From my own experience I can bear witness against this assertion, with historic proof to the contrary.

In February 1917, at the fall of the last Tsarist regime, Alexander Kerensky and the members of his Provisional Revolutionary Government spent the first hectic days of the new order in the Tauride Palace in Petrograd (now Leningrad). Formerly the Duma parliament had held its sessions in the palace, but there was no food in the building, and the city was besieged by warring factions, so for 5 days the men who were attempting to shape Russia's destiny lived in their closely guarded stronghold—and starved.

The situation finally became known to an outside friend who informed Peter Eliseef, proprietor of Petrograd's fanciest grocery store. Eliseef at once loaded a droshky with his largest containers of caviar—40 pounds of it—and sped to the relief of the hungry statesmen. With great difficulty the grocer persuaded the soldiers to pass him through the gates of the palace. "The government,' shouted Eliseef, "must eat!"

In he went, and until conditions became more normal, the members of the Provisional Government ate nothing but caviar, caviar morning, noon, and night. Most of them dined at my house later on, and not one of them would touch caviar in any form. They said their 7-day caviar diet would be enough, thank you, for years to come.

HERRING (SELODKA)

In our protocol of the zakooska table, herring occupies a place of first importance. Our Russian word for herring is *selodka*. When we serve only one appetizer with our before-dinner vodka, herring is the one we serve.

Five days in the week, the Russian who takes a glass or two of vodka before the main meal will bite the vodka down, as we say, with a snack of herring. The herring will be served merely with oil and vinegar, or with no dressing at all.

On the other two days of the week a somewhat fancier herring treat will appear. If not, the plain herring will be attended by a few slices of sausage or Swiss cheese in small separate dishes. Even in summer the herring is always there on the zakooska table for the vodka drinkers, but with a seasonal addition of sliced fresh cucumbers or radishes served separately in sour cream.

At good delicatessen stores in this country you can usually buy fillets of Matjes herring from Iceland or Scotland. Some fish stores stock them, too, and I recommend them especially since they come already boned and skinned. So does the Scandinavian type of Matjes herring, but this is sweeter and spicier, darker in color, reddish brown instead of silvery pink. While the Scandinavian herring doesn't taste quite as good with vodka, it does provide an excellent zakooska item.

The Schmaltz herring can generally be found here, and its flavor is right with vodka, but Schmaltz herrings are sold whole, which makes them rather troublesome to prepare. They should be soaked 3 hours in water, another 3 hours in milk or cold tea. Then split the fish open, remove the bones, take off the skin, and divide the herring lengthwise into 2 fillets.

A herring fillet always means half a herring, divided the long way.

American grocery stores and delicatessens now stock many varieties of ready-dressed herrings in glass jars or tins. As a rule these are too vinegary or too sweet to be perfectly adapted for zakooska purposes, yet they can be counted upon as an emergency substitute, for you can purchase them almost everywhere and they do present the work-saving convenience of being neatly cut up, all set to go straight from the container to the table.

It is much more satisfactory, however, to fix your own *selodka* fillets if you possibly can do so.

How to Prepare Herring Fillets

To adhere to correct Russian practice at your zakooska spread, serve the herring fillets in a long narrow dish. Have the fillets laid side by side, skin side up. Slice across them diagonally at 1-inch intervals, so that the herring is cut in 1-inch pieces. Real Russian herring-lovers lay the cut-off heads and tails on the serving dish, but I imagine you will be wise to dispense with that little touch of naturalism.

When your herring fillets are arranged and sliced, dress them with any of the following sauces or garnishes:

Herring with Oil and Vinegar Dressing

1 tbsp. olive (or salad) oil   2 prepared herring fillets
½ tbsp. vinegar

51

Mix the oil and vinegar. Pour over the herring and let stand 15 minutes.

If you like, you can add 1 tablespoon of finely chopped white onion after the herring is dressed with oil and vinegar. Or you can sprinkle the dressed herring with 1 tablespoon of any one of the following: minced parsley, chopped fresh dill, minced scallions, or chopped chives.

Herring with Mustard Sauce

2 tbsp. olive oil	1 tsp. water
1 tbsp. prepared mustard	2 prepared herring fillets
1 tsp. sugar	

Stir the oil into the mustard, adding drop by drop, as for mayonnaise. Add the sugar and water. Let stand 15 minutes before using. Pour on the herring and serve.

Herring with Roe Sauce

1 herring milt (soft white roe)	Lemon juice
2 tbsp. sour cream	2 prepared herring fillets
1 finely sliced onion	

Press the roe through a sieve. Mix with the sour cream. Add the onion and a squeeze of lemon juice. Cover the herring with this sauce and chill for ½ hour.

Herring with Vegetable Garnish

2 prepared herring fillets	2 cold cooked beets, sliced
1 cold cooked potato, sliced	1 dill pickle, sliced

Surround the herring fillets with slices of potato, beet, and dill pickle. Dress the herring with oil and vinegar or with mustard sauce (see preceding recipes). Use no dressing on the vegetables and pickle.

Herring Salad with Beets

2 prepared herring fillets	1 chopped dill pickle
1 cup diced beets	1 cup sour cream
1 cup chopped apple	1 tsp. vinegar
1 tsp. minced onion	1 tbsp. salad oil
1 tsp. minced dill (optional)	Pepper

Dice the herring fillets. Mix with all the other ingredients. Chill for 1 hour.

Chopped Herring with Eggs

1 slice white bread	2 hard-cooked eggs
2 tbsp. water	1 apple, grated
1 tsp. vinegar	1 small onion, grated
2 prepared herring fillets	1 tbsp. heavy sour cream

Remove the crust and soak the bread in the water and vinegar. Squeeze the bread dry. Cut up the herring and eggs and put them twice through a meat grinder. Add the bread, apple, onion, and sour cream. Mix thoroughly. Arrange in a mound. Chill.

ZAKOOSKA SPECIALTIES

From the innumerable varieties of cold zakooskas served in different parts of Russia, I am here introducing 10 char-

53

acteristic recipes that have become nation-wide favorites. The Pickled Mushrooms and the Salad Olivier are regarded by Russians as extra-special delights.

Pickled Mushrooms

1 lb. small mushrooms	5 peppercorns
1 cup wine or cider vinegar	½ bay leaf
2 cloves	1 tbsp. salt
½ cup water	1 tbsp. vegetable oil

When you find small mushrooms in the market, put them up in Mason jars, covering them with a spoonful of vegetable oil. They will keep for months in your refrigerator.

Wash the mushrooms before pickling. Cut off the stems close to the cap. Drop caps into boiling water and cook 20 minutes. Drain 1 hour in a sieve, then pack in a sterilized jar. Combine water, vinegar, cloves, bay leaf, peppercorns, and salt. Simmer 15 minutes. Strain, cool, and add to mushrooms. Pour the vegetable oil on top. Cover tightly and place in the refrigerator. Keep 1 week before serving.

Salad Olivier

1 cooked breast of chicken	3 tbsp. mayonnaise
3 boiled potatoes, medium	1 tomato, sliced
2 small dill pickles	6 large olives
1 tsp. Worcestershire sauce	2 hard-cooked eggs cut in wedges

Of all zakooska salads, this is the most renowned. It was invented and served for the first time at the Winter Palace to Tsar Nicholas II by his French chef, Monsieur Olivier. Unlike his royal employer, the chef escaped from Russia after the Revolution and prospered as the proprietor of a Berlin restaurant. Make his famous salad as follows:

The breast of a cold boiled chicken is preferable, though cold roast chicken can be used. Trim off all skin and fat. Slice the meat evenly in very thin strips. Slice the potatoes in ¼-inch slices. The dill pickles must be peeled and sliced thin. Mix the Worcestershire sauce into the mayonnaise, then combine very carefully with the chicken, the potato, and the dill pickle, lifting with a fork to avoid breaking. Place the salad in a zakooska dish. Decorate with 6 egg wedges, 6 slices of tomato, and 6 olives.

This salad can also be made with cold duck.

Kilki on Egg Slices

Cut rounds of pumpernickel bread the size of a slice of hard-cooked egg. Spread the bread with unsalted butter and cover each round with a cross-wise slice of hard-cooked egg.

Now get your kilki ready.

Kilki are Norwegian anchovies—small spicy fish that come in wooden tubs and can be bought at Scandinavian delicatessen stores. They must be rinsed in cold water, split open and cleaned, and the bones removed. This is a task, you may think, but we Russians believe the result is worth the work.

Curl up one of your kilki on top of each slice of egg. They look very attractive and always get snapped up very soon, so that you never have any left over. You can use anchovies if you don't care to take the trouble of fixing the kilki, but anchovies won't taste the same. And they won't be truly Russian.

Eggplant Caviar

This is a favorite summer zakooska, made entirely with vegetable ingredients. It gets its name from the fact that we think it looks like caviar.

1 large eggplant	2 tsp. lemon juice
2 small onions, minced	2 tsp. salt
4 tbsp. olive oil or vegetable oil	Pepper
4 tbsp. tomato purée	

Drop the whole eggplant into a pot of boiling water. Cook about 25 minutes. Take out and let cool sufficiently to handle. Cut off the stem end; remove the skin; chop the eggplant *very* fine. Simmer the onion 10 minutes in a little of the oil, without browning. Add the chopped eggplant, the tomato purée, and 1 tablespoon of oil. Cook slowly for 15 minutes over gentle heat, uncovered, stirring from time to time. Continue cooking, gradually adding oil till quite thick. The cooking time depends on the eggplant, some being drier than others. About 1 hour should give the required consistency. Now add the lemon juice, salt, and a dash of freshly ground pepper.

For the oil, use at least 1 tablespoon olive oil to 3 of vegetable oil if possible. Olive oil improves the flavor.

Serve well chilled.

Chopped Chicken Livers

1 lb. chicken livers	2 hard-cooked eggs
2 tbsp. butter (or substitute)	1 tbsp. chicken fat
2 small onions, minced	Salt
4 chicken gizzards	Pepper

Sauté the livers quickly in hot butter, taking care not to brown them too much. Remove the livers and sauté the minced onion in the same pan. Simmer the gizzards in just enough water to cover them, till tender—about 1 hour. Trim off the hard parts of the gizzards, cut them into small pieces. Cut up the livers and eggs, then put gizzards, liver, and eggs through a meat grinder twice, or if the mass is not finely enough ground, put it through the grinder a third time. Mix in the chicken fat, previously melted, add salt and pepper sparingly. Shape the liver mixture into a neat mound and serve at room temperature.

Pickled Mackerel

4 fillets fresh mackerel	2 sliced onions
½ cup milk	1 small can tomato purée
2 tbsp. flour	1 tsp. sugar
1 tsp. marjoram	1 tsp. salt
2 tbsp. vegetable oil	1 tbsp. vinegar

Choose medium-sized fish and have the fishman fillet them for you. Wash and dry the fillets, cut them across in 2-inch pieces. Dip them in milk, then in flour and marjoram, and brown lightly in hot oil. Drain the pieces well on paper and lay them neatly in the dish you will use to serve them in. Simmer the onions in the oil you used for the fish, add the tomato purée, sugar, salt, and vinegar. Cook for 15 minutes. Pour the sauce over the fish, then set aside to cool for several hours before serving. Do not serve too cold—the fish loses its flavor from overchilling.

Smelts can also be prepared this way, but the fish must be left whole.

Salmon Vinaigrette

½ lb. smoked salmon slices
2 cold potatoes, diced
1 tbsp. capers
1 tbsp. minced onion
¼ cup sliced pitted olives

1 tbsp. minced scallions
1 tbsp. vinegar
2 tbsp. salad oil
1 tsp. prepared mustard
Pepper

Cut the smoked salmon into strips or small squares. The salad will present a better appearance if the slices are not cut too thin in the store when you buy them. The onion must be minced very fine, the scallions not quite so fine. Prettier that way. Mix the salmon, potatoes, capers, onion, olives, and scallions very carefully with a fork. Arrange in a dish and pour over the dressing, previously mixed. Don't stir it into the salad. It will run down anyway, and if you don't mix it in the potatoes and salmon will stay in shape better. Chill before serving.

Pashtet of Liver (Baked Liver Loaf)

1 carrot
2 small onions
2 sprigs celery leaves
1 sprig parsley
1 bay leaf
1 lb calves' liver
½ lb. pork liver

2 slices bacon
2 slices white bread
Salt
Pepper
½ tsp. nutmeg
2 small eggs

Put the vegetables and bay leaf in a pot with 3 cups of water and cook for ½ an hour. Add the liver and bacon, bring to a boil, then diminish heat and simmer gently for 20 minutes. Take out the liver, bacon, and carrot. Discard the other vegetables and the bay leaf. Cut up the liver, carrot, and bacon and put through the meat grinder twice. Cut the crusts from the bread slices, soak in a little water, squeeze dry, and add to the liver mixture. Mix in salt and pepper to taste, the nutmeg, and the eggs—whole. Mix very thoroughly, gradually adding ½ cup of the stock in which the liver was cooked. Pack the mixture in a well-greased loaf-shaped pan and bake in a moderate oven for 40 minutes. Serve cold, cut in slices.

Calves' Brains in Mayonnaise

1 pair calves' brains	1 sprig celery leaves
1 tsp. salt	2 tbsp. mayonnaise
1 tbsp. vinegar	1 tbsp. chopped chives

Soak the brains for 1 hour in cold salted water to cover. Remove all membranes and cover with boiling water. Add the vinegar and celery leaves, bring to a rapid boil, then simmer slowly for 20 minutes. Remove the brains, drain, and dry on a towel. When quite cold cut in thin slices and cover with the mayonnaise to which the chives have been added.

Veal and Cucumber Salad

½ cup mayonnaise	1 cup diced cucumber
½ cup sour cream	½ cup diced dill pickle
1 tsp. Worcestershire sauce	1 cup diced tart apple
2 cups cold diced veal	2 cups diced cold potato

Mix the mayonnaise with the sour cream and Worcestershire sauce. Add all other ingredients and toss carefully. Serve very cold.

HOT ZAKOOSKAS

Hot zakooskas make or break the reputation of a Russian cook. They're what the French call *le clou,* "the nail," in the zakooska menu. In American vernacular we probably would say the hot zakooska is the peg on which the party hangs.

Russians always use butter in the preparation of a hot zakooska, but this is not imperative, although a small amount of butter added to a good butter-substitute will improve the flavor of your zakooska dish.

Frankfurters in Tomato Sauce

8 frankfurters	½ tbsp. sugar
2 cups cream sauce	Pepper
3 tbsp. tomato purée	

Cook the frankfurters, drain them, take off the skin, and cut the franks in 1-inch pieces. Cut them across, not lengthwise. Mix the tomato purée into the prepared cream sauce and cook a few minutes till the tomato is well incorporated. Add the sugar and pepper to taste. Put the sausages into the sauce. Let stand on low heat till needed. Serve in a casserole.

Mushrooms in Sour Cream

1 lb. mushrooms	½ tsp. lemon juice
3 tbsp. butter (or substitute)	Salt
1½ tbsp. flour	Pepper
1 cup sour cream	

Peel the mushrooms and slice them not too thin. Sauté 10 minutes in butter. Sprinkle with flour and continue cooking another 5 minutes, stirring carefully with a wooden spoon. Add the sour cream and the lemon juice. Keep the heat low and cook for 15 minutes more. If the sauce seems too thin, sprinkle in a little flour. If it seems too thick, add a little water. Some mushrooms are drier than others, which may change the consistency of the sauce, so you must act accordingly to keep the sauce like thick cream. Season lightly with salt and pepper.

These mushrooms can also be served au gratin—in a fireproof dish sprinkled with grated cheese on top and lightly browned in the oven.

Dragomir Forshmak

2 small onions, chopped	2 drops Tabasco Sauce
3 tbsp. butter (or substitute)	2 cooked potatoes
1 tbsp. flour	2 cups ham cut in thin strips
½ cup consommé	2 small dill pickles
½ cup sour cream	Grated cheese
1 tsp. Worcestershire Sauce	

Simmer the onion in butter till soft (do not brown). Add the flour. Cook 5 minutes, then add the consommé, sour cream, Worcestershire sauce, and Tabasco. Continue cooking 10 minutes over low heat. Slice the potatoes very thin and sauté them 5 minutes in butter.

Trim the fat from thin slices of ham and cut the ham in strips about 2 inches long, ½ inch wide. Peel the pickles and slice them very thin. Mix all the ingredients with the onion sauce, using a fork to mix. Do not break the potatoes. Place all together in shallow ovenproof dish. Cover with grated cheese. Place in hot oven till nicely browned.

Chicken Livers in Madeira Wine

1 lb. chicken livers	1 cup Madeira wine
3 tbsp. butter	1 tsp. Worcestershire sauce
1½ tbsp. flour	Salt

Have the livers carefully prepared with all ends of skin trimmed away. Wipe dry with a cloth. Sprinkle lightly with flour and sauté 5 minutes in hot butter. Lift out the livers. Sauté 1 tablespoon flour 10 minutes in the same pan. Add the Madeira and let come once to a boil. Add the Worcestershire. Salt to taste. Serve at once.

YOUR ZAKOOSKA PARTY

A zakooska party can be as simple or as elaborate as you care to make it. The first point to decide is whether you're going to serve zakooskas and then serve a regular dinner after them, or if you are going to make a complete meal of the zakooskas, as a sort of Russian-American buffet supper. The buffet-supper idea has much to be said for it nowadays, since zakooskas followed by a dinner would be a lot more food than most people would want to eat.

I advise you to give your guests fair warning if you intend to start them off with vodka and zakooskas, and then feed them another meal. One evening I had a small dinner party in New York for an English friend of mine who loves zakooskas. The friend was H. G. Wells, and with the other guests he lingered long around the zakooska table in my living room. Eventually I suggested that we move on to the dining room and eat.

"Eat?" howled H. G. "Eat dinner on top of this? I thought

this was all we were going to get. I *can't* eat dinner now!"

He did, though. It was hard work, but he did it.

When you serve zakooskas before a dinner, 5 cold snacks and 1 hot dish are plenty. In my opinion the dinner should start with a clear soup, then should include nothing more than a very simple meat course, and a dessert.

For a zakooska buffet supper you can extend the variety of cold dishes and have 2 hot dishes of a substantial kind. In Russia today, official Soviet entertaining often follows this buffet-supper version of the zakooska hour, and it is extremely popular with foreign diplomatic and military guests.

The ingenious style of setting the table is worth copying. The table should be long. Divide the surface into 3 general areas. Devote one end of the table to the zakooska snacks, the plates, forks and napkins, the trays holding the carafes of vodka and the small vodka glasses.

Reserve the center of the table for the more spectacular dishes, the hot zakooskas in casseroles, pickles and relishes, perhaps a cold roast turkey or a whole baked ham, and more plates and forks.

At the other end of the table put the desserts, cakes and candies, fruit and sweet drinks. Madeira and port and liqueur cordials, again with appropriate china and glass and silver.

Whatever kind of zakooska party you plan to have, I advise you to start getting ready for it well ahead of time. You can save yourself a great deal of work and trouble by making friends with the boss of a good delicatessen store—either Russian or Jewish or Scandinavian. The delicatessen man can teach you a lot about the different varieties of smoked fish and salted fish, and about the salads and sausages and breads. By means of carefully selected delicatessen purchasing, you can cut down your own kitchen-work to one or two special dishes.

Menus for Your Zakooska Party.—Each of these 4 combinations of zakooskas is suitable to be served at a zakooska hour which will be followed by a regular dinner.

But any one of these menus may also be used as the basis for a zakooska buffet supper. You can do so by increasing the size of the hot zakooska dish, and by adding 1 or 2 extra salads from one of my other zakooska menus. Or you can add a second hot zakooska. Or you can include a standard buffet-supper specialty such as baked ham, cold roast turkey, or cold roast beef, with any popular salad. Of course you will want cake or dessert of some kind, and coffee.

There is one other typically Russian delicacy that you will always find welcome at a buffet supper. This is a good big stack of warm *piroshki*—Russian pastry rolls stuffed with meat. Everyone likes them so much they vanish very rapidly. You will find the recipe for *piroshki* in Chapter IV.

Now here are my 4 sample menus for a zakooska hour:

First Zakooska Menu

1. Shrimp or lobster in mayonnaise (add no vegetables)
2. Smoked tongue or reindeer meat in thin slices
3. Small globe artichokes, pickled (as sold in glass jars)
4. Caviar
5. Sliced fresh cucumbers or radishes in sour cream
6. Hot chicken livers in Madeira-wine sauce

Second Zakooska Menu

1. Herring fillets with mustard sauce
2. Pickled mushrooms
3. Veal-and-cucumber salad

4. Slices of smoked sturgeon
5. Liver loaf
6. Hot sliced sausages in tomato sauce

Third Zakooska Menu

1. Eggplant caviar
2. Brains in mayonnaise
3. Herring-and-beet salad
4. Slices of Swiss cheese
5. Kilki on egg slices
6. Hot Dragomir Forshmak

Fourth Zakooska Menu

1. Salad Olivier
2. Pickled mackerel or pickled smelts
3. Sliced salami or other sausage
4. Chopped chicken livers
5. Slices of smoked salmon
6. Hot mushrooms in sour-cream sauce

CHAPTER 3

SOUPS

Statisticians and students of social economy or social justice have a way of presenting the world with figures of per-capita wealth, thereby proving the living standard of this country or that. In my opinion the average housewife, without the aid of per-capita finance figures, is just as good a judge of living standards, once she knows what constitutes a nation's basic meal. I believe you can judge Russia's living standard pretty accurately from our Russian soups.

"Dinner" and "soup" are synonymous words for millions of Russians. Soup *is* dinner. Soup is the basic meal of any characteristic Russian family. It always has been, and it is today. If the family happens to be in fairly prosperous circumstances, the soup will have a piece of meat in it. Otherwise it will just be vegetable soup with the addition, perhaps, of a small piece of pork fat. Very obviously Russia is a *poor* country.

Some day when a history of the Russian Revolution is written in factual truth untinged by the prejudice of political theories and isms, it will become apparent that the meat served to Russian army recruits during the early years of the First World War was as responsible as anything else for the eventual fall of tsardom. Young peasant rookies from all over Russia began to have meat in their soup every day, instead of only 2 or 3 times a year, as they had in their own homes. The government provided meat soup for the soldiers. And the soldiers argued that if the Tsar and his government could afford to give them soup every day with meat in it, then surely the peasant families back home should be able to earn enough to have meat soup at least once a week, if wealth were more equally distributed.

The Soup Dinner.—A Russian-style soup dinner is a great time-saver for any housewife. In the Russian cuisine our meat soups take the place of meat stews, which we seldom serve.

A Russian soup simmers for hours without attention, and the baked grain *kasha* that goes with the soup needs no watching after it is in the oven. Come dinnertime, the meat is taken out of the soup, either to be sliced and put back in the soup when the tureen is brought to table, or to be served as a separate course accompanied by dill pickles.

The soup can always be prepared beforehand. Russians claim that borsch or *s'chee* made yesterday and reheated today tastes even better than when eaten the same day it is made. Borsch is beet soup; *s'chee* is cabbage soup.

In poor Russian homes the soup pot goes straight from the stove to the table, or the soup may be served at times in a large peasant bowl of lacquered wood. There are no individual soup plates. Everyone at the table takes turns dipping into the family soup. You dip in with your spoon, which is also made of lacquered wood. Under the spoon, while you are slowly conveying it from the family soup bowl to your mouth, you carefully hold a thick slice of dark rye bread. It is considered extremely bad manners to spill a single drop of soup during the transit. This age-old custom of communal soup dipping is discouraged nowadays as being highly insanitary, yet it lingers in many families too poor to buy individual plates or bowls.

Cabbage soup, *s'chee,* rates first and foremost among the popular soups of Russia. It has several variations and is made either with fresh cabbage or with sauerkraut. During Lent dried mushrooms are used instead of meat. The chief features of the soup are the slow cooking and the diversity of the vegetables it has in it. When making *s'chee,* the cook is in fact at liberty to throw in whatever she has handy.

Our Russian folklore tells a classic story to illustrate the ingenuity that can be employed in contriving a good pot of *s'chee....* A discharged soldier is tramping the country roads, bumming a meal where he can. He knocks at the door of a neat little cottage that seems to him a likely prospect. But the old peasant woman who lives there says she hasn't a bite of food in the house By the door the soldier sees a hatchet and some wood for the stove. The soldier says, "All I need is that hatchet. I can make wonderful soup with nothing but a hatchet. Let me show you the magic trick."

Of course the old dame's curiosity is aroused. She permits the soldier to chop kindlings, to start a fire, to fill a pot with water and put the pot on to boil. The soldier drops the hatchet into the pot. As soon as the water starts to bubble, he tastes it. He smacks his lips, says the soup tastes fine already. All he needs now is a pinch of salt to make it perfect. Old woman donates salt. The soldier tastes his soup again. It will be done in a jiffy, but a few cabbage leaves, he admits, might improve the flavor slightly. The old woman gives him the cabbage leaves, then a carrot, an onion, and so forth. In the end the soup contains all the ingredients of a good hearty *s'chee.* Together the soldier and the old woman eat it up with gusto. When the soldier has departed on his vagabond way, the old woman tells her neighbors what a fine soup she has learned to make with nothing but a hatchet.

So in Russia the expression *soop iz topora,* which means "hatchet soup," has become a byword for any kind of improvised cooking when supplies are low. When my Russian friends want to compliment me on being a thrifty housewife, they call me a "hatchet-soup cook."

Next to *s'chee,* borsch rates high in Russian soup popularity. Cold borsch, either clear or with vegetables, is getting to be nearly as well liked here as in Russia. Consequently I am giving you, among my borsch recipes, a good quick-order borsch that I find specially suitable for the menu of a busy American housewife. This particular recipe is vastly simplified by the use of canned consommé and canned beets, and it tastes equally good hot or cold.

Russians are very fond of clear consommé or bouillon. We serve this in cups. Other Russian soups are always served in large deep soup plates, ladled out of an enormous soup tureen. Real Russian connoisseurs of good meat bouillon insist that 12 pounds of the finest beef are absolutely necessary to make a broth of the right strength for 6 people! I have omitted the recipe for this 12-pound bouillon. Its "extra" flavor is much too strong to suit most of us.

Instead, I give you our 3 classic Russian recipes for consommé. One we call White Consommé; another we call Yellow Consommé; the third we call Red Consommé. Each can be served as is, or with some simple garnish. These 3 consommés also supply the base for innumerable other soups. The excellent canned consommés and bouillons available in this country can be substituted in many cases for the homemade Russian consommés.

Black bread, the dark Russian pumpernickel, is always served with soup in Russia. But the more interesting pastries, the little *piroshki* and the big turnover pies called *pirogs* or *kulebiaka,* are also considered part of the soup course. And we sometimes have *grenki* with the soup. *Grenki* are pieces of French roll spread with cheese and toasted.

In the following section I have listed the various soup accompaniments. Recipes for *piroshki, pirogs, grenki, kulebiaka,* and baked grain *kasha* are in Chapter IV.

Russian cream soups and soups of the purée type are of French origin, not sufficiently representative of native Russian cooking to be included in a book of this kind. The same is true of our fruit soups, which Russians like very much, but which with one or two exceptions are identical with the fruit soups of Scandinavia or Germany. I give only one fruit-soup recipe, one that is more truly Russian than most.

On the other hand, cold soups are a distinctive feature of Russian eating. I have modified some of the cold-soup recipes to accommodate American ingredients, and in a number of instances have found the flavor improved. All of them can be made here just as well as in Russia.

WHAT TO SERVE WITH EACH KIND OF RUSSIAN SOUP

For most Russian soups you have a choice of one or more different accompaniments, but only one should be served. With any of them you also serve black bread.

With S'chee

1. *Piroshki* made with any of the *piroshki* fillings except cabbage, fish, or mushrooms
2. Any of the baked grains

With Borsch

1. *Vatroushki* with pot-cheese filling
2. *Piroshki* with any filling except cabbage or fish
3. Boiled potatoes
4. Any of the baked grains

With Consommé or Bouillon

1. *Piroshki* or *pirog* filled with braised cabbage, carrots, mushrooms, or meat
2. "Delicious" *piroshki* made with liver and Madeira wine
3. *Grenki*

With Mushroom Soup

1. *Piroshki* or *pirog* filled with mushrooms, carrots, onions, or scallions
2. "Delicious" *piroshki*—the Russian word for them is *privkoosniya*
3. *Grenki*

With Sorrel Soup

1. *Vatroushki*
2. Boiled potatoes
3. *Piroshki* or *pirog* filled with meat, carrots, onions, or scallions

With Chicken Bouillon

1. Old-fashioned Russian chicken pie
2. *Piroshki* with chicken filling

3. "Delicious" *piroshki*
4. *Piroshki* with carrot, onion, or scallion filling

With Rassolnik

1. *Piroshki* or *pirog* filled with meat, carrots, onions, or scallions.

With Fish Soups

1. *Piroshki* or *pirog* with fish filling, or with a filling of fish and cabbage combined
2. *Piroshki* with a filling of riced potato and onion

Golden Chicken Bouillon

4-lb. fowl	1 clove garlic, chopped
2 carrots, sliced	4 white peppercorns
1 onion, sliced	1 tsp. salt
1 leek, chopped	1½ tbsp. butter
2 sprigs parsley, chopped	7 cups water

Put the chicken and giblets, except liver, into a pot with cold water to cover. Heat slowly till it boils, then skim and cook very slowly. Brown the sliced carrots and onions slightly in hot butter, then add the chopped leek, garlic, and parsley. If you like you can also add 1 small stalk of celery, but be very careful not to put in too much celery as it spoils the taste of the bouillon. Add the vegetables, bay leaf, and peppercorns to the pot with the chicken. Simmer gently for 1½ hours, or longer if the chicken is still tough. Put the salt in half an hour before the soup is done. Strain the bouillon through several layers of cheesecloth, skim off the fat, and serve with a light sprinkle of minced parsley, or plain.

White Consommé

2 lb. lean beef	2-inch root of Russian parsley
1 lb. lean veal	2 sprigs fresh dill
8 cups cold water	1 large onion
2 stalks celery	6 white peppercorns
4 sprigs parsley	1½ tsp. salt
2 sprigs Russian parsley	

Wash the meat and dry it. Bring it to a boil with the water in a heavy pot with a close-fitting lid, then skim carefully. Repeat this boiling and skimming process 3 times. After the third skimming, add the vegetables cut in large pieces, add the peppercorns and salt. Cover the pot and simmer gently for 3 hours, preferably over an asbestos mat. Cook very slowly or your meat will be ragged. When the meat is tender, take it out and set it aside for later use. Now strain the soup through a fine sieve lined with a piece of scalded linen or 4 layers of cheesecloth. When the consommé is cold, skim off all the fat. There should be 6 to 7 cups of consommé.

Yellow Consommé

3 lb. beef	4 sprigs parsley
1 marrow bone	4 sprigs Russian parsley
1 large onion	2-inch piece of Russian parsley root
1 leek	2 sprigs fresh dill
2 carrots	1 bay leaf
3 stalks celery	12 peppercorns
½ cup celery leaves	1½ tsp. salt
1 small turnip	10 cups cold water
	2 tbsp. fat

Proceed with the meat as in the recipe for White Consommé. Cut the vegetables in large pieces. Simmer for 15 minutes in a little butter or butter substitute, or fat cut from the beef. Add them to the pot with the meat and put in the bay leaf, peppercorns, and salt. Cover and simmer slowly for 3 hours. Discard the bone. Set the meat aside. Strain the liquid through a fine sieve lined with a piece of scalded linen or 4 layers of cheesecloth. When the consommé is cold, skim off all the fat, then return 2 tablespoons of the fat to the consommé. There should be 6 to 8 cups of consommé.

Red Consommé

3 lb. beef	5 sprigs parsley
1 lb. cracked bones	3 sprigs fresh dill
2 large onions	½ cup celery leaves
2 carrots	1 bay leaf
2 stalks celery	12 peppercorns
1 small turnip	8 cups cold water
1 small parsnip	1½ tsp. salt

The beef should be lean with a layer of fat on one side. Heat a heavy pot. Lay the meat in it fat side down and sear well as for pot roast, turning till all sides are browned. Now lay the bones around the meat. Have the vegetables cut in large pieces and lay them on the bones. Add the spices and 4 tablespoons of water. Cover and cook 30 minutes over medium heat, stirring the bones and vegetables from time to time to prevent burning. Turn the meat also. Now add the remaining water. Bring to the boil. Skim. Bring again to the boil and skim again. After the second skimming, add the salt and simmer slowly 2 to 3 hours, until the meat is tender but not overcooked. Set the meat aside. Strain the liquid through a sieve lined with a piece of scalded linen or 4 layers of cheese-cloth. Cool and skim off all fat. There should be 6 cups of consommé.

Garnishes for White or Yellow Consommé

Either white or yellow consommé can be served with any of the garnishes listed below. With the exception of the first and second on the list, all these garnishes must be cooked before-hand in a little water, then drained and added to hot con-sommé. The amount of garnish given in each case is for 6 cups of consommé.

4 tbsp. minced parsley
2 tbsp. finely minced parsley and 2 tbsp. minced fresh dill
1 cup cooked vermicelli
1 cup cooked pearl barley
1½ cups cooked carrots, turnips, and celery knobs, mixed
1½ cups cooked green peas and string beans, mixed
1½ cups flowerets of cooked cauliflower

Garnishes for Red Consommé

The amounts given in the list below are for 6 cups of red consommé. Do not cook the consommé after adding the garnish.

3 tbsp. Madeira or sherry wine
1½ cups cooked asparagus tips
1½ cups cooked diced carrots and green peas, mixed
2 tbsp. finely minced fresh dill

Rice and Lemon Soup

6 cups white (or canned) consommé

3 tbsp. cooked rice

6 thin slices lemon

1 tbsp. minced parsley

Heat the consommé. Add the rice. Cook gently for 10 minutes, then add the lemon slices. Keep on the stove for 3 minutes, but do not let the soup boil after the lemon is added. Serve in cups. Sprinkle with parsley.

Russian Sorrel Soup

¾ lb. sorrel

½ lb. spinach

1 small onion

3 tbsp. butter (or substitute)

½ cup sour cream

1 tbsp. flour

6 cups white or yellow consommé

1 cup lean cooked ham, shredded

Sorrel is usually called sourgrass in American markets. I think sorrel sounds nicer, so this is Sorrel Soup.

Wash the greens thoroughly, shake them dry, and snip off the coarse stems. Take up a small bunch of the leaves, press them tightly together, and shred them very fine with a sharp knife. Do all the sorrel and spinach this way. Mince the onion and simmer 10 minutes in 2 tablespoons of hot butter. Do not brown. Add the shredded sorrel and spinach. Cook uncovered over low heat till quite soft. Add the sour cream, which should be at room temperature. Stir well. Warm the consommé and thicken it with the flour browned in 1 tablespoon of butter. Add slowly to the sorrel-spinach mixture. Keep the pot hot but not boiling. The ham should be cut in fine matchstick strips with all fat trimmed off. Add this to the soup 5 minutes before serving.

RUSSIAN CABBAGE SOUPS

S'chee

2 lb. fresh cabbage	1 large onion, sliced
2 carrots	6 or 8 cups white or yellow
2 stalks celery	(or canned) consommé
1 celery knob	1 tbsp. flour
3 tomatoes or 1 tbsp. tomato	½ tsp. salt
purée	1 tbsp. minced parsley
3 medium-sized potatoes	1 tbsp. minced dill
3 tbsp. butter (or bacon fat)	1 cup sour cream

Cut a firm white cabbage in quarters, discarding the hard core and any very hard ribs of the leaves. Pour boiling water over the cabbage to scald it; rinse off with cold water and set aside to drain well. Chop coarsely when drained. Cut the carrots and celery in 1-inch pieces; cube the celery knob; peel and seed the tomatoes; cut the potatoes in halves. Add these vegetables (not the onion or cabbage) to the consommé and boil up once, then simmer gently. In another pot simmer sliced onion for 5 minutes in 2 tablespoons of butter or bacon fat. Add the cabbage; cover the pot and braise gently for 20 minutes. Add the consommé to this, a couple of spoonfuls at a time, and continue cooking for 30 minutes. The cabbage should become pinkish in color. Brown the flour in the remaining tablespoon of butter or bacon fat, thicken the soup with this, then add the cabbage and salt. Boil up. Cook for 20 minutes.

If you are serving S'chee the Russian way, you must have a large tureen well heated. Slice the meat left from making the consommé. Put the meat in the tureen and sprinkle it with the minced parsley and dill. Pour in the soup and serve meat and soup together, scalding hot. The sour cream is passed at table. When the meat is to be served as a separate course, it is heated in the soup for 20 minutes before serving, then cut up at table.

Lazy S'chee

1 lb. soup meat	2 onions
10 cups cold water	2-lb. head of cabbage
1 clove garlic	3 large potatoes
1 bay leaf	3 carrots
1 tbsp. minced dill	1 small turnip
2 tbsp. minced parsley	3 stalks celery, with leaves
2 lb. lean beef	1½ tsp. salt
3 tomatoes or 1 tbsp.	1 tbsp. flour
tomato purée	1 tbsp. butter (or substitute)

Lay the soup meat in a heavy pot. Add the water, garlic, bay leaf, dill, and parsley. Boil up and continue cooking fast for 15 minutes. Add the lean beef, peeled tomatoes, and onions cut in halves. Bring to a boil, then simmer for 1 hour. Have the cabbage cut in eighths, the potatoes in halves, the celery, turnip, and carrots in large pieces. Put all these in the soup and cook gently for 1½ hours more. Half an hour before the soup is served, add the salt and the flour browned in butter. Skim off the excess fat. Serve a bowl of sour cream on the side.

Sauerkraut S'chee

2 or 3 dried mushrooms	1 tbsp. tomato purée
1½ lb. sauerkraut	1 tbsp. flour
¾ lb. uncooked ham	½ cup sour cream
2 onions minced	
6 cups consommé, white, yellow, or canned	

Soak the mushrooms 4 hours in 1 cup of water. Rinse the sauerkraut in cold water and drain well. Trim the fat from the ham and put the fat in a pan to melt down. When you have 2 tablespoons of hot liquid fat, add the minced onions and simmer for 5 minutes, then put in the sauerkraut and the ham cut in 1-inch cubes. After cooking 10 minutes, add a few tablespoons of the consommé, cover, and simmer for 30 minutes. Now slice the mushrooms and put them in the remaining consommé along with the tomato purée and mushroom water, and let simmer for 1 hour.

Mix the flour to a smooth paste with a little cold water. Add the cream and a little hot consommé. Pour this into the simmering mushrooms and consommé, boil up once, then add the cabbage and ham. Keep hot but do not boil again. Serve minced dill on the side in a separate dish.

Soldiers' S'chee

2 lb. beef flank	2 stalks celery
8 cups cold water	3 large potatoes
1 tbsp. minced dill	2 onions, minced
1 tbsp. minced parsley	2 tbsp. bacon fat
1 bay leaf	1½ lb. sauerkraut
2 carrots	1 tbsp. flour
1 turnip	Polish sausage or 4 frankfurters

Place the beef in a pot with the water, dill, parsley, and bay leaf. Bring to a boil. Let simmer 1 hour, then add the vegetables cut in large pieces. Continue simmering for 1 hour. Rinse the sauerkraut in cold water; drain well. Sauté the minced onion in the hot bacon fat for 5 minutes; add the sauerkraut to this; cover and braise 20 minutes, then add to the pot with the meat. Mix the flour to a smooth paste with a little cold water and add it to the soup. Now put in the sausage cut in 1-inch pieces. Boil up once, then simmer for 15 minutes. Skim off excess fat before serving the soup. Serve a bowl of sour cream on the side.

Rassolnik Soup

2 onions	4 sour gherkins
2 tbsp. butter (or substitute)	6 large olives
1 veal kidney	6 pickled mushrooms
1 tbsp. flour	12 pickled cherries
6 cups consommé, white or canned	Pepper
2 small dill pickles	

The pickled mushrooms and cherries make this soup very special, but it can be made without them, in which case you add 1 teaspoon vinegar instead. If you want to make pickled mushrooms and pickled cherries to have on hand, I have given recipes for them in Chapter 14. Now for the Rassolnik:

Mince the onions and simmer 10 minutes in hot butter or substitute, then add the kidneys sliced thin and free from fat and gristle. Sauté the kidneys 2 minutes, being careful not to brown them, then cover and cook very gently for 10 minutes. *Do not let them boil.* Now sprinkle in the flour, stirring all the time to prevent lumps. Bring to a boil for 1 minute; add the warm consommé; simmer very gently for 30 minutes. Peel the dill pickles and squeeze the juice from them into the soup. Remove the seeds and dice the flesh. Slice the gherkins thin; cut the olives in fine slivers. Add these to the soup with the dill pickle, mushrooms, and cherries. Heat thoroughly. Put in a dash of freshly ground pepper and serve.

Pass a dish of minced fresh dill. A sprinkle of dill really adds a great deal to this soup.

Rassolnik Soup with Pearl Barley

2 tbsp. pearl barley	2 tbsp. butter (or substitute)
6 cups consommé or chicken broth	1 veal kidney or 5 lamb kidneys
2 cups diced potatoes	1 tbsp. flour
2 small dill pickles	2 tbsp. minced parsley
1 large onion, minced	½ cup sour cream

This is a simpler version of the Rassolnik. It is extremely popular for family dinners. Either white, yellow, or canned consommé may be used, but the soup has a more delicate flavor when made with chicken broth. If the chicken broth is homemade and you have some cooked giblets, these can be minced and added to the soup.

Cook the pearl barley till soft in 1 cup of water and drain. Parboil the potatoes in the consommé, then add the pearl barley and keep hot. Sauté the minced onion in hot butter. Add the kidneys, thinly sliced and free from fat and gristle. Sauté for 2 minutes. Sprinkle in the flour; cook 2 or 3 minutes; cover and simmer gently for 10 minutes. Add a little consommé; boil up and keep hot. Peel the dill pickles, squeeze the juice into the consommé, remove seeds, and dice flesh.

Put the kidneys and dill pickles into the consommé. Boil up once, then simmer for 15 minutes.

Pour the sour cream into a soup tureen and thin it with some consommé, stirring well to avoid curdling. Pour in the rest of the soup. Serve sprinkled with minced parsley and freshly ground pepper.

Mushroom Soup with Wine and Sweetbreads

1 sweetbread	½ cup sweet cream
1 tbsp. flour	2 egg yolks
3 tbsp. butter	½ cup Madeira wine
5 cups yellow consommé	¼ cup sherry wine
½ lb. mushrooms	2 slices lemon

Soak the sweetbread ½ hour in cold water, then poach 15 minutes in a small amount of acidulated water. Make a paste of the flour and 1 tablespoon of the butter. Dissolve this with a little consommé, then add it to the rest of the consommé. Boil up once and keep warm. Rinse the sweetbread with cold water, dry, and slice thin. Slice the mushrooms and simmer till soft in 2 tablespoons of butter with the lemon slices for about 15 minutes. Discard the lemon. Beat the egg yolks slightly; add the cream and 4 tablespoons of consommé. Stir briskly while adding liquids. Warm up till hot. *Do not boil.* Mix with the consommé very carefully.

Lay the sliced sweetbread and mushroom slices in a hot soup tureen. Pour in the wines. Add the consommé and stir with fork. Serve at once.

For a super-luxurious touch, you can put in 6 small slices of truffle.

Mushroom Cream Soup

1 lb. fresh mushrooms	1 stalk celery, minced
4 tbsp. butter	4 scallions, minced
½ tsp. salt	1 tbsp. minced parsley
6 cups cold water	1 cup sour cream
4 small raw potatoes, thinly sliced	Pepper
2 onions, minced	

Slice the unpeeled caps of the mushrooms. Chop the good parts of the stems. Melt 3 tablespoons of the butter in a pot. Add the mushrooms and minced onion. Cook slowly for 20 minutes; add the salt, water, and sliced potatoes. Bring to a boil, then simmer from 20 to 30 minutes. The potato slices should be tender but remain whole. Now sauté the minced celery, scallions, and parsley in the remaining tablespoon of butter for 15 minutes. Cool slightly. Add the sour cream diluted with a little broth from the mushrooms. Boil up once and add to the pot. Just before serving, dust the soup with a very little pepper. Minced fresh dill usually accompanies this.

BORSCH

Of the 3 borsch recipes I am now going to give you, the Ukrainian borsch is the one that makes a complete soup meal —and a good hearty meal it is. The other 2 recipes are for more elegant varieties of borsch, particularly the one made with braised beets.

Excellent to serve cold in cups is the clear borsch made with canned consommé and the juice from plain canned beets—not pickled beets. On very hot summer days I like to pep it up with a small amount of diced fresh cucumber. From the view-

83

point of classic Russian cuisine, this cucumber addition of mine is not strictly according to Hoyle, but I find it always meets with approval at my table.

Now to begin with I'll give you the robust Ukrainian borsch that serves as a whole dinner:

Ukrainian Borsch

1½ lb. soup meat	3 large potatoes
1 lb. lean fresh pork	6 tomatoes or 1½ tbsp. tomato
½ lb. smoked pork	purée
10 cups cold water	1 tbsp. vinegar
1 bay leaf	1 tsp. sugar
6 peppercorns	1 clove garlic
1 bunch soup greens	5 frankfurters
8 medium-sized beets	1 tbsp. butter
1 cup shredded cabbage	1 tbsp. flour
2 large onions	½ cup cooked navy beans

Any kind of smoked pork is good for this soup, but the best flavor is obtained from "smoked backs." These are inexpensive and wonderfully flavorsome, but have almost no meat on them. They can't be served in the soup. If you use smoked backs, you'll need 1 lb. instead of ½ lb.

Put your soup meat and your 2 kinds of pork in a large heavy pot with the water. Bring to a boil. Skim, then add the bay leaf, peppercorns, garlic and soup greens. The soup greens should include parsley, Russian parsley, a carrot, celery, and a leek. Cover and simmer 1½ hours.

In the meantime cook 7 beets, unpeeled, till tender. Grate 1 raw beet and mix with 3 tablespoons of cold water. This is to use for coloring. When the 7 cooked beets are done, peel them and cut each beet in 8 pieces.

Take the meat out of the soup pot. Discard the smoked backs, if that is what you have used. If you have used a more meaty cut of smoked pork, take it out and put it aside.

Strain the soup; pour it back in the pot; add the beets, cabbage, and the onions and potatoes cut in quarters. Peel and seed the tomatoes before putting them in. Add the vinegar and sugar.

Now put in all the pieces of meat. Boil up. Let simmer for 1 hour. Add cooked navy beans. Cut the frankfurters in thick slices. Add them to the soup 20 minutes before serving.

When you're ready to eat, skim the excess fat from the soup. Thicken the soup with the flour browned in butter. Add the juice of the raw beet mixed with water. Salt if needed. Cut all the meat in thick slices and put back in the soup. Serve piping hot, with a bowl of sour cream on the side. Very fancy Russian gourmets add strips of cold roast duck to this borsch a few minutes before serving.

Borsch

6 cups consommé, white, yellow, or canned	1 tbsp. vinegar
	1 tbsp. flour
6 medium-sized beets	½ cup sour cream
2 tbsp. butter (or substitute)	

If you are using canned consommé, the best flavor is obtained by mixing 2 cans of consommé with 1 can of bouillon and 2 cups of water, cooked 30 minutes with 1 large cabbage leaf cut in big pieces, 1 onion, and 6 peppercorns. Strain and keep hot.

Peel the beets. Cut them in matchstick strips or thin slices, or shred on a coarse grater. Set aside 1 heaping tablespoon of the raw beets mixed with 3 tablespoons of water. This is for coloring. It will give the borsch that rich ruby glow! The fine red color is essential to a good borsch.

Heat the butter, or substitute, in a pot. Put the beets in. Stir for 3 minutes, then add the vinegar and continue cooking gently for 30 minutes. Sift in the flour, stirring well to avoid lumps. Let cook a few minutes, then add 3 or 4 tablespoons of warm consommé. Boil up once and add the remainder of the consommé when the beets are tender. The exact time depends on the age of the beets. Thin the sour cream with a little of the hot soup, then add the cream to the soup and serve immediately.

Quick Borsch

2 cans consommé
1 can bouillon
1 cup water
1 tsp. vinegar

½ tsp. Worcestershire sauce
½ cup juice from canned beets
½ cup sour cream

Mix the consommé with bouillon and water. Bring to a boil. Add the vinegar, Worcestershire sauce, and beet juice. Put in a pinch of sugar if the beet juice doesn't give the soup a slightly sweet taste. *But be very careful not to oversweeten!* Stir the sour cream smooth with 1 tablespoon of water, then add the consommé, a little at a time. Reheat but do not boil.

When you serve this borsch cold, do not add the sour cream before chilling. Instead, put the sour cream in just before serving. This borsch should always be sprinkled with finely chopped parsley when you serve it either hot or cold.

FISH SOUPS

Russians are crazy about fish soup, especially the clear fish broth we call *ooha*.

We prefer our fish soup to be made with fresh-water fish, and always with several different varieties of fish. Because fish from the sea is so much easier to get in most parts of America, I have specified sea fish instead of fresh-water fish in the following fish-soup recipes. But if fresh-water fish is handy for you to get, you can substitute it—except in the recipe that calls for sturgeon. For *that* one you *have* to use sturgeon.

Ooha (Fish Broth)

3 lbs. any white-fleshed fish	1 small carrot
7 cups cold water	1 bay leaf
2 onions	5 white peppercorns
3 stalks celery	1 tsp. salt
1 small root Russian parsley	Dash of nutmeg

Use at least 2 kinds of white-fleshed fish—haddock, cod, flounder, and butterfish are all suitable. A small eel adds considerably to the flavor. Have the fish trimmed but not skinned or boned. Put it in a pot with the water, sliced vegetables, and spices, being careful to use only a *very little* nutmeg. Bring to a boil, then simmer for 2 hours. Strain through a fine sieve lined with a piece of scalded linen. Reheat before serving. Minced fresh dill should accompany the Ooha. If you like you can add 2 tablespoons of dry white wine just before serving,

87

along with 2 chopped scallions sautéed in butter with a little minced parsley.

Sturgeon Champagne Soup

2 lb. white-fleshed fish
6 cups cold water
2 small onions
2 stalks celery
1 small root Russian parsley

½ bay leaf
4 white peppercorns
1 tsp. salt
1 lb. fresh sturgeon, sliced
1 cup dry champagne

Haddock or cod is good for the basic stock for this soup, which tastes much better if you add some other fish, heads and bones included. In a pot with the water place the fish, onions, celery, parsley root, bay leaf, peppercorns, and salt. Boil up. Skim, then cook for 1½ hours over medium heat. Skim twice during this time. When ready, strain through a fine sieve lined with a piece of scalded linen.

Have the fresh sturgeon washed, trimmed, and cut into 6 pieces. Wipe dry. Bring the broth to a boil; drop in the pieces of sturgeon; reduce the heat and simmer very, very gently from 20 to 25 minutes.

Heat the champagne in a separate pan. Add it to the soup just before serving.

When you take up the pieces of fish, be very careful not to break them. Put one piece of sturgeon into each well-heated plate. Pour the broth over the sturgeon. Serve immediately.

On a separate dish have a mound of minced young scallions or chives surrounded with wedges of seeded lemon. Serve this with the soup.

Russians use a fish knife and fork, as well as a spoon, to eat this soup. Personally I think it is far better to have the sturgeon in smaller pieces, with the skin and bones removed before serving.

Selianka

¾ lb. fillet of haddock or any other firm white-fleshed fish

4 thin slices smoked salmon

1 tbsp. tomato purée

1 tbsp. butter (or substitute)

1 tbsp. flour

6 cups fish broth

1 cup sweet cream

2 tbsp. minced sour gherkins

1 tbsp. minced capers

½ lb. cooked shelled shrimps

1 tbsp. minced parsley

Pepper

Poach the fillet of haddock 10 minutes in 1 cup water. Take up and drain well. Drop the slices of smoked salmon in the same water and boil up for 1 minute. Drain the salmon slices and cut them in 1-inch squares. Fry the tomato purée in the butter; add flour; add some fish broth. Boil up. Add cream very carefully to prevent curdling. Break up the filet in medium-sized pieces and put in the soup along with the salmon, the gherkins, capers, and shrimps. Heat but do not boil. Garnish with minced parsley and dust with freshly ground pepper.

COLD SOUPS

In Russia our cold soups of meat or fish, or meat-and-fish combinations, are generally made with a slightly fermented drink called *kvas*, a sort of beer brewed from either white bread or black bread. *Kvas* is also popular to drink with meals.

Since there isn't any *kvas* in this country, I make my cold

89

soups with wine and consommé and water, a small amount of sparkling water, and a little lemon juice or vinegar. Personally I like these cold soups better this way, for I do not like *kvas* at all, and neither do any Americans of my acquaintance who have tasted *kvas* in Russia. Fortunately we can get along very well without it in the following recipes:

Okroshka

2 cups cold diced meat
3 tbsp. minced scallions
1 tsp. minced tarragon
1 tbsp. minced dill (optional)
1 tsp. salt
1 tsp. sugar
Freshly ground pepper
3 tbsp. sour cream
1 tsp. prepared mustard
1 tbsp. lemon juice

1 tsp. vinegar
2 small cucumbers, diced
½ dill pickle, diced
2 cups consommé, white or canned
1½ cups dry white wine
½ cup ice water
1 cup sparkling water
1 cup crushed ice
2 hard-cooked eggs, chopped

The Russian word *okroshka* really means "minced."

Of all our cold soups, this one is served most frequently, for almost any kind of cold meat can be used—beef, veal, tongue, ham, chicken, or duck. Or you can mix 2 kinds of meat in it.

Begin by putting the minced scallion, tarragon, and dill in a large bowl. Add the salt, sugar, a dash of pepper, then mash well with a wooden spoon. Now add the mustard, sour cream, lemon juice, and vinegar. Stir thoroughly. Put in the diced meat, the cucumbers and pickle, peeled and diced, the consommé, the wine, and the ice water. Chill at least 4 hours.

Add the sparkling water, the crushed ice, and the hard-cooked eggs just before serving.

Botwinia

1 lb. sorrel (sourgrass)
½ lb. spinach
3 small cucumbers, diced
3 tbsp. minced scallions
1 tsp. prepared horse-radish or mustard
1 tbsp. lemon juice
1 tbsp. vinegar from pickled beets
1 tsp. salt

½ tsp. pepper
2 cups dry white wine
½ cup ice water
1 cup cold cooked salmon—or 6 slices smoked sturgeon
2 cups consommé, white or canned
¼ cup sparkling water
1 cup diced cold meat (optional)

Wash the sorrel and spinach till entirely free from sand. Cut off the stems. Cook the leaves without water for 12 minutes, then rub through a sieve. Set aside to cool. Peel and dice the cucumbers, which should have very small seeds. If the seeds are large, discard them. Mince the scallions very fine and add to the sorrel-spinach purée. Also add the horse-radish (or mustard), the lemon juice, vinegar from the pickled beets, salt, pepper, wine, and ice water.

Have the salmon flaked in large flakes, free from bones and skin. Or if you use smoked sturgeon, cut it in 1-inch squares. The fish must be well chilled. Add it to the soup together with the sparkling water, just before serving. Allow 1 ice cube per plate—6 cubes in all.

Use beef or veal if you want to add cold meat, and put it in at the same time with the fish.

91

Hlodnik

6 small beets	1 tsp. vinegar
1 lb. young beet tops	3 cups chicken broth or consommé
1 cup water	½ lb. shelled cooked shrimps
3 tbsp. minced scallions	3 small cucumbers
½ tbsp. minced dill	3 hard-cooked eggs
1 tsp. salt	1 cup diced cold veal, beef, or pork
1 cup sour cream	6 thin slices lemon
2 tbsp. lemon juice	Pepper

Hlodnik is actually a Polish soup, but it is served so widely in Russia that it belongs among our Russian recipes.

Peel the beets and cut them in eighths. Put them to cook with the beet tops in 1 cup of water. Cook 20 to 25 minutes, till tender. Reserve the water. Chop the beets and beet tops *very* fine. Crush the scallions and dill with a wooden spoon and add to the beets. Add the salt, sour cream, lemon juice, vinegar, water from the beets, and the chicken broth or consommé. Chill in refrigerator at least 4 hours.

Chop the shrimps. Peel and dice the cucumbers (discarding the seeds if large). Cut the eggs in quarters. For serving, mix all the ingredients except the eggs; add a little freshly ground pepper; pour into chilled plates with 1 tablespoon of crushed ice in each plate. Garnish each plate with 2 egg quarters and 1 slice of lemon. Serve at once.

Fruit Soup

4 cups hulled strawberries	4 cups cold water
1 cup sugar	1 cup claret wine
1 cup sour cream	

If the berries aren't sweet, you may need more sugar, but you will be wise to make this soup only with very ripe, sweet strawberries.

Rub the berries through a fine sieve. Add the sugar, then the sour cream. Mix well. Add the water and wine and heat very slowly over a low flame. Stir *with a wooden spoon* while heating. Do not boil. Serve warm or chilled, as you prefer. When served cold, this soup is garnished with a few whole berries. Thin wafers go with it.

Raspberries are used in the same way, either by themselves or mixed with strawberries or red currants.

CHAPTER 4

PIROGS AND PIROSHKI

The English have an old legend about the Devil, and it could easily be transplanted to Russia because it applies perfectly to one of our Russian culinary folkways.

The Devil was in Devonshire, says the legend. The Devonshire people were trying to drive him across the county line into Cornwall—westernmost English county where the island of England terminates at Land's End, on the coast of the Atlantic Ocean.

But the Devil didn't want to be driven into Cornwall. It was well known, he argued, that the Cornish housewives were famous for their pasties, and that they would put *anything* in a pasty—anything they could lay their hands on. If he went to Cornwall, declared the Devil, as sure as fate he'd be nabbed to fill some Cornish housewife's pasty, and that was no fitting finish for the Devil.

Our Russian housewives also have a reputation for putting anything they can lay their hands on into the envelope of dough we call a pirog. A pirog is the same shape as a Cornish pasty. In America you would call it a turnover pie. It is usually made large enough to serve 6 or more people.

When a Russian cook makes a meat pirog, she chops the meat very fine with two long, sharp, murderous-looking knives. Meat chopped with knives has more juices left in it than meat which has been put through a grinder. The sound of chopping

94

can nearly always be heard coming from any Russian kitchen, for Russian cooks love to chop things. In our more hurried modern life, however, ground meat or vegetables make perfectly good fillings for pirogs, and for the smaller piroshki.

When the pantry contains no meat at all—either fresh or left over from making broth—then you make your fillings for the pirog with cabbage or carrots, or a few mushrooms mixed with leftover grain from the pot of baked buckwheat. The same is true of the fillings for piroshki. And some people like the cabbage filling better than anything fancier. Strangely enough in my own home, where I cater to the taste of a New England husband, the urgent requests for pirog filled with cabbage come from him, though a fondness for cabbage pirog is supposed to be a straight 100-per-cent Russian partiality.

I am telling you this in case you hesitate to try any of the very characteristically Russian dishes on your own American husband. You never can guess what any husband will fall for! Nineteen years ago, when mine and I were first married, he told me that he detested sour cream. Yet he found no fault with the sauces I made; in fact, he said they were dandy. He didn't know they had sour cream in them. By the time he discovered it, he was self-sold on the subject of sour cream.

Cooks shouldn't give secrets away too soon.

Pirogs.—Pirogs are the pappies of the piroshki. A pirog is a large and well-filled envelope of piecrust, whereas piroshki are small individual bite-and-a-halfs of rolled-up piecrust and filling.

The filling for a pirog may be any one of a number of succulent combinations of meat, fish, cabbage, mushrooms, or carrots. Nothing sweet ever goes into a pirog. Piroshki sometimes have sweet fillings. (The word *piroshki* is *pirojok* in the

95

singular. One pirojok, two piroshki, seven dozen piroshki.)

The standard shape for all pirogs is rectangular. Actually a pirog is a big, flat, straight-sided folded-over pie. In size they start from about 12 inches by 8 inches, and the largest are about 18 by 10. Most Russians like the big ones best, with 2 or sometimes 3 different fillings. For example, one end will be stuffed with braised cabbage, while the other end is divided in half again, one corner having a carrot filling, the other corner a filling of rice and mushrooms.

When the hostess serves one of these pirogs she has to cut a slice and peek under the crust before she portions it out so that everybody gets a share of each kind of filling. Russians have never invented any other way of knowing which filling is where in the internal geography of the pirog. It seems as though some code of marks on the crust could be devised, but none ever has been.

Ordinarily a pirog is not a dinner dish. It is usually served at lunch with a cup of consommé. It takes less time to make a pirog than it does to make dozens of small piroshki, which have the same fillings a pirog has but are rolled up and served individually.

Americans have generally become more familiar with piroshki than with our larger Russian pirogs. That's because you seldom get a pirog at any restaurant in this country. You get piroshki quite often on a Russian menu here.

Apropos of the word pirog, there is a certain type of sailboat in the South Sea Islands which is called a "pirogue." I am no etymologist, but surely I think there must be some link between those two words. In a sketchy sort of way the shape of a pirog resembles a pirogue boat.

When the crust of a pirog is made of raised dough, the part where the folded-over edges of the dough are sealed together must be underneath. You have to do the folding on top, then turn the pirog over before you slide it onto the baking pan. The turning process bothers inexperienced pirog makers, but it really isn't difficult. The trick lies in rolling out the dough on a heavy cloth, well floured. Roll your dough out to form a rectangle about 24 inches by 16 inches. Cut away small squares from the corners. Lay the filling on the center of the dough. Don't put the filling any closer than 4 inches to the edge. All edges must be free of filling. Bring up the long sides first and pinch them together at the center of the pirog, then smooth the pinch marks out of the dough. Now bring the short sides up and pinch their edges together, taking care that the dough is well sealed.

Have a cookie sheet lightly greased and floured. Lay it on top of the pirog, then by gently lifting the cloth on which the pirog has been made, you can ease the pirog over onto the cookie sheet, upside down, so that the folded edges of the pirog dough will be on the bottom. Better get someone to help you the first time you tackle this. Later you'll do it alone and think nothing of it. When you have your pirog safe on the cookie sheet, pat and coax it into a nice neat rectangular shape. Cut two slits in the top and brush the top over with the yolk of an egg slightly beaten and diluted with a little cold water. All this is for making a pirog of raised dough.

For making a pirog of short pastry, the method is somewhat different. The shortened dough is more fragile, so you don't turn this kind of pirog over.

Roll the dough on a well-floured board, then lay the filling on it just as you did for the raised-dough pirog. Pinch the pastry together in a neat ridge along the center of the pirog, and along the corners diagonally. Cut slits; brush with egg yolk. Lift up the pirog with the aid of 2 pancake turners or broad spatulas. Ease the pirog tenderly onto the cookie sheet. Here again practice and taking your time about it will eventually give you dexterity.

You can also make a pirog in the shape of a slightly flattened jelly roll. Lots of pirogs are made that way, but mostly by commercial bakers, not in private Russian homes. The sealed part of the pastry should be underneath, whatever kind of pastry you use for this shape.

Then there's the *kulebiaka*, still another kind of pirog, made like a jelly roll. A *kulebiaka* has a very short crust. The filling is either of fish or a combination of cabbage and chopped eggs.

For serving, a rectangular pirog should be cut through the center lengthwise, then sliced across each half to divide into portions. The jelly-roll pirogs are sliced across, just as you slice a jelly roll.

However rich the pirog may be, Russians like to lift up the top crust of their piece on their plate and stick a dab of unsalted butter inside. When a pirog accompanies the soup, the slices of pirog should be served on small separate plates.

Here in America I find most people like a pirog best when it comes after the soup and constitutes the main course of the meal, with pickles or a vegetable salad.

The real Russian way to bring a pirog to the table is to cover a wooden chopping board with a clean napkin and place the pirog on the napkin.

Piroshki.—Piroshki should be about 3 inches or 3½ inches long, and about 2½ inches thick across the middle. The ends taper off, like finger rolls.

The easiest way to shape piroshki correctly is to pinch off a piece of dough or pastry about the size of an egg. Flatten

98

ıt, then roll it into an oval shape. Lay 1 or 1½ tablespoons of filling in the center of the pastry oval, leaving a border free from the filling all the way round.

If you use raised dough, bring up the edges of the pastry and smooth them together, then when the dough is well sealed, turn the piroshki over so that the unfolded side is on top. Plump them up with your hands and set them aside before brushing them over with egg yolk mixed with water.

When you make them with another kind of dough, pinch the pastry together in a neat ridge along the center of the piroshki. By cutting the dough in rounds of generous size, you can also make piroshki circular or crescent-shaped. The classical shape, however, is the long tapering finger.

Make your piroshki smaller and use a rich pastry when you intend to serve them as hors d'œuvres. Make plenty of them because they always vanish quicker than you expect.

Raised Dough for Piroshki or Pirogs

1 yeast cake	2 tsp. sugar
1 cup lukewarm milk	3 large or 4 small eggs
4½ to 5 cups sifted flour	½ cup butter, melted
1 tsp. salt	1 extra egg yolk

Crumble the yeast cake and dissolve it in the lukewarm milk. Stir in 1 cup of flour. Let rise 1 hour in a warm place. Then add the salt, sugar, 3 eggs slightly beaten, the butter melted but only lukewarm—since it will prevent the dough from rising if the butter is too hot—and the rest of the flour. The exact quantity of flour depends on the kind of flour you use. Mix well and knead energetically, as for bread dough. Form the dough in a large ball; place it in a lightly greased

99

bowl; cover with a towel and set away to rise in a warm place where there's no draft. Do not put it in a *hot* place. This dries the outside of the dough and prevents it from rising. It will take from 3 to 4 hours to rise, by which time it should be springy. You must watch the dough carefully. Only experience will teach you the exact moment when it has risen enough and not too much.

When it is ready, pinch off small egg-sized pieces if you are making piroshki. Flatten them and roll each piece to an oval shape about ¼ inch thick. Lay 1 tablespoon of filling along the center of the oval. Carefully close the edges; turn the roll over and plump it slightly so it is broader at the middle, with tapering ends. Let the piroshki rise for 15 minutes. Brush them over with egg yolk diluted with water. Set them on a cookie sheet of heavy metal, lightly greased and floured. Bake 15 minutes in a hot oven (400°), then lower the heat a little and bake for 20 minutes more.

Piroshki made with this dough can also be fried in deep fat like doughnuts. In this case the piroshki usually are made round in shape, and of course you don't brush them with egg yolk.

Another Raised Dough

1 yeast cake	1 tsp. salt
1 cup lukewarm milk	⅓ cup butter, melted
2 tbsp. sugar	1 egg, beaten
4 cups sifted flour	2 egg yolks

Crumble the yeast in the lukewarm milk. Stir till smooth. Add 1 teaspoon of sugar and allow to stand 10 minutes. Sift the flour and salt into a large bowl; make a well in the center of the flour and pour the yeast mixture in. Mix lightly. Have the melted butter lukewarm and combine it with the remaining sugar, the beaten egg, and the egg yolks. Stir this into the flour and yeast mixture and beat hard for 15 minutes. The dough should be smooth and elastic. Put in a warm place, covered with a towel, and allow to rise from 3½ to 4 hours. Form into piroshki as in the previous recipe. Bake 20 to 30 minutes in moderate oven (375°).

Short Pastry

2 cups sifted flour

½ tsp. salt

½ cup butter

1 tbsp. rum

½ cup ice water (approximately)

Sift flour and salt together; work in the butter, which should be very cold, using the finger tips or a pastry blender till the flour resembles coarse meal. Mix the rum with a little less than the ½ cup of water and mix with the flour. The dough should be rather stiff, but this will depend somewhat on the quality of flour used. It may require the full ½ cup of water. Roll out to ¼-inch thickness. Proceed with filling as in previous recipes. Brush over with egg yolk diluted with water. Piroshki made with this dough must be baked on a greased cookie sheet, 15 minutes in a hot oven (400°). A pirog of the same dough will require 25 to 30 minutes' baking, the heat being lowered a little after 12 minutes.

Sour-Cream Pastry for Vatroushki or Piroshki

3½ cups sifted flour

1 tsp. baking powder

1 tsp. salt

½ cup butter

2 eggs

1 cup thick sour cream

101

Sift flour with baking powder and salt. Work in the butter with the finger tips or a pastry blender. Beat the eggs very slightly; mix with the sour cream; then add to the flour and stir till dough is thoroughly mixed. It should be quite smooth but not too stiff to handle. Roll out to less than ¼-inch thickness. Brush over with diluted egg yolk. Bake on greased and floured cookie sheet. For piroshki, 15 minutes in moderate oven (375°). For a pirog, 25 minutes.

Puff Pastry

3 cups sifted flour	½ tsp. salt
½ cup plus 1 tbsp. butter	1 tsp. lemon juice
½ cup plus 1 tbsp. lard	⅔ cup water (approximately)

This recipe is for so-called "rough" puff pastry, which is much easier to make than the complicated puff pastry of classic formula.

Sift the flour onto a pastry board. Divide the butter and lard into pieces the size of a hazlenut. Without breaking them, lightly mix the pieces of butter and lard with the flour. Make a mound of the flour and shortening. Poke a hole in the center of the mound. Into this hole put the salt and the lemon juice mixed with 1½ tablespoons of water. Combine lightly, adding the remainder of the water till a stiff dough is formed. You may not need all the water. Sprinkle flour on the board and roll the dough gently into a long narrow strip. Fold the strip in 3. Turn it round so the folded edges are to the right and left of you, then roll again into a long narrow strip. Repeat the folding and rolling 3 times, then chill for 1 hour. Roll out again when chilled to ¼ inch in thickness, or thinner if possible. This will depend on how well you have chilled the dough. For piroshki, bake 12 minutes on a cookie sheet in a hot oven (425°). This dough is so delicate it is rather difficult to make a pirog with it unless you're an expert. A pirog will take 20 to 25 minutes' baking.

Quick Russian Pastry

2½ cups sifted flour	½ cup vegetable shortening
1½ tsp. baking powder	2 tbsp. butter
1 tsp. salt	1 egg
	Ice water

Sift the flour, baking powder, and salt together. Work in the vegetable shortening and the butter till the flour is like very coarse meal, with some bits of the shortening the size of small peas. Beat the egg slightly and add enough ice water to make ½ cup of fluid. Mix this quickly into the flour and shortening, adding a little more ice water if needed. The dough must be very soft and light. Sprinkle over with flour. Roll on a well-floured board. Bake 15 minutes on greased and floured cookie sheet in a medium oven (375°). Pirogs will take 30 minutes.

Meat Filling

1 large onion	Pepper
4 tbsp. butter	2 tbsp. minced parsley or dill
1 lb. ground beef	1 tbsp. flour
Salt	2 hard-cooked eggs

Chop the onion very fine; sauté 5 minutes in 1 tablespoon of the butter; then add the remainder of the butter, heat, and add the meat. Brown the meat. Salt and pepper to taste. Add

103

the minced parsley or dill, or a mixture of both if you like. Remove the meat from the pan. Brown the flour slightly in the pan. Add 2 tablespoons of water, boil up, and mix with the meat. Cool and add the chopped eggs.

On each piece of pastry for piroshki use 1 to 1½ tablespoons of filling. Any of the pastry recipes can be used, but the raised dough is the standard pastry for this.

Filling of Cooked Meat and Anchovies

3 cups ground cooked beef	¼ cup gravy or thickened
2 onions, chopped	consommé
3 tbsp. butter	1 tbsp. minced parsley
4 anchovy fillets, minced	2 hard-cooked eggs

Beef from which the consommé was made can be ground up for this filling. Sauté the chopped onion in the butter. Add the meat and cook for 5 minutes. Add the gravy or consommé, the anchovies, and the parsley. Cool and add chopped eggs.

Sour-cream pastry, short pastry, or the quick Russian pastry will be best for these piroshki.

Meat and Rice Filling

2 onions, chopped	½ cup cooked flaky rice
4 tbsp. butter	2 tbsp. minced parsley or dill
¾ lb. ground beef or 2½ cups	Salt
ground cooked beef	Pepper
2 tbsp. sour cream	2 hard-cooked eggs, chopped
½ tsp. Worcestershire sauce	

104

Sauté the chopped onion in butter. Add the ground beef and brown 5 to 7 minutes. Add the sour cream, Worcestershire sauce, rice, and parsley or dill. Salt and pepper to taste. Cool and add chopped eggs. Use short pastry or raised dough as preferred.

Add a little gravy or consommé if you increase the amount of rice in this recipe.

Egg and Mushroom Filling

1 lb. mushrooms	Pepper
1 large onion or 4 scallions chopped	Salt
1½ tbsp. butter	1 tbsp. minced parsley
1 cup finely crumbled stale bread	1 tbsp. minced dill
3 tbsp. sour cream	2 hard-cooked eggs

Cook the mushroom caps, unpeeled, in boiling water for 15 minutes. Drain well and chop very fine. If the stems are good they can also be used. Sauté the chopped onion or scallions in butter. Add the mushrooms, bread crumbs, and sour cream. Salt and pepper to taste. Cook gently for 10 minutes, till the mixture thickens. Cool and add the finely chopped eggs, parsley, and dill. Use sour-cream or puff pastry.

Mushroom Pirog

2 lbs. mushrooms	Salt
3 sprigs parsley	Pepper
5 tbsp. butter	1 tbsp. flour
6 scallions, chopped	5 hard-cooked eggs
¾ cup sour cream	

105

Use only the caps of the mushrooms. Peel them and cut them in thin slices. Simmer about 20 minutes in covered pan with the parsley in 4 tablespoons of the butter. Take out the parsley when the mushroom slices are soft. Put in the chopped scallion, the green part as well as the white. Add the sour cream. Salt and pepper to taste. Cook uncovered for 10 minutes. Rub the flour smooth with the remaining butter. Add this and boil up once. The mixture should be fairly thick. If it seems too thin, cook it a little longer, or add just a little more flour. Be careful with the flour, as the mixture must not be too sticky. Cool till barely lukewarm.

Use sour-cream or quick Russian pastry. Roll out the pastry for 2 piecrusts to fit a glass pie dish. Lay half the mushrooms on the lower piecrust. Cover with a layer of chopped egg and the remainder of the mushrooms. Place the top piecrust over the filling. Pinch the edges of the upper and lower piecrusts together. Cut 2 slits in the top. Decorate with pastry trimmings and chill the pie 1 hour. Brush the top with egg yolk diluted with water. Bake 15 minutes in a hot oven (425°). Lower the heat and bake for another 10 to 15 minutes.

"Delicious" Piroshki—Privkoosniya— with Calves' Liver and Madeira Wine

1 lb. sliced calves' liver	½ tsp. nutmeg
1 slice salt pork	1 tbsp. butter
1 large onion, sliced	3 tsp. Madeira wine
½ tbsp. pepper	1 tsp. rum
1 thick slice 2-day-old bread	

Have the liver at room temperature. Dry it thoroughly. Cut the salt pork in 1-inch squares—you should have 4 or 5 of these. Put the pork in a heavy pan with liver, sliced onion, and pepper. Cover and place over very strong heat. Cook till the liver is brown, stirring to prevent burning. Cut the liver up, then put it twice through a meat grinder. Trim the crusts from the bread, soak the bread in a little water, and squeeze dry. Mix the ground liver with the bread, butter, wine, and rum. Stir with a wooden spoon till very smooth, or force the mixture through a sieve *if* you have the patience. Add nutmeg. Chill before using to fill piroshki made with puff pastry.

Cabbage Filling

5 cups chopped cabbage	4 tbsp. butter (or substitute)
2 tbsp. salt	1 tbsp. minced dill or parsley
2 onions, chopped	2 hard-cooked eggs, chopped

Use the tender inside leaves of firm white cabbage. Chop fine. Mix with the salt and let stand 15 minutes, then squeeze out the excess water. Put the cabbage in a colander, pour boiling water over it, and leave 30 minutes to drain. Sauté the chopped onion in butter. Add the cabbage to the onion and braise 30 minutes. Do not brown. Add the minced dill or parsley and the chopped eggs. Use 1½ full tablespoons of this filling for each portion. Cabbage piroshki should have a little more filling than other kinds. Use either short pastry or raised dough.

Carrot Filling

12 large carrots	1½ tsp. salt
4 tbsp. butter	½ tsp. pepper
2 tbsp. thick sour cream	3 hard-cooked eggs, chopped

107

Scrape the carrots and cook them whole in salted water, then chop very fine and sauté 10 minutes in the butter. Add the sour cream. Boil up once. Stir well and cool. Add the seasoning and chopped eggs. Use either short pastry or raised dough.

Carrot and Béchamel Piroshki

2 egg yolks	3½ cups finely chopped cooked carrots
1 cup cream sauce	1 tsp. salt
2 tbsp. minced chives	¼ tsp. nutmeg

Mix the egg yolks into the thick cream sauce while still warm. Add the chives, carrots, salt, and nutmeg. Chill well before using to fill piroshki made with puff pastry.

Fillet of Fish and Smoked Salmon Piroshki

1 lb. fillet of haddock or flounder	Pepper
	Dash of nutmeg
2 tbsp. butter	1 tbsp. sour cream
3 tbsp. minced parsley	8 thin slices smoked salmon
Salt	

Sauté the fish fillets 12 minutes in butter, then chop very fine. Add the minced parsley, salt, pepper, and a very sparing dash of nutmeg. Mix the sour cream into the chopped fish. If it seems too dry, moisten with a little water or consommé. Lay this filling on pieces of short pastry or raised dough. Divide the salmon so there will be 1 slice of salmon for each pirojok. Lay a slice of salmon on top of each portion of fish filling and pinch the pastry together. When you use raised dough, put the salmon on first and the fish filling on top of it, since these piroshki will be reversed when baked.

Fish and Rice Filling

1 lb. fillets of haddock or cod
Salt
Pepper
2 onions, chopped
3 tbsp. butter

2 tbsp. minced parsley
¾ cup flaky cooked rice
1 cup thick cream sauce
2 hard-cooked eggs

Wash and dry the fish. Sprinkle with salt and pepper. Wrap in a towel and let stand 1 hour. Slice the fish thin; sauté the chopped onion in 2 tablespoons of the butter; add the fish and cook 10 minutes; then add the parsley. Cool the fish. Mix with the rice, the cream sauce, the chopped eggs, and the remaining tablespoon of butter, melted. Do the mixing with a fork so the fish will be flaky and not too finely broken up. Use raised dough for your pirog or piroshki.

Vatroushki to Serve with Borsch

1 lb. pot cheese
1 tbsp. thick sour cream
2 eggs

½ tsp. sugar
1 tsp. salt
1 egg yolk

Wrap the pot cheese in cheesecloth and place it in a sieve with a plate on the cheese and a weight on top of the plate. Leave it 3 to 4 hours to press out the excess water. When the cheese seems quite dry, rub it through a fine sieve. Add the sour cream. Stir till smooth. Add the sugar, salt, and 2 whole eggs. Mix thoroughly. Set aside to chill for ½ hour.

Roll out sour-cream pastry to ¼-inch thickness. Stamp out rounds about 3 inches across. On each round of pastry put 1½ tablespoons of the cheese filling. Pat the filling flat, leaving a

109

border of pastry. Turn the border up and pinch in scallops. These vatroushki are like small open tarts. Brush the cheese filling with the yolk of an egg diluted with 1 tablespoon water, then prick lightly with a fork and place on a slightly greased cookie sheet. Bake 15 minutes in a hot oven (400°). Serve immediately.

Minced Chicken Piroshki

1 small onion, minced	2 cups minced cold chicken
2 tbsp. butter	Salt
1 tbsp. flour	Pepper
4 tbsp. sour cream	Nutmeg

Sauté the minced onion in the butter. Add the flour. Cook 10 minutes. Add the sour cream and boil up once. Mix with chicken. Add the seasonings sparingly, particularly the nutmeg. Cool before using. Make the piroshki with puff pastry or sour-cream pastry.

Old-Fashioned Kurnik
(Russian Chicken Pie)

2 onions	½ cup thick cream, sweet or sour
1 stalk celery	2 tbsp. minced parsley
1 clove garlic	1 tsp. lemon juice
6 peppercorns	¼ tsp. nutmeg
2 cloves	1 cup rice
1 bay leaf	1 lb. mushrooms
5 cups water	2 tbsp. butter
3-to-4-lb. chicken	5 hard-cooked eggs, chopped
1½ tsp. salt	

Put the onions, celery, garlic, peppercorns, cloves, and bay leaf in a spice bag or tie them together in a piece of gauze. Put them in a pot with the water and bring to a boil. Put the chicken in and simmer for 1 hour. Add the salt and continue cooking for 30 minutes. The chicken should be tender but not overcooked. If it needs additional cooking, be careful not to cook it too long. Take the chicken out and slice the breast in thin slices. Chop the rest of the meat, discarding all skin and gristle. Skim the fat from the chicken broth. Mix 1½ cups of the broth with the cream and simmer very slowly till reduced to 1 cup. Add the minced parsley, lemon juice, and nutmeg, then mix with the chopped chicken.

Wash the rice well and cook it 10 minutes in boiling salted water. Throw the rice in a sieve and rinse with cold water. Put the rice to cook in 3 cups of boiling chicken broth. Cook till just done. The rice mustn't be too soft. Slice the mushrooms and sauté them in butter.

Use a deep round pie dish. Ovenproof glass is best. Roll out sour-cream pastry so you will have 1 piece big enough to line the dish, with an extra margin to bend in a little at the top. The other piece must be a round piece cut to fit the top of the dish exactly.

Put half of the rice on the bottom crust, then a layer of chopped eggs, and some of the chopped chicken and mushrooms. Now another layer of eggs, then another layer of chicken and mushrooms. On this layer of mushrooms arrange the slices of chicken breast and cover with the remainder of the rice. Press the filling down evenly. Put on the top piece of pastry. Turn the margin of the lower crust over it and crimp the edge. Cut a good-sized hole in the center of the pie. Decorate around it with leaf-shaped pieces of pastry.

Brush over with lightly beaten egg yolk. Bake 15 minutes in hot oven (400°). Reduce the heat and continue baking till the pie bubbles where the crusts are joined. This should take about 30 minutes. Serve very hot.

Other Fillings for Piroshki and Pirogs

1. Chopped scallions simmered in butter
2. Chopped scallions simmered in butter and mixed with an equal quantity of cooked rice. Add 2 tablespoons sour cream to 1 cup rice.
3. Mushrooms and onions simmered in butter and mixed with an equal quantity of baked buckwheat kasha
4. Onions browned in butter and mixed with riced potato, $\frac{1}{3}$ onions to $\frac{2}{3}$ potato
5. Equal quantities of braised cabbage and fish cooked in butter
6. Fish cooked in butter with equal amount of braised sauerkraut and onion
7. Mushrooms simmered in butter mixed with buckwheat kasha, $\frac{1}{3}$ mushroom, $\frac{2}{3}$ kasha

Russian-American Fillings

1. Corned-beef hash with browned chopped onions
2. Equal quantities of riced potato mixed with chopped green peppers and onions cooked in butter
3. Minced cold ham and chopped green peppers cooked in butter
4. Cold cooked finnan haddie simmered in butter with scallions, with 1 tablespoon sour cream added to each cup of filling

Baked Buckwheat Kasha

1½ cups coarse buckwheat groats   Boiling water
 1 tbsp. butter   1 tsp. salt

Heat the butter in a heavy skillet. Add the buckwheat groats and fry for 10 minutes over medium heat, stirring constantly to prevent the groats from browning. Put the groats in an earthenware or fireproof casserole. Add salt and sufficient boiling water to cover the groats with 1 inch of water over them. Cover the casserole. Place in hot oven (400°) for 30 minutes. Remove the cover and add a little water if the kasha seems too dry. Continue cooking for 30 minutes or longer in a slow oven (325°). The kasha should be moist with every grain separate. It should not be mushy.

Baked Millet Kasha

Follow the recipe for Baked Buckwheat Kasha, but bake the Millet Kasha a little longer.

Steamed Buckwheat Kasha

1 cup fine buckwheat groats   1 tbsp. butter of chicken fat
1 egg, slightly beaten   1 tsp. salt
2 cups boiling water

Stir the groats into the slightly beaten egg. Place in a skillet on a hot fire, stirring briskly for 5 minutes until each grain is separate and dry. Now place the cooking pot over the fire for a few moments before you put in the buckwheat, salt, and boiling water. The water must be boiling. Cover the pot, slip

113

an asbestos mat under it, and cook 30 minutes on very low heat. Add the butter or chicken fat 15 minutes before kasha is ready.

Coarse unsplit groats can also be cooked this way, but they take about 10 minutes longer.

CHAPTER 5

RUSSIAN PANCAKES

A well-made Russian pancake is actually the same thing as a well-made American pancake, yet in other respects the pancake customs of Russia and America are far apart.

In Russia the word for pancakes is *blini,* and most Russians prefer them made of buckwheat flour, or wheat and buckwheat mixed. Hot off the griddle, light and fluffy and nicely browned, without a suspicion of grease about them, they are as popular from Moscow to Kamchatka as they are from Maine to Kalamazoo.

But there is a world of difference between the "fixings" you eat with your American pancakes and those that we eat with our Russian blini.

You eat yours with butter spread on them like bread, and then syrup, honey, molasses, sugar, etc. We never put anything sweet on ours. Nor do we eat them with sausage or bacon, as you do.

Russian blini are eaten with melted butter and smoked fish, pickled fish, salted fish, or caviar. Blini with caviar have become an internationally famous delicacy. On top of the fish goes a dab of sour cream.

Having no baking powder in Russia, or any ready-prepared pancake flour, we make most of our blini with yeast-raised batter. In size, the standard Russian blini are slightly smaller than the standard American pancake. The expert Russian cook turns blini over by tossing them in the air, exactly as it is done by flapjack artists in the American West. I regretfully admit that I still turn mine at griddle altitude, although I have had impressive lessons in pancake tossing. Clark Gable tried to teach me how, and he was an accomplished pancake chef, but I just couldn't seem to learn the trick.

The pancake recipes I give in this chapter are regulation Russian. If you would rather not make yeast-raised batter, simply go ahead with your own favorite recipe, but keep the pancakes small and thin when you prepare them to serve as blini. They should be about 3 inches across.

Maslyanitsa, the carnival week before Lent, is the great season for blini in Russia. Literally translated, the word *Maslyanitsa* means "butter festival." That's when everyone eats valiant quantities of blini.

The way to serve them and eat them is as follows:

Bring your small buckwheat pancakes to the table piled on a hot platter. Put a bowl of melted butter on the table and a bowl of sour cream. The cream should be at room temperature, not chilled. Also on the table have a dish of smoked salmon cut in thin slices; a dish of sliced kippered salmon; a dish of smoked whitefish; a dish of cut-up salt herring; and, last but not least, the caviar. If possible, use the best grade of black caviar. However, there is nothing wrong with red caviar or the black pressed caviar.

Start by putting butter on your pancake, then a piece of fish or some caviar, then a spoonful of sour cream on top. Some Russians double the pancake over on their plate, others don't. There's no rule of etiquette about this. Eat your blini the way you like best.

Many Russians drink straight vodka with blini pancakes.

Buckwheat Blini

2 cups milk	3 eggs, separated
1 cup water	2 tbsp. softened butter
1 cake yeast	1 tsp. sugar
2 cups sifted buckwheat	1 tsp. salt

Warm ½ cup of the milk mixed with 1 cup water. Crumble the yeast into this liquid and stir till smooth. Add enough flour to make a thick sponge—about 1 cup. Cover the bowl of dough with a cloth and set in a warm place away from drafts to rise for 2½ or 3 hours. Beat the egg yolks till frothy, then combine them with the rest of the milk, the butter, sugar, and salt. Mix well and add this to the sponge, along with the rest of the flour. Whip the egg whites quite stiff. Fold them carefully into the batter. Let stand 45 minutes without stirring.

Ladle the batter out in small quantities. Use small frying pans very lightly buttered, and fry the pancakes till brown on both sides. Keep melted butter in a sprinkle-top jar, or use a small feather brush to butter the pan. The pancakes should be buttered lightly on the uncooked side before they are turned. Serve very hot.

Blini Made with White and Buckwheat Flour

1 yeast cake	3 eggs, separated
½ cup lukewarm water	½ tsp. salt
1½ cups sifted fine buckwheat flour	1 tsp. sugar
1 cup sifted white flour	3 tbsp. melted butter
2 cups scalded milk	3 tbsp. thick sour cream

Crumble the yeast and dissolve it in water. To this add half the buckwheat flour, all of the white flour, and half of the milk. Beat well. Put in a large bowl, cover with a cloth, and set in a warm place—not hot—to rise for 3 hours. Then beat again, add the rest of the buckwheat flour, and let rise again for 2 hours. Now add the remaining cup of milk and mix till smooth. Add the egg yolks slightly beaten, the salt, sugar, melted butter, and cream. Whip the whites of the eggs very stiff and fold into the batter. Let stand 30 minutes without stirring. Fry the pancakes as is described for Buckwheat Blini above.

White-Flour Blini

½ yeast cake
2 cups scalded milk, cooled
2 tsp. sugar
3 cups sifted flour

3 eggs, separated
5 tbsp. softened butter
1 tsp. salt

Crumble the yeast in a deep bowl with the lukewarm milk and stir till smooth. Stir in the sugar and 1½ cups flour. Cover the bowl with a cloth and set it in a warm place for 1½ hours for the sponge to rise. Beat the egg yolks with the butter, adding the salt and the rest of the flour, then mix this with the sponge. Beat well and put aside to rise again for another 1½ hours. Stir the stiffly whipped egg whites into the batter with a fork. Let stand 10 minutes before making your pancakes.

Quick Blini

1 cup sifted white flour
1 tsp. baking powder
1½ cups milk

1 tsp. sugar
2 tbsp. sour cream
2 eggs

Sift the flour and baking power together. Add the sugar, milk, and sour cream. Beat the eggs till frothy, put them in, stir well, then let stand 20 minutes. Fry your small pancakes in very hot butter. Drain on paper before serving.

Blini Made with Prepared Pancake Flour

When you make Russian blini with any of the American ready-mixed pancake flours, follow the directions on the package given for waffle-style pancakes made with eggs.

Sirniki
(Cottage-Cheese Cakes)

3 lb. cottage cheese	Salt
4 egg yolks	Flour
1 egg	Sour cream
1 cup flour	

Drain the cheese for 4 hours before using. Wrap it in a cloth or in several layers of gauze and hang it up to drip. Or place it in a colander with a weight on top to squeeze the liquid out.

When dry, rub the cheese through a sieve. Mix in the egg yolks. Beat the whole egg and add that. Salt to taste. Beat the mixture till thoroughly blended, then shape into rolls about 2 inches in diameter. Chill for 1 hour. Cut in slices about 1 inch thick. Dust these with flour and fry brown in hot butter or vegetable shortening. Drain on paper. Serve hot with a bowl of sour cream.

This is one of Russia's most popular luncheon dishes. It is served at all times of the year, but most frequently during Lent.

CHAPTER 6

FISH

An international distinction is shared by the respective waters of the United States and Russia; this being the exceptional variety of fishes that swim therein.

When I set out to write this book I had no notion of such lore, but tracking down English-language names of Russian fishes led me to the American Museum of Natural History in New York, where I was delighted to renew acquaintance with Francesca La Monte, Assistant Curator of Ichthyology, whom I hadn't seen since the years when we both were schoolgirls in London. We talked old times, then we talked fish; and I was surprised to learn that ichthyologists find some knowledge of the Russian language a great help because there are so many different kinds of fish in Russia that science has to identify. I owe Miss La Monte a debt of gratitude for her scholarly advice in the work of selecting American fishes for these Russian recipes.

For example, the seeg, a fish greatly admired by Russians, is called "whitefish" in America. There is a long narrow Russian seeg from the cold deep water of Lake Ladoga that is unlike the American whitefish, which is shorter and broader, yet I am informed that in some lakes in midwestern United States there is a type of whitefish that is an exact replica of the Lake Ladoga seeg.

To me the most interesting result of my fish research is

the data I picked up on the history of the crayfish, a table treat common enough in Russia, though very rare in America generally. My pursuit of crayfish information leads back to earliest youth when my father, a scientist of authority on the glacial period, was forever teaching me about that dismal era in our planet's past. Now Dr. Willard G. Van Name, Assistant Curator Emeritus of Invertebrates at the American Museum of Natural History, offers me a theory explaining why we have fresh-water crayfish in some parts of America and not in others.

During the ice age the great glacial cap over the northern and eastern regions of this continent destroyed most of the fresh-water shellfish in the lakes and rivers, sweeping them into the sea. The rivers and lakes of the midwestern and southern states—or what we now know as such—were not engulfed as completely by the glaciers. According to this theory, after the ice age many fresh-water crustaceans, including the crayfish, had survivors enough to revive the species in what is now Wisconsin, Illinois, Indiana, Louisiana, etc.; whereas the glaciers finished the crayfish off forever along the northeast coast.

It does seem to me that with the tremendous wealth of fish in America people here have every reason to be enthusiastic fish-eaters. Russians, with a similar abundance of fish, are experts at cooking it. I hope these recipes from Russia will add to the pleasures of fish lovers in America.

FRESH STURGEON

Russians are sturgeon snobs. We think Russian sturgeon is the best in the world, and sturgeon of any other nationality is regarded by us in a very stuck-up manner. We tell everyone our Russian sturgeon is infinitely superior. Condescendingly we exclaim, "*Konetchno!*" which means, "That goes without saying!"

Naturally we believe our magnificent sturgeon deserves to be presented with a great flourish. So at big dinner parties in Russia, on the most gala occasions, a 7-to-10-pound sturgeon is cooked and served whole on a giant platter surrounded with assorted vegetables and garnishes. It makes an imposing and appetizing sight. The wreath of garnishes includes sliced crayfish simmered in butter; potatoes cut in the shape of olives and sprinkled with drawn butter and minced chives; potatoes decorated with finely chopped brown onions; mushroom caps simmered in butter; chopped cooked celery. Then there are pickled mushrooms as well as the fresh mushrooms; slices of dill pickle; sour gherkins cut lengthwise to form dainty little greenfans. A sauce is served separately to go with this monumental sturgeon dish.

One of our favorite sauces for sturgeon is a very rich tomato-cream sauce made with tomato purée, cream, and the yolks of eggs.

You can buy excellent sturgeon in American markets, where it is usually sold already skinned, happily eliminating a bothersome kitchen task, for skinning a sturgeon is no fun! Extralarge sturgeon are caught in various parts of this country. There is a California record, from the year 1855, of a sturgeon that weighed 354 pounds and measured 9 feet 8 inches in length. But the American sturgeon you will encounter at your market is a much smaller fish as a rule, and is all the better for being smaller, and younger. The old sturgeon that grows to enormous size are less delicate in flavor. The flesh of the sturgeon sold here is of a light red color resembling beef, and the fat is pale yellow.

Sturgeon Steaks Baked with Parmesan Cheese

3 lb. fresh sturgeon steaks	1 tbsp. butter
Salt	1½ cups sour cream
4 yolks hard-cooked eggs	Dry bread crumbs
¼ cup white vinegar	5 tbsp. grated Parmesan cheese
Nutmeg	2 tbsp. olive oil or salad oil
Pepper	Juice of ½ lemon

The sturgeon steaks should be about 1 inch thick. Rub them with salt and let them stand 2 hours. Do not put them in the refrigerator.

Rub the egg yolks through a fine sieve, then mix smooth with the sour cream. Add the vinegar, a good pinch of nutmeg, pepper, and softened butter. Mix well.

Wipe the fish dry. Lay the fish in a shallow fireproof dish, lightly greased. Cover with the sour cream mixture. Sprinkle with dry bread crumbs, then with the cheese, and lastly with the olive oil or salad oil and the lemon juice.

Bake 12 minutes in hot oven (400°). Lower the heat and cook for another 25 minutes. Serve in the baking dish.

Don't try sprinkling with parsley for eye appeal. The taste of parsley doesn't blend well with the Parmesan cheese and the delicate flavor of the sturgeon.

Sturgeon in Pastry Ring

3 lb. fresh sturgeon	3 tbsp. sour cream
Salt	4 tbsp. grated Parmesan cheese
Pepper	½ tsp. marjoram or thyme
Flour	Bread crumbs
Butter	½ lb. mushrooms
2 cups thick cream sauce	Puff pastry or sour-cream pastry

Have the sturgeon cut in steaks 1 inch thick. Dust with salt and pepper and roll in flour. Fry 12 minutes in hot butter, 6 minutes on each side. Cool the fish slightly. Cut each steak in 2 pieces and remove the bones. Prepare your cream sauce with fish stock, and with *cream* if possible. When the sauce is ready add the sour cream to it, then 2 tablespoons of the cheese, and the marjoram or thyme.

Make a border of pastry about 2 inches wide, 1½ inches high. Make this pastry border on a pie plate or fireproof earthenware dish. Roll the pieces of sturgeon in the bread crumbs and the remaining cheese, then put them in the center of the pastry ring. Pour the sauce over the fish. Bake 10 minutes in hot oven (400°). Reduce to 350° and continue cooking for 15 to 20 minutes, until the pastry is done and the sauce slightly browned. Sauté the mushroom caps in butter. Garnish the center of pastry ring with them just before serving.

Salmon is excellent done in this manner. You can use almost any fish if it isn't dark-fleshed and hasn't too many bones.

Sturgeon Steaks in Madeira Wine

6 fresh-sturgeon steaks	3 sprigs parsley
Salt	1 dill pickle
4 tbsp. butter	Pepper
1 cup Madeira wine	1 tbsp. flour
1 cup water	1 tbsp. minced capers
1 bay leaf	1 tbsp. shredded olives
	1 cup chopped cooked celery

Scald the sturgeon steaks by pouring plenty of boiling water over them. Drain them well. When thoroughly dry, rub with a little salt and set aside for 1 hour. Put 3 tablespoons of the butter in a pan. Add the wine, water, bay leaf, parsley, and half the dill pickle, peeled and cut in slices. Boil up, add the fish and a little pepper. Cover and simmer gently for 15 minutes. Take the fish up carefully with a fish slice so that all liquid drains off. Lay the fish on a platter and keep warm. Strain the broth; thicken it with the flour and the remaining tablespoon of butter. Boil up, then add the capers and olives and celery, and the other half of the dill pickle, peeled and minced. Pour over the fish and serve.

This should be accompanied by boiled potatoes generously buttered with unsalted butter and sprinkled very sparingly with chopped chives.

Fish Poached in Wine

3 lb. any white-fleshed fish	1½ cups dry white wine
3 tbsp. butter	½ tsp. pepper
1 lemon	1 tsp. salt

This is one of our classic Russian fish recipes. Use haddock, flounder, or any white fish fillets. Cut the fillets in pieces about 3 inches square.

Wash the fish and dry well on a towel. Cut the lemon into eighths and remove all the seeds. Leave the rind on the lemon sections. Put the lemon and butter and wine in a pan large enough to hold all the pieces of fish in a single layer, not on top of each other. Sprinkle the fish with salt and pepper and put in the pan. Cover and place over strong heat. Bring to a boil, then reduce the heat and cook from 8 to 15 minutes, depending on the fish. A soft fish such as flounder takes only

125

8 minutes, while a firmer fish like haddock or cod will take longer. Pick up the fish with a fish slice; drain; place on a hot platter. Remove the lemon from the sauce in the pan. Thicken with a little flour and butter. Serve the sauce in a gravy boat.

Baked Yellow Pike with Rice-and-Egg Stuffing

4 lb. yellow pike	6 tbsp. butter
2 cups cooked rice	Flour
6 anchovy fillets, finely chopped	Bread crumbs
4 hard-cooked eggs, chopped	Salt
2 egg yolks	Pepper

If you live near the Great Lakes you can easily enjoy this delicious fish. Yellow pike is harder to get in other parts of the country, so I suggest that you substitute haddock if necessary, but I don't for a moment claim it will taste the same as a yellow pike.

The original Russian recipe also calls for vesiga in the stuffing. Vesiga is the dried marrow from a sturgeon's backbone, rather like leaf gelatine in appearance. We don't have vesiga here. Anchovies do not actually take its place, but they give very much the required flavor to the rice stuffing.

Mix your cooked rice with the chopped anchovy fillets, the chopped hard-cooked eggs, a dash of pepper, 1½ tablespoons of butter, and the raw egg yolks. Rub the inside of the fish with salt. Put in the stuffing. Sew the fish up. Rub it over with flour. Cover it well with bread crumbs and place it in a greased baking dish. Melt the rest of the butter and pour over the fish. Put 2 tablespoons of water in the baking dish and

126

place the dish in a medium oven (350°). Bake about 45 minutes. Baste with the juice in the dish during the baking.

Fish Cutlets

1 lb. fillet of any white-fleshed	¼ tsp. nutmeg
fish (haddock, hake, flounder)	¼ tsp. pepper
2 slices stale bread	1 egg white
3 tbsp. cream	Dry bread crumbs
1 onion, sliced	Butter, or substi-
1 tbsp. butter	tute, for frying
½ tsp. salt	

Cut up the fillets of fish and put through the meat grinder twice. Cut the crusts from the bread and soak the bread in the cream. Sauté sliced onion in 1 tbsp. butter, then chop the onion very fine. Mix the fish, bread and cream, chopped onion, salt, pepper, and nutmeg. Add the butter in which the onion was cooked and blend the mixture well, mashing as you blend with a wooden spoon. When it is quite smooth, add the unbeaten white of egg and mix again till thoroughly blended. Chill for at least three hours.

Sift the bread crumbs onto a piece of waxed paper. Take up small amounts of the fish mixture, roll into a ball between your hands, drop onto the bread crumbs, flatten slightly to form oval cutlets. See that each cutlet is well coated with bread crumbs and work quickly so that the fish remains ice cold. Fry the cutlets in plenty of very hot fat until they are nicely browned. Serve sizzling hot, accompanied by a cream sauce spiked with minced chives and mixed pickles, and a dash of sherry wine.

Cutlets of Salt Herring

4 fillets of Schmaltz or	2 tbsp. sour cream
Matjes herring	2 eggs
Milk	Dry bread crumbs
3 slices stale bread	Egg yolk
1 chopped onion, minced	3 tbsp. butter (or substitute)

Soak the fillets 2 hours in milk. Dry and chop very fine. Soak the bread in a little milk, then squeeze dry. Sauté the chopped onion in 1 tablespoon butter. Mix the minced onion with the herring, the bread, sour cream, and eggs, working till quite smooth. Form into cutlets. Dip the cutlets in yolk of egg and roll in bread crumbs. Brown in hot butter. Serve with boiled potatoes sprinkled with melted butter and minced dill.

Forshmak of Herring and Meat

3 or 4 fillets of Schmaltz or	½ cup sour cream
Matjes herring	1 tbsp. softened butter
Milk	Pepper
3 slices stale bread	Nutmeg
3 cups ground cooked meat	1 egg
3 hot cooked potatoes	Dry bread crumbs

Soak the herring fillets 2 hours in milk. Dry and chop very fine, or put through a meat grinder. Soak the bread in milk or in water, then squeeze dry. Mix the bread and herring and meat together; rice the hot potatoes and add to the mixture, also the sour cream, the butter, pepper, and a little nutmeg. Stir till very smooth, then add the unbeaten egg. Grease a fireproof casserole; dust it with bread crumbs; put the mixture in and sprinkle bread crumbs on top. Bake 30 minutes in medium oven (375°). Serve in the casserole. A finely minced onion simmered in butter can be added to this forshmak if you like.

Cod with Saffron Sauce

½ tsp. saffron	4 sprigs parsley
1 tbsp. lukewarm water	1 leek
3 lb. fresh cod	2 stalks celery
Salt	1 bay leaf
1 cup white wine	6 peppercorns
½ cup vinegar	1 tbsp. sugar
½ cup raisins	1 lemon
2 onions	Flour
1 carrot	Butter

Soak the saffron in the lukewarm water. Wash and dry the fish and rub it with salt. Let stand 1 hour. Again dry it well, then cut it in individual portions for serving. Place the pieces of fish in a pan with just enough wine and vinegar barely to cover. Add the raisins, the vegetables cut in pieces of medium size, the spices, and half the lemon, sliced and seeded. Cover the pan. Bring quickly to a boil, then simmer for 20 minutes. Take up the fish; drain and place on a hot platter. Drain the vegetables and raisins and surround the fish with them on the platter, removing the bay leaf and peppercorns. Strain the broth, adding to it any remaining wine and vinegar. Thicken the sauce with flour and butter. Add the water from the saffron and the half lemon in slices. Pour the sauce over the fish. Serve with plain boiled potatoes.

CRAYFISH

My telephone rings and I hear the excited voice of some Russian friend of mine saying, "Wonderful news, Sasha! Listen..."

I am Sasha. In the Russian language Sasha is a diminutive either for Alexandra or Alexander.

My friend goes on, "What do you think Moura has done?"

It may be Moura or Varya, Annoushka or Ellena of whom I am about to hear the wonderful news. The same thing happens to so many Russians in America.

"What is it?" I ask. "Has she gone into the movies? Has Moura had another baby? What has she done?"

"Well, you know she and her husband went to live in the country, somewhere in Illinois."

"Yes, yes! So what?"

"I have just received a letter from her. You'll be as excited as I am when I tell you what Moura and her husband have done!"...Long dramatic pause..."They have found crayfish —CRAYFISH, my dear, in a river only a few miles from where they live! Oh, isn't America marvelous? Crayfish just like in Russia! Crayfish, can you imagine? Moura says we must go to visit her. She and her husband catch crayfish every week end. Sasha, when can we go? We will eat crayfish every day!"

Moura may be living in a remote corner of Illinois, Wisconsin, Ohio, Indiana, or Louisiana. Does that discourage her Russian friends in New York from planning week-end trips to eat crayfish with Moura? Certainly not. Distance is powerless to dim the optimism of our nostalgic Russian longing for crayfish.

Russians in Russia are simply crazy about crayfish. And in

America, any prospect of eating crayfish aways touches our
Russian hearts.

I am sorry to say we seldom carry out our impetuous ambition to visit Moura and eat her crayfish. We stay where we are,
and eat shrimps—which we can buy in any market—instead.
But we know how to prepare our shrimps exactly as we would
cook them if they were crayfish. Here is how we do it:

Shrimps Cooked Like Crayfish

2 lb. large fresh shrimps	1 tsp. thyme
1 cup white wine	½ tsp. salt
2 cups sour cream	

Buy jumbo shrimps if possible. Wash them well and drain
them. Mix the wine and sour cream. The sour cream shouldn't
be too cold. Add the salt and the thyme, powdered or fresh.
Bring to a boil. Add the shrimps. Cover and simmer very
gently for 20 minutes. Serve very hot—with a generous helping of paper napkins.

Extracting the meat from a sauce covered crayfish or shrimp
is quite a business. In this country, where complications at
table aren't popular, you may prefer to precook your shrimps,
remove the shells, then heat the shrimp meat up in the prepared sauce. In this case cook the sauce 15 minutes; add the
shrimps and *do not boil.*

Porgies Baked in Saffron Cream

6 porgies	½ cup milk
½ tsp. saffron	1½ cups sour cream
1 tbsp. water	Dry bread crumbs
3 tbsp. butter	Salt
2 tbsp. flour	Pepper

131

The porgies should weigh about ½ lb. each, so that 1 porgie is enough for each person.

Soak the saffron 1 hour in the water. Wash the fish and dry it in a towel. Roll it in 1 tbsp. flour seasoned with salt and pepper. Fry quickly in 2 tablespoons of hot butter; 3 minutes for each side of the fish will be about right. Make a cream sauce of 1 tablespoon flour, the butter and the milk, then add the sour cream, and the water from the saffron strained through a sieve. Lay the fish in a greased ovenproof dish, in which it will be served at table. Pour the sauce over the fish; sprinkle with bread crumbs; put in hot oven till sauce has browned—about 15 minutes. Serve sizzling hot.

Butterfish or pompano can be prepared in this way. A salad that goes particularly well with this dish is one of cooked green peas and diced fresh cucumber, the flavors blending nicely with the saffron in the sauce.

Butterfish or Porgies Fried in Sour Cream

6 to 12 butterfish or porgies	2 eggs, beaten
Salt	1 tbsp. prepared mustard
Pepper	Dry bread crumbs
1 onion, chopped	2 cups sour cream
3 tbsp. butter	2 tbsp. minced parsley

Wash the fish and dry on a towel. Rub with salt and pepper. Fry the onion in 1 tablespoon of the butter till a golden brown. Cool and mince very fine. Mix the beaten eggs with the mustard and minced onion. Dip the fish in the egg mixture; roll in bread crumbs and fry in hot butter, 3 minutes on each side. Add the sour cream to pan. Cook over brisk heat for another 6 to 8 minutes. The sour cream should be slightly browned by this time. Sprinkle with minced parsley before serving.

For this dish, Russians like to use a shallow skillet of copper and serve the fish at table in the skillet. Since such utensils are scarce in American kitchens—my own included—I fry the fish in an ordinary frying pan, then transfer it to a dish of fireproof glass or to an earthenware pie plate, placed over an asbestos mat. Finish cooking the fish, and serve it at table straight from the pie plate. Fillets of flounder or haddock can be prepared this way. Cut very large fillets in half, cutting across, not lengthwise.

Fillets of Flounder with Sweet Cream and Scallions

2 lb. fillets of flounder	½ cup water
Salt	1½ cups sweet cream
1½ tbsp. butter	4 tbsp. minced scallions
4 tbsp. bread crumbs	Pepper

Sprinkle the fillets with salt; let stand 1 hour; then dry thoroughly and cut each fillet in 2 or 3 pieces, cutting across the fish, not lengthwise. If the fillets are small, leave them whole. Cook the bread crumbs 5 minutes in hot butter. Add water. Stir till smooth. Add the cream and cook another 5 minutes. Put the fillets into the cream-and-bread-crumb sauce. Add the minced scallions and a little pepper. Simmer gently for 15 minutes. Serve in the cooking dish.

Fillets of sea trout, haddock, or bass can be prepared this same way. Just before serving, if you want to "fancify" this very tasty simple dish, you can decorate it with cooked shrimps warmed in a little butter and peeled halves or quarters of small tomatoes sautéed in butter.

Carp Poached in White Wine

3- to 4-lb. carp, whole
2 celery hearts, chopped
1 root Russian parsley, chopped
3 dill pickles, sliced
½ tsp. nutmeg
½ cup dill-pickle marinade

1 tbsp. butter
1 tbsp. flour
1½ cups dry white wine
Salt
Pepper

Have your fishman skin the carp for you, in addition to cleaning, but don't forget to say that you want the roe. Cut the fish in slices 1 inch thick. Slice the roe also. Lay slices of fish and roe in a deep pan. Surround with chopped celery and parsley root and sliced dill pickles. Season with nutmeg, a very little salt, but a generous sprinkling of pepper. Add the marinade from the dill pickles, or if you can't get the marinade, use enough water and wine barely to cover the fish. Cover and cook 30 minutes over a slow fire. Take up the fish. Lay on a hot platter. Surround with the vegetables. Thicken the broth with flour and butter and add the rest of the wine if you didn't use it all. Boil up and pour over the fish. Some Russian cooks put a tablespoon of chopped raisins in with the vegetables during the cooking.

Haddock, Bass, or Perch Stuffed with Buckwheat Kasha

2 onions, chopped
4 tbsp. butter
2 cups cold buckwheat kasha
3 hard-cooked eggs
1 whole fish, 3 to 4 lb.
Salt

2 tbsp. flour
Pepper
½ cup dry bread crumbs
½ cup water
1 cup sour cream

Simmer the onions in 2 tablespoons of the butter. Add the cold cooked kasha and chopped eggs. Rub the inside of the fish with salt; stuff it with the kasha, sew it up or close it well with wooden toothpicks. Lay the fish in a greased baking dish. Sprinkle with flour, pepper, and bread crumbs. Melt the other 2 tablespoons of butter and pour it over the fish. Add the water to the baking dish. Bake 12 minutes in hot oven (400°), then reduce the heat to 350° and continue cooking for 25 minutes. Baste the fish from time to time with liquor from the pan. If the pan gets too dry, add a little boiling water. When the fish is ready, transfer it to a serving platter. Add sour cream to the baking dish; boil up and pour around the fish. Garnish with parsley and serve.

If you serve the fish in the dish in which it was baked, add the sour cream 10 minutes before serving. Leave in oven 10 minutes, then garnish and serve.

Fillets of Fish with Mushrooms

2 lb. fish fillets	Salt
½ lb. mushrooms, sliced	Pepper
2 onions, chopped	1½ cups dry white wine
2 tbsp. minced parsley	2 egg yolks, slightly beaten
1 tsp. minced lemon rind	2 tbsp. flour
3 tbsp. butter	

Any good white-fleshed fish is suitable for this. Haddock, flounder, etc.

Sauté the mushrooms and onions together in hot butter. When they are soft, add the minced parsley and lemon rind. Cut the fillets in pieces about 3 inches square. Rub with salt

135

and pepper and add to the mushrooms and onions. Boil up the wine. Pour it over the fish. Cover and simmer very slowly for 20 minutes. Lift the fish out. Lay it on a hot platter. Thicken the sauce with flour diluted in a small amount of water. Boil up. Add the egg yolks and pour over the fish.

Fillets of flounder or sea trout should be cooked only 12 minutes when done like this.

Hot Salmon with Horse-Radish Sauce

3 lb. salmon	Court bouillon
Salt	Horse-radish sauce (p. 212)

Have the fish in one piece. Rub with salt and let stand 1 hour. Wipe dry. Plunge in boiling court bouillon (p. 141). Boil up, then simmer 20 to 30 minutes, depending on the thickness of your piece of salmon. Remove the skin before serving. The horse-radish sauce can be served either warm, cold, or in frozen form.

Salmon Steaks in Madeira with Shrimp Sauce

6 salmon steaks cut thin	1 cup Madeira wine
Salt	1 bay leaf
Pepper	2 tbsp. grated Parmesan cheese
2 tbsp. butter	

Shrimp Sauce

¾ lb. shrimp	1½ tbsp. flour
1½ cups water	2 tbsp. minced parsley
3 sprigs fresh dill	1 tbsp. lemon juice
2 tbsp. butter	3 tbsp. sweet or sour cream

Prepare your sauce first. Cook the shrimp in the water with the dill for 15 minutes. Boil up once, then simmer. Keep 1 cup of this water when you drain the shrimp. Remove the shells and take out the black thread from the back of each. Chop the shrimp and sauté 3 minutes in hot butter. Add the flour. Cook 5 minutes more, then add the shrimp water and cook till thickened. Now add the parsley, lemon juice, and cream. Keep warm.

Rub the salmon steaks lightly with salt and pepper. Put the wine and bay leaf in a pan. Add the fish. Cover and bring rapidly to a boil, then simmer very gently for 15 minutes.

Place the fish on a hot platter. Remove the bay leaf from the wine broth; add the shrimp sauce; heat; then add the cheese. Stir till the cheese is melted and the sauce quite smooth. Do not boil. The sauce may be poured over the fish or served separately in a sauce boat.

Broiled Salmon Steaks with Caviar Sauce

2 thick salmon steaks (3 lb.)	2 egg yolks
Salt	1 tsp. lemon juice
Pepper	2 tbsp. anchovy butter
Olive oil or salad oil	2 tbsp. fresh caviar
1½ cups thick cream sauce	1 tbsp. butter

Have the salmon steaks about 1½ inches thick. Rub them with a little salt, but with plenty of pepper. Brush them over with oil. Broil 10 minutes on each side.

Make a rich cream sauce; add the egg yolks and lemon juice, and keep warm. When the fish steaks are ready, spread the top side of each steak with anchovy butter. To the cream sauce add the caviar and butter and stir till smooth. Cover the steaks with this sauce. Serve at once.

For the anchovy butter, chop 4 anchovy fillets very fine, then pound smooth and mix with 2 tablespoons of butter. Chill before using.

Crusty Salmon Cutlets

2 lb. salmon	2½ cups very thick cream sauce
Salt	Bread crumbs
Pepper	Fat for deep-frying
2 tbsp. butter	Cream

Remove bones and skin from the salmon. Cut in pieces about 2 inches square and 1 inch thick. Lay the pieces of fish in a pan; pour boiling water over them and let stand 2 minutes. Take up and drain well, then dry on a towel. Dust with salt and pepper and sauté 6 minutes in hot butter, carefully turning each piece once. Cool the fish.

Make the cream sauce extra thick, preferably using a mixture of cream and meat consommé. Flavor with a little lemon juice and 1 teaspoon of Worcestershire sauce. Chill 1½ cups of your cream sauce for 1 hour, then coat the pieces of fish with the chilled sauce. Lay the coated pieces of salmon on a platter so they are all in one layer, not on top of each other, and put in the refrigerator for 2 to 3 hours. When you are ready to serve dinner, cover the cream-coated pieces of fish with bread crumbs and fry them 6 to 8 minutes in plenty of very hot deep fat, just as you fry crullers. Drain on paper and serve. Thin the remaining sauce with a little cream, add another dash of Worcestershire, and serve with the fish.

Salmon Steaks with Green Peas, Shrimp, and French Toast

6 small salmon steaks	2 tsp. butter
Salt	1 tsp. flour
Pepper	½ lb. shelled cooked shrimp
2-3 cups green peas	3 slices French toast

This is a dish of gourmet rating which can be prepared very quickly by any American housewife who has the tremendous advantage of being able to buy quick-frozen peas and ready-cooked shrimps.

Dust the salmon steaks with pepper and salt. The steaks may either be broiled or pan-fried.

Cook the peas with a very thin slice of onion, a pinch of sugar, a pinch of salt. Keep the water from the peas. You'll need about ½ cup, thickened with the butter and flour. Keep 6 shrimps whole. Chop the rest of the shrimps. Mix the chopped shrimps with the peas and the thickened water from cooking the peas. Season with pepper and keep hot.

Prepare the French toast, using 2 eggs. Lay the salmon steaks in a ring on a hot platter. Fill the ring with the shrimps and peas. Cut the slices of French toast in half diagonally and use to garnish, arranging on top of the peas, with a whole shrimp on each piece of toast. Dust with paprika and serve at once.

Instead of fresh salmon, you can use kippered salmon heated with a very little water in a closed dish in the oven.

TROUT

Forelle, the French word for trout, is the word we use for this delicate fish in the Russian language, and we are in favor of preparing our trout along classic lines. We steam or simmer it in a court bouillon or cook it *au bleu,* as a rule. Of course both these methods are superlatively gourmet, yet in my humble opinion they can't touch a freshly caught trout rolled in corn meal and plain pan-fried in a skillet with bacon fat. No doubt this statement will cause me to be classified among the vandals, for the amateurs of French-style trout are as high hat as the ruddy-duck lovers. Nevertheless I rashly declare that for me a pan-fried trout in a crisp brown corn-meal jacket is heavenly trout perfection. That, however, is an American taste of mine, and this is a Russian cookbook.

So here is a trout recipe over which our Russian connoisseurs invariably rave:

Trout Steamed in Mixed Wines

3- to 4-lb. trout	½ cup Madeira wine
1 small onion	½ cup light rum
½ bay leaf	½ cup fish stock or water
4 peppercorns	3 tbsp. sweet butter
1 cup white wine	Flour-and-water paste

Place the cleaned fish on the rack of a fish kettle. Lay the onion, bay leaf, and peppercorns around the fish. Fill the lower part of kettle with the wines, rum, and the fish stock or water. The liquid should just barely reach the fish. Add the butter in large pieces. Cover the kettle, then seal around the edges with a thick paste of flour and water. Bring quickly to a boil on top of the stove, then place the kettle for 45 minutes in a slow oven (325°).

Break off the dough. Lift up the rack with the fish and let all the liquid drain off. Remove the spices and onion. Transfer the fish very carefully to a hot platter. Strain the broth from the kettle; thicken slightly with butter and flour, and pour this sauce over the fish. Surround with small boiled potatoes. Decorate with lemon wedges and parsley.

Court Bouillon for Fish

1 onion	1 bay leaf
1 carrot	4 cups water
1 root Russian parsley	6 white peppercorns
1 stalk celery	Fish trimmings and head

Cut the vegetables in large pieces and put them in the cold water with the spices, fish trimmings, and head. Bring to a boil. Skim, then simmer for 30 minutes. Strain through cheese-cloth and a fine strainer.

For cooking fish, the court bouillon may be used lukewarm, or it may be brought to a boil. Some cooks do it one way, some prefer the other. Most Russian cooks believe the fish tastes best when it is put into lukewarm court bouillon.

CHAPTER 7

MEAT

By the time you've looked through the recipes in this chapter it will not surprise you, I think, to learn that well-to-do Russians who ate continually and copiously of these succulent dishes always spent a month or so every year at some curative resort where they took the waters for the sake of their liver.

I must point out, however, that the ordinary Russian family has never gone in for fancy cooking as an everyday practice. In the average home our meat and poultry dishes were usually as simple as they are here in America—roast, broiled, or boiled. The more elaborate methods were for special occasions. The plain family stand-bys, such as pot roast or meat balls or breast of veal, have always been prepared and are still prepared today according to the standard Russian recipes I give in this chapter.

I hope these will be of use to the American housewife who wants to vary her menu without committing herself to a Russianized cuisine.

Perhaps the frequent mention of sour cream as an ingredient may appear somewhat excessive. At the beginning of this book I deemed it advisable to say that sour cream *is* one of the characteristic features of Russian cooking, and now I suggest again that when you use sour cream, your wisest course may be to refrain from speaking of it unless somebody asks you. The chances are ten to one everybody will like what they're

142

eating, and nobody ever will guess it has sour cream in it.

Our internationally famous *Bœuf à la Stroganoff* is a perfect example of this. Very few people realize that sour cream is used in the sauce.

Beef Stroganoff—to translate it into English—was named for a noted Russian gourmet, Count Paul Stroganoff, who flourished in the Gay Nineties of the last century. He was a dignitary at the court of Tsar Alexander III and a member of the Imperial Academy of Arts in St. Petersburg. The record doesn't tell us whether it was he himself who invented the delectable treat which has immortalized him, or whether his chef conjured it up. At any rate, the name Stroganoff has become familiar throughout the world to lovers of fine food—whereas it is a name virtually unknown to casual readers of Russian military history. Yet long before Count Paul won celebrity from his dish of beef, a peasant-born Stroganoff earned *his* spurs as one of the fighters who helped Ivan the Terrible conquer the vast territory of Siberia.

Beef Stroganoff

1½ lb. fillet of beef or lean part of the tenderloin	1 cup consommé
1½ tsp. salt	1 scant tsp. prepared hot mustard
2 tsp. pepper	1 onion, sliced
3 tbsp. butter	3 tbsp. thick sour cream
1 tbsp. flour	

There are several modified variations of Beef Stroganoff, but this is the classic Russian recipe. The secret of the sauce is the mustard in it.

Remove all fat and gristle from the meat. Cut it in narrow strips about 2 inches long and ½ inch thick. Dust the strips of beef with the salt and pepper, then set them aside for 2 hours. Do not put them in a cold place.

Melt 1½ tablespoons of the butter and blend in the flour. Add the consommé and boil up. Stir in the mustard.

Now in another pan brown the strips of meat very quickly with the sliced onion in the remaining 1½ tablespoons butter.

Have the sour cream at room temperature. Add it to the mustard sauce and boil up once, then add the meat to the sauce. Don't put the onion in. Cover the pan and keep hot for 20 minutes, taking care it doesn't boil or even simmer. Set the pan over brisk heat for 3 minutes just before serving. Serve immediately.

Even this classic recipe for Beef Stroganoff has undergone local changes during the past 20 years. Through the south of Russia 1 tablespoon of tomato purée has crept into the sauce. Or a few cooked mushrooms, sliced, may be introduced. In America the tomato purée and the mushrooms are both added. The result is tasty, I admit. But it *isn't* Beef Stroganoff.

I have known ultra-conservative Russian gourmets who even prefer to leave the mustard out of the sauce. They substitute a few drops of lemon juice. Others permit a few drops of strong mushroom ketchup, which is termed "mushroom essence" in Russia.

Russian Pot Roast Cooked with Wine

4 slices salt pork	3-4 lb. beef
1 large onion, sliced	Pepper
1 tbsp. chopped scallions	¾ cup sour cream
1 large carrot, sliced	Flour
¾ cup dry red wine (claret or burgundy)	1 tbsp. vinegar or lemon juice

Lay the slices of salt pork on the bottom of a heavy pot which can be put in the oven. Into the pot put the onion, scallions, and carrot. Use any cut of meat that you prefer for pot roast. Rub the meat with pepper and lay it in the pot. Set the pot over a strong flame and brown the meat for about 20 minutes, turning it several times. When the meat is thoroughly browned, add the wine and the sour cream. The sour cream must be at room temperature. It will toughen the meat if it is too cold.

Place a couple of slices of salt pork on top of the meat. Cover the pan and cook from 2-2½ hours in a moderate oven (325°-350°). Tender meat won't require longer cooking, but if the beef is not very tender it may need 3 hours.

Skim off all fat from the gravy and take the salt pork out. Thicken the gravy with flour. Add the vinegar and boil up. Strain. Russians serve the meat already sliced, with some of the gravy poured over it.

Pot Roast with Special Gravy

The gravy prepared as follows will turn a plain home pot roast into a special company treat. Do the pot roast according to your customary American recipe. It will be best without tomatoes or tomato purée in this case. I assume you'll have your pot roast really well browned, cooked so the gravy in the pot is dark and very meaty in flavor. Skim off the fat. Thicken the gravy with flour, adding whatever amount of water may be necessary.

Have ready 2 tablespoons of shredded olives. Also 2 tablespoons of the juice from spiced peaches, spiced pears, spiced plums or crab apples or cherries. Add the shredded olives and the spiced fruit juice to the gravy. Boil up. Then at the last moment before serving, add ¼ cup dark rum. This gravy really is something to write home about! Don't let it boil for even the briefest instant after adding the rum.

Pot Roast with Mushroom Gravy

Cook the pot roast according to your usual American recipe. Then when you make the gravy, put in 3 tablespoons of thick sour cream, 1 tablespoon of lemon juice, and ½ pound of fresh mushrooms sliced and simmered in a little butter. This gravy is very rich, but not a spoonful of it ever gets left over at my house. Two guests, a senator and a congresswoman, once flipped a coin for the privilege of scraping the bottom of the gravy boat.

Beef Kidneys with Dill Pickles and Potato Slices

2 beef kidneys	12 large slices potato ¼ inch thick
2 onions, chopped	¾ cup sour cream
4 tbsp. butter	1 bay leaf
2 dill pickles	Salt
1 cup consommé	Pepper
1½ tbsp. flour	1 tbsp. minced dill (optional)
2 tbsp. minced parsley	

Have the kidneys skinned. Soak them 2 hours in water, then put them in a pan of cold water and bring to a boil. Take out, rinse with cold water, and slice thin. Sprinkle the slices with flour but do not salt them. Sauté the onion till golden brown in hot butter. Add the sliced kidneys. Fry for 10 minutes, stirring till all the slices are nicely browned.

Peel the dill pickles. Squeeze the juice from them into the

146

frying pan with the kidneys. Add ½ cup of the consommé, cover the pan, and simmer very gently for 20 minutes, adding 1 or 2 tablespoons more of the consommé from time to time. In 20 minutes the kidneys should be tender. Try them with a fork, and continue cooking a little longer if necessary. When the kidneys are ready, add the dill pickles cut in slices, the potatoes, and the rest of the consommé. Continue cooking slowly until the potatoes are tender. Now add the sour cream, stirring it carefully with a fork. Season with pepper and a little salt. Quickly boil up once. Sprinkle with minced dill and serve.

Jellied Corned Beef

2 onions, sliced	3 lb. lean corned beef
1 carrot, sliced	2 pigs' feet or 2 cans consommé
4 sprigs parsley	1 tbsp. vinegar
6 peppercorns	1 hard-cooked egg, sliced
3 sprigs fresh dill	1 dill pickle, sliced
2 bay leaves	

Put the onions and carrot in a pot with the parsley, dill, bay leaves, and peppercorns. Put the corned beef in the pot and barely cover it with lukewarm water. Bring to a boil. Skim. Let simmer for 2½ hours. Then take the corned beef out and let it cool. Trim off all fat. Slice the meat very thin.

Now cook the pigs' feet 2 hours with an onion, some celery leaves and peppercorns, in just enough water to cover. When cool, skim off all fat and strain the liquid. This should give you 3 cups of liquid with which to make the jelly. Or you can get your jelly by cooking 2 cans of consommé 30 minutes with onion and celery leaves, then straining and adding water enough to make 3 cups. Dissolve 2 tablespoons of gelatine; reheat the consommé; pour it over the gelatine and cool till half jelled. Whichever liquid you use—the consommé or stock from pig's feet—add the vinegar to it *before* chilling.

Rinse a mold in cold water. Pour in a little of the liquid. Decorate with slices of peeled dill pickle and hard-cooked egg. Chill till set.

When set, lay the thin slices of corned beef in the mold. Have the rest of the liquid ready in a half-jellied condition. Stir it with a fork and pour it in the mold. It should be just thin enough to pour, but not so thin that the slices of beef float to the top. Chill the mold for at least 5 hours. Unmold and serve surrounded with sliced beets. On the side serve mustard and a sauce of horse-radish (see Chapter 11).

KOTLETI (Russian Meat Balls)

Kotletki is another word for meat balls. The average meat-eating Russian eats them at least 4 days out of 7. Foreigners visiting Russia for the first time nearly always get the impression that Russians eat kotleti *every* day. Kotletki means "little kotleti," but the difference in size is quite slight. It is true that kotleti and kotletki are faithful stand-bys to which most Russian cooks resort more than half the time, year in year out—so a smart Russian cook dresses them up by serving them with various sauces.

The standard sauce, as in my recipe, is made by stirring sour cream into the pan-thickened gravy. Variations of this are made by adding any one of the following:

Sliced mushrooms simmered in butter
Finely chopped cooked celery
Tomato purée
Creamed chopped onions with a strong flavoring of thyme

Onions simmered in butter with a little sugar and vinegar
Chopped raisins, vinegar, and sugar

Everyday Kotleti

1½ lb. lean beef	½ tsp. pepper
¼ lb. kidney fat	2 egg yolks or 1 whole egg
3 slices stale bread	4 tbsp. butter
1 small onion	Sifted dry bread crumbs
¾ tsp. salt	

Put the meat through your meat grinder. Cut up the kidney fat in small pieces, add them to the beef, and put through grinder a second time. The stale bread gives best results when at least 2 days old. Remove the crusts. Soak the bread in a little cold water, squeeze dry, and add to the meat. Mix thoroughly, till there are no lumps whatever. Grate the onion into the meat and bread mixture, using the finest grater. Add salt and pepper, mix in well, then add the egg or yolks and stir at least 3 minutes. Now shape the mixture into meat balls. You should have 12 of them. Roll them in bread crumbs and flatten them to oval shape. Criss-cross them with the back of a knife. Heat 3 tablespoons of the butter very hot. Brown the kotleti quickly, 6 minutes on each side. They will be best if you fry only 4 of them at a time. As they get done take them up and place them on a hot platter. When all are done and out of the platter, put the rest of the butter in the frying pan in one lump. Heat quickly. Add 2 tablespoons of consommé or water. Boil up and pour over the kotleti. Serve at once.

Russians usually add 2 tablespoons of sour cream to the gravy, but it isn't obligatory.

149

Baked Kotleti with Cream Sauce

1½ lb. ground lean beef
3 or 4 tbsp. butter
1 tsp. salt
Pepper
1 tbsp. minced dill or parsley

3 slices stale bread
2 eggs separated
Flour
1 cup consommé or water
3 tbsp. sour cream

Put the meat through your grinder once. Add 1 table-spoon of softened butter in small pieces. Put in the salt and season with pepper to taste. Add the minced dill or parsley, and the bread soaked in water then squeezed nearly dry. Mix thoroughly by hand. Add the egg yolks and mix again. Whip the whites of the eggs till they stand stiff, and add to the mixture, stirring in with a fork. Make 12 oval-shaped kotleti. Fry in very hot butter, 5 minutes on each side. Now place the fried kotleti in a casserole. Add a little flour to the frying pan and let cook a few minutes, then put in the consommé or water. Boil up. Add the sour cream and stir well. Pour this sauce over the kotleti in the casserole. Cover and bake 25 minutes in a medium oven (350°). Serve in the casserole.

If you like you can add 1 teaspoon of Worcestershire to the sauce.

Braised Kotleti with Horse-Radish

2 lb. ground beef
2 eggs
Salt
Pepper
4 tbsp. dry bread crumbs

1 onion, minced
3 tbsp. freshly grated horse-radish
3 tbsp. butter (or substitute)
1 tbsp. flour
1 cup water or consommé

Mix the ground meat with 1 whole egg and 1 egg yolk. Season with salt and pepper. Sauté the bread crumbs in 1½ tablespoons hot butter with the minced onion and the horse-radish. Form the meat into slightly flattened cakes. Roll them in the mixture of bread crumbs, horse-radish and onion. Sprinkle them with flour and brown them in the rest of the butter. When they are well browned, add the water or consommé. Cover the pan and simmer gently for 20 minutes. Take up the kotleti and place them on a hot platter. Strain the sauce, which may be poured over the kotleti or served separately. Plain boiled potatoes and dill pickles are the usual accompaniment for this dish.

Meat Loaf with Three Kinds of Meat

1 lb. ground beef	2 tbsp. minced parsley
1 lb. ground veal	Salt
1 lb. ground pork	Pepper
4 slices stale bread	Nutmeg
Cream	2 eggs
1 large onion, finely chopped	Sifted dry bread crumbs
1 tbsp. butter	3 slices bacon
	½ cup sour cream

Have your butcher put the 3 kinds of meat twice through the grinder. Remove the crusts and soak the bread in the cream. Mix with the meat. Simmer the chopped onion in the butter and add to the meat mixture. Add the parsley, salt, pepper, a little nutmeg, and the eggs. Don't beat the eggs. Stir well till all ingredients are thoroughly incorporated. Shape to loaf form in a baking pan. Cover generously with bread crumbs. Lay the slices of bacon on top. Cook 20 minutes in hot oven (400°), then reduce the heat and cook slowly for 40 minutes. Baste at least twice during cooking. Remove the loaf to a hot platter. Discard the bacon. Skim the fat from the gravy in the pan and thicken with very little flour. Add the sour cream and a little water. Boil up. Serve this gravy in a sauce boat with the meat loaf.

The same combination of three kinds of meat can be used for meat balls, which are very good with the gravy of onion and thyme that I mentioned in my introduction to kotleti recipes.

Golubtsi
(Meat Wrapped in Cabbage Leaves)

12 cabbage leaves	Salt
1 lb. ground round steak	Pepper
½ lb. ground pork	4 tbsp. butter (or substitute)
1 cup cooked rice	2 tbsp. flour
2 tbsp. minced parsley	1 cup tomato juice
1 egg	1 cup water
1 large onion, chopped	½ cup sour cream

Buy a large head of cabbage. Separate the leaves and pick out 12 perfect leaves. Cut away the hard part at the bottom of each leaf. Scald your 12 perfect leaves in salt water for 10 minutes. Take them up, spread them out on a towel, and let them dry while you prepare the stuffing.

Mix the ground beef and pork with the cooked rice and parsley, the egg (unbeaten), and the chopped onion simmered previously in a little butter. Salt and pepper to taste. Stir the mixture well. Divide into 12 portions. Make little rolls of the meat and wrap them in the cabbage leaves, folding the leaf all around the meat to make a neat little package.

Tie each package with fine string or thread. Fry in hot butter till brown, then cover the pan and cook gently for 30 minutes. Carefully remove the string so the cabbage-meat packets stay neatly shaped. Keep them warm. Add the flour to the pan in which they were fried. Cook 5 minutes, then add the tomato juice and water. Boil up. Add the sour cream and salt to taste. Boil up again. The gravy may be poured over the cabbage rolls or served separately.

In Russian the word *golubtsi* means pigeons. These rolls of cabbage and meat get their name for their rotund shape, which resembles that of a pigeon.

Kidneys in Madeira
(Potchki V Madeiry)

The last Tsar of Russia spent much of his time with his family at his palace in Tsarskoe Selo. Literally translated, Tsarskoe Selo means "the Tsar's village." Since the Revolution this place has been renamed Dyetskoe Selo, "the Children's Village," and the Soviet Government has established educational homes there for children.

Before these changes the railway restaurant at the Tsarkoe Selo station was far-famed for its cuisine. It catered to an endless cortege of official notables who had state business with the Tsar. At the station restaurant they ate to fortify themselves before the royal audience, then they ate there afterward to celebrate their success or console their failure. Lesser mortals also discovered the excellence of that station restaurant. Some Russian gourmets went to Tsarkoe Selo for no other reason but to enjoy the famous specialty of the railway-station chef—kidneys in Madeira. Never have I seen a restaurant patronized by so many bald-headed customers, all wearing decorations, all looking as though the fate of the world depended upon them. While they were missing the train of progress they enjoyed many a dish of kidneys in Madeira, made as follows:

2 veal kidneys
Flour
2 tbsp. butter
1 tbsp. sour cream

½ cup Madeira wine
Salt
Pepper

Skin the kidneys. Remove all fat and gristle. Slice very thin. Powder lightly with flour. Sauté in very hot butter 2 tablespoons of sliced kidneys at a time. Cook for 4 minutes only. Take up the kidneys. Put the sour cream in the pan, add the wine, and boil up. Season lightly with salt and pepper. Pour over the kidneys and serve.

Veal Chops with Brains

1 pair calves' brains
6 veal chops
4 tbsp. butter
Dry bread crumbs
Salt
Pepper

1 onion minced
3 tbsp. minced parsley
3 tbsp. sour cream
1 tbsp. flour
2 egg yolks

Cook half of the brains in salted acidulated water. Cool and cut in slices ¼ inch thick. Pound the chops a little with the edge of a plate. Sauté them on 1 side only in 2 tablespoons of hot butter. Arrange the chops neatly in a large baking pan. Cover each chop with a slice of the cooked brains. Dust with

154

salt, pepper, and bread crumbs. Sprinkle with a little melted butter. Cook 25 minutes in moderate oven (375°).

Cook the minced onion in hot butter. Do not brown. Add the parsley. Now take the remaining half of the brains, uncooked, rub them through a coarse sieve, and add them to the pan with the onion and parsley. Into this put the flour and sour cream, stirring over a moderate heat till you have a thickened sauce. Season with salt and pepper. Cool a few minutes, then stir in the egg yolks diluted with a little water. Pour the sauce over the veal chops. Sprinkle with bread crumbs. Return chops to the oven, cook 15 minutes.

This recipe is best when prepared in a flat fireproof dish which can be served at table.

Veal Chops Braised with Wine and Mushrooms

½ lb. mushrooms, sliced
½ onion, sliced
Butter
1 tbsp. flour
1 cup consommé
1 cup sour cream

1 tbsp. tomato purée
Salt
Cayenne pepper
½ cup Madeira wine
6 veal chops

Sauté the sliced mushrooms and onion in butter. Add the flour and cook for 5 minutes. Then add the consommé, sour cream, tomato purée, salt, and a little Cayenne pepper. Boil up. Now add the wine.

Dust the chops with a little flour and fry in hot butter till nicely browned. Lay the chops in a deep pan. Pour the mushroom sauce over them. Cover and cook 30 minutes over very slow heat. Do not cook fast or you will ruin this dish! Serve as follows: Make a ring of the chops on a large platter. Pour the sauce over them. Heap the center with French-fried potatoes and decorate with a sprig of parsley in the middle.

A few drops of lemon juice may be added to the sauce if a more piquant tang is desired. You can tenderize the chops by rubbing them with fresh lime juice and salt, or fresh lemon juice and salt, 2 hours before cooking. After that keep the chops at room temperature until you cook them.

Roast Veal with Ripe Cherries

4-lb. roast of veal	2 tsp. pounded cardamon seeds
Salt	1½ tbsp. flour
1 lb. ripe cherries	½ cup Madeira wine
¼ lb. butter (no substitute!)	½ cup cherry syrup
½ tsp. ground cinnamon	1 cup consommé

Do not attempt this recipe unless you have a great deal of patience and time.

The veal must be boneless and cut from the leg of a very young calf. In Russia such a cut is called a "fricandeau." Wipe the meat, rub it with salt, and let it stand 1 hour. Now, with a very sharp small knife make incisions for larding all over your piece of veal. There should be about 25 incisions. Into each incision insert 1 ripe cherry, pitted. Cook the rest of the cherries in a little water with sugar. Strain and save the syrup. You will need it later.

Place the veal in a greased roasting pan. Over it pour 2 tablespoons of melted butter. Powder with the cinnamon and ground cardamon. Cook about 20 minutes in hot oven (400°) till the meat is slightly browned. Pour on 2 more tablespoons of melted butter; sprinkle with flour; cover and cook 45 minutes in medium oven (350°). Now add the Madeira wine, the cherry syrup, the consommé, and the rest of the butter. Replace the cover. Continue cooking for 1 hour, basting every 15 minutes. Skim the fat from the gravy. Add a few table-spoons of water or consommé. Thicken very slightly. Boil up the gravy and serve in a gravy boat with the sliced veal. The cherries which were cooked in the syrup may be added to the gravy.

New potatoes and a cucumber salad go perfectly with this masterpiece of Russian meat cookery.

Braised Veal with Caviar Sauce

¼ lb. salt pork
3- to 4-lb. roast of veal
1 onion
1 carrot
4 sprigs parsley
2 stalks celery, with leaves
3 bay leaves

3 cloves
1 tbsp. minced lemon rind
1 cup white wine
Pepper
2 tbsp. fresh black caviar
Lemon juice

Slice the salt pork fairly thin. Lard the veal in a few places with very small slivers of pork. The veal should be boneless, cut from the leg. In a heavy pot lay the sliced pork and vege-tables with the spices and lemon rind. On these lay the veal, and set the pot on a strong heat for 20 minutes to brown the veal, taking care not to let the pork burn. Sprinkle with pepper, add the wine. Cover the pot and braise 1½ hours over low heat, turning the veal 2 or 3 times. When the veal is tender, take it out and place it on a hot platter. Strain the gravy; skim off the fat; thicken with flour; then add the caviar and a squeeze of lemon juice in a little water. Boil up once, pour over meat, and serve.

If the veal is good quality the sauce should be dark and tasty enough. But veal is sometimes watery and doesn't brown as it should. In this case enrich the sauce with 2 bouillon cubes dissolved in a little water, and put 1 teaspoon of butter in at the last minute.

Breast of Veal in Lemon Sauce
With Shrimps and Cauliflower

4 lb. breast of veal	1 lb. shrimp
Salt	1 cauliflower
3 onions, sliced	2 tbsp. butter
1 carrot, sliced	2 tbsp. flour
4 sprigs parsley	2 tbsp. lemon juice
Pepper	3 tbsp. dry white wine
Rind of ½ lemon	

The veal can be half breast and half shoulder if you prefer. Have the meat cut in pieces as for veal stew. Drop the pieces of veal into 3 cups of boiling salted water, bring to a boil, and cook for 2 minutes. Take out veal. Through a fine sieve strain the water in which veal was cooked. Now put the strained water in a clean pot with the sliced carrot and onion, the parsley, pepper, lemon rind, and butter. Add the veal and simmer till tender, about 1½ hours. When the veal is ready, take it up and keep it warm.

The shrimp should be cooked and shelled, the cauliflower cooked and divided into flowerets.

Discard the vegetables from the veal pot. Strain the gravy, thicken it with flour, add the lemon juice, boil up, and cook for 10 minutes, then put the veal in with the wine and shrimps. Arrange the veal and shrimps on a deep platter. Surround with cauliflower. Pour gravy over all. Serve extra gravy in a gravy boat.

This dish may also be garnished with asparagus spears between the flowerets of cauliflower, and with crescents of baked puff paste.

It is an inexpensive dish that makes a grand showing of elegance and tastes delicious.

Breast of Veal with Cream Sauce and Raisins

Follow the preceding recipe, leaving out the shrimps and cauliflower. To the gravy add 1 teaspoon sugar, ½ cup scalded and chopped raisins, 1 tablespoon fresh or sour cream.

Breast of Veal with Gherkins and Worcestershire

Cook the breast or shoulder of veal as in the 2 preceding recipes. Make the sauce as follows:

Thicken with flour. Add 3 bouillon cubes, and when they are dissolved add 2 teaspoons sugar, 12 sour gherkins cut in quarters lengthwise, ½ cup sauterne wine and 1 teaspoon Worcestershire sauce.

Shashlik

Originally this Caucasian way of broiling lamb came from the oriental parts of Russia where the people live very much in the Turkish or Persian manner, but shashlik has long since become a general favorite, a Russian national specialty. It is a very simple and delicious way of preparing lamb. You need long steel skewers. These can be bought in most good stores that stock kitchen equipment. The price of the skewers is quite moderate.

A shashlik skewer is flat, about ¼ inch wide and 11 inches long. One end is sharply pointed. The other end of the metal skewer forms a loop for convenient handling.

With the present-day popularity of cooking on outdoor grills, shashlik broiled over hot embers makes an ideal dish, much enjoyed by the men, who have fine sport playing chef with this easy culinary job.

For those of us who do our broiling indoors—under the flame instead of over it—I prescribe the use of a wide broiling rack, or even a wire rack of the kind used for cooling cakes. Place the rack in a roasting pan. It is handy to rest the skewers across the rack, and the result is better than when the skewers loaded with meat are placed directly in the pan.

Traditional accompaniment for shashlik is a generous quantity of fluffy boiled rice and a bowl of chopped scallions.

Here are the ingredients required for making shashlik:

3 lbs. boned leg of lamb	6 crushed peppercorns
1 large onion, chopped	1 cup diluted vinegar
1 clove garlic, chopped	½ cup red wine
¼ tsp. ground cloves	½ cup salad oil
¼ tsp. ground cinnamon	Salt

Cut the lamb in pieces about 1½ inches thick and 2 inches square. Trim off excess fat. Save some of the fat and cut it in thin slices. Place the pieces of lamb in a bowl with the chopped onion and garlic. Mix well.

Boil up the spices in the vinegar diluted with water. Let cool, then add the wine and pour over the meat. Cover and

160

let stand 4 hours or more at room temperature. This is very important.

Dry each piece of lamb carefully. Brush the pieces all over with oil and thread them on the skewers, with 1 thin slice of the fat between each piece of lamb and the next piece. Broil 12 minutes under or over very strong heat, turning once or twice. If you use a gas-stove broiler, have the shashliks as close to the flame as possible and baste at least once with the fat that runs down into the roasting pan below. Salt the shashliks lightly just before serving. A cube of bread at the pointed end of the skewer keeps the meat from sliding off when handled. Brush the bread with oil.

The correct way to serve shashlik is to slip the meat off the skewer onto the plate of the person being served and lay the skewer aside. Waiters in Russian restaurants make a big show of performing this rite with a flourish.

Shashlik Variations

1. The pieces of lamb may be marinated in the juice of very ripe pomegranates. This is done in the Caucasus.
2. On each skewer the pieces of lamb may alternate with any of the following:

   First a piece of lamb, then a thick slice of ripe tomato, then another piece of lamb, then another slice of tomato, etc., etc. (with thin slices of fat between each of the pieces of lamb and tomato).

   Or mushroom caps instead of the tomato slices.

   Or slices of eggplant salted for several hours and drained before use.

   Or slices of ham.

   Or slices of peeled fresh cucumber cut lengthwise.

Veal can be substituted for lamb, but in this case a slice of kidney fat is alternated with each piece of meat, and either mushrooms or tomatoes should always be used, since the broiled veal by itself is much less tasty than the lamb.

Siberian Pelmeny

Every housewife in Siberia always makes a lot of these little meat turnovers during the cold winter months. Some are cooked and eaten right away, but others are hung in a bag out of doors to freeze stiff. Frozen, they keep for weeks, can be taken on journeys or hunting expeditions, and are said to be better than ever when defrosted and cooked after a long glacial wait. The ingredients for the filling are:

1½ lb. best ground beef	3 tbsp. water
¼ lb. kidney fat	1 tsp. salt
1 onion, chopped	½ tsp. pepper

Put the beef and kidney fat through a meat grinder. Chop the onion very fine. Mix the meat, onion, and water. Season with salt and pepper.

The ingredients for the dough are:

2 cups sifted flour	3 egg yolks
1 tsp. salt	½ cup water (approximately)

Sift the flour and salt together. Mix with the egg yolks and water enough to make a stiff paste. Knead well. Set aside for 1 hour. Roll as thin as possible without tearing. Stamp out rounds or squares of paste, about 3 or 3½ inches across. On each piece of pastry lay 1 heaping teaspoon of the filling to form a small mound. Moisten the edges of dough with white of egg; fold the edges over to form crescents or triangles;

162

pinch together firmly. Your pelmeny are now ready for cooking. They look a good deal like Italian ravioli.

Throw them into a large pot of boiling water—not too many at a time. Cook them for 15 minutes. They will float to the top when done. Take them out and drain them. Place them on a hot platter. Serve very hot. In Siberia a bowl of mild vinegar goes with this dish, but melted butter or sour cream may suit your taste better.

Sometimes the pelmeny are cooked with consommé in a smaller pot. Then the consommé is eaten as soup when the pelmeny are ready.

Other fillings for Pelmeny are:

1. Ground ham with cooked dried mushrooms and fried onions, finely minced.
2. Ground raw pork mixed with finely ground game, raw or cooked.

Lamb Pilaf

3 lb. leg of lamb	1 onion, sliced
Pepper	2-2½ cups consommé or water
Salt	¾ cup rice
3 tbsp. butter	½ bay leaf

Cut the lamb in slices about ½ inch thick. Rub with plenty of pepper and a little salt. Brown the meat well in hot butter, add the sliced onion, and continue cooking gently for 10 minutes. Add 1 cup of consommé or water. Cover the pan and simmer for 20 minutes.

Wash the rice thoroughly. Scald it with boiling water and let it stand 10 minutes in the hot water. Drain. Rinse with cold water. Drain again, then put the rice on top of the lamb. Add the bay leaf, more salt, and the rest of the consommé or water, which should be lukewarm. The liquid should just barely cover the meat and rice. Cover and cook 45 minutes, in a moderate oven (325°). The rice should come out soft, each grain separate. The cooking time depends on the kind of rice used—it may take a little less than 45 minutes or a little longer. The best rice for this dish is the long-grain unstripped rice.

Russian-Style Turkish Pilaf

Follow the recipe for Lamb Pilaf, adding some half-cooked prunes and a few thin slices of lemon to the rice. Remove the pits from the prunes, the seeds from the lemon slices. You can substitute chopped raisins for the prunes, or use both prunes and raisins. About ½ cup raisins. About 6 or 8 cut-up prunes.

Pilaf with Tomato and Raisins

Follow the recipe for Lamb Pilaf, adding ½ cup scalded raisins to the rice. Heat 1 tablespoon tomato purée in a little butter and stir it very carefully into the rice with a fork when the rice is done. Let stand 10 minues before serving.

Suckling Pig

In Russia a boiled suckling pig served cold with horse-radish sauce is considered the perfect thing for a banquet or buffet supper. It is also a family dish, though roast suckling pig with stuffing and baked buckwheat groats is the specialty reserved for gala dinners at home. I have often wondered why suckling pig is served so rarely in America, where so many hogs are raised. To feed a large party, cold boiled suckling pig is an extremely good dish, easy enough to prepare.

Suckling Pig with Creamed Horse-radish Sauce

1 suckling pig, about 6 lb.	2 cups sour cream
10 cups cold water	Salt
½ cup freshly grated horse-radish	

Put the cleaned and scalded suckling pig in cold water without salt, spices, or soup greens. Barely bring to a slow boil, then reduce the heat *immediately*. Cover and simmer from 1½ to 2 hours. The suckling is ready when a long-pronged kitchen fork pierces the meat easily. *Do not overcook!* Let stand 15 minutes after removing from the heat. Take the suckling up, let it drain, place it on a platter. Let it cool, then chill it.

Mix the grated horse-radish with the sour cream and salt. Add a few drops of lemon juice if the cream isn't tart enough. Spread over the suckling pig, decorate with parsley, and serve.

An 8-lb. suckling isn't in the same class with a young porker of 6-6½ lbs. The larger suckling is usually cut into joints before cooking. In this case the cooking time isn't more than 1½ hours.

Roast Stuffed Suckling Pig with Kasha

1 suckling pig, about 6 lb.	Baked buckwheat groats (p. 113)
3 tbsp. butter	Salt
	Pepper

Have the suckling split in half lengthwise. Place the 2 halves side by side in your baking pan. Brush over with melted butter. Salt very lightly. Place in a hot oven (400°) for 20 minutes, or until the outside of the meat is browned. Add ½ cup of water to the pan after 15 minutes. Lower the heat and continue cooking for 45 minutes. Baste often.

Have the buckwheat groats ready. The groats must be hot. If they were cooked previously, warm them up in a pan with a little butter. Skim the fat from the roasting pan. Into this fat blend 1 scant tablespoon of flour, adding water to make about 1 cup of pan gravy. Put the buckwheat kasha on a large platter. Pour the gravy over the kasha. Lay the 2 halves of the roast suckling pig on top and serve. The meat may be cut in portions before laying on the platter. Spiced plums, peaches, cherries, or pears should go with this dish.

Roast Fresh Ham, Moscow Style

5-6 lb. fresh ham	1 tbsp. tarragon vinegar
2 tsp. ground allspice	½ cup Madeira wine
2 tsp. ground pepper	Salt
1 tsp. ground cinnamon	8 medium-sized onions
½ tsp. ground cloves	3 apples, chopped
2 tsp. ground marjoram	

Carefully choose a fresh ham from a young pig, plump but not too fat. Have the skin removed and some of the outer layer of fat trimmed off. Mix the spices together and rub the ham all over with them. Let stand 3 to 4 hours at room temperature. Prick the ham in several places with a kitchen fork. Place in a large roasting pan with 2 tablespoons of water, the tarragon vinegar, and 4 tablespoons of the Madeira wine.

Sprinkle the ham with salt. Put in a very hot oven (450°) for 20 minutes. Lower the heat to about 375° for 45 minutes. Baste 2 or 3 times.

Have the onions previously cooked for 15 minutes in salted water. When the ham has roasted for 45 minutes, place the onions and the chopped peeled apples around it. Return to the oven and continue cooking for 1 hour. Baste frequently.

If the ham is from a young pig and doesn't weigh more than 5 lb., the complete cooking time will be 2 hours. If it weighs more, allow another 20 or 30 minutes. In this case don't add the onions and apples until 1 hour before the meat will be ready. The onions should be served whole around the meat. Skim the fat from the pan gravy before thickening slightly with flour. Rub the gravy through a sieve and add the rest of the wine. Serve the gravy separately. Serve it boiling hot.

Breaded Pork Chops with Prune or Cherry Sauce

6 trimmed pork chops	1 tsp. minced lemon rind
Flour	½ tsp. ground cinnamon
Dry bread crumbs	¼ tsp. ground cloves
1 tbsp. butter (or substitute)	½ cup water
1 cup purée of stewed prunes or cherries	½ cup port wine

Put the chops in boiling salted water. Reduce the heat and simmer for 15 minutes. Take up the chops and let them cool, then dust them with flour and roll them in bread crumbs. Sauté them in the hot butter, 5 minutes on each side, then cook them gently for 20 minutes, turning once.

Have the prunes or cherries cooked, rubbed through a

sieve, and sweetened. Add the lemon rind, spices, and water if the fruit purée seems too thick. Cook 10 minutes. Add the wine. Boil up once. Pour over chops and serve very hot.

Boujenina
(Fresh Ham Cooked with Hay and Beer)

I introduce this recipe more as a curiosity than as a practical suggestion for your dinner table. In old Russia, when a young pig was killed, the ham prepared in this manner used to be a treat served at fine rural estates. I tasted it once at a big country place a couple of miles from the town where Lenin was born. The ingredients and the methods are as follows:

1 fresh ham	2 cloves
2 generous handfuls of hay	2 peppercorns
2 pints dark beer	Bay leaves
Soup greens	Salt

Wash the ham. Tie it loosely in a cloth and put it in a large pot of cold water, adding the 2 generous handfuls of fresh clean hay. Bring twice to a boil. Cook 10 minutes. Take out the ham. Take off the cloth, rinse the ham in warm water, and place it in another pot together with the beer, soup greens, spices, and salt. Cover the pot and simmer slowly for 2½ hours, till the meat is tender. Skim the fat from the liquid in the pot, then thicken it with a little paste of flour and water. Boil up. Boiled potatoes, braised cabbage, spiced cherries or plums, and a purée of chestnuts are served with this ham. The hay really does give it a nice aromatic flavor.

CHAPTER 8

POULTRY AND GAME

In Russia the average family eats a good deal of chicken, usually cooked in one of the plain ways that are customary throughout America and other countries—roast chicken, broiled chicken, boiled or stewed chicken. Fried chicken has never been popular in Russia. I don't know why.

Since there is nothing particularly characteristic about Russia's plain chicken cooking, I have devoted this chapter to special recipes of a more different and uniquely Russian type.

Wherever ducks and geese are plentiful in Russia, they are served frequently, plain roasted as a rule, but with the distinctive Russian stuffing of buckwheat kasha.

Plain roasting is also the favorite Russian way to cook game birds. This becomes monotonous, however, because wild birds are so numerous as to constitute an everyday food supply in nearly all parts of Russia. For this reason you may think us very lavish when you see our game recipes, in some of which we use only the breasts of the birds, tossing all else into the soup pot.

I believe there are still a few districts in this country where wild game gets to be tiresome as a steady diet, and those Americans who live there will readily understand our Russian need for fancified game dishes. On the other hand, game is far from abundant in the more populous communities here, so out of kindness I have omitted many of our Russian game specialties, knowing they could only make game-lovers feel deprived.

I recommend the following chicken recipes for party dinners:

Chicken with Liver-and-Walnut Stuffing

4- to 5-lb. roasting chicken	Mace
½ lb. calves' liver	½ lb. shelled walnuts
2 tbsp. butter	2 eggs
3 slices stale bread	1 tsp. sugar
Salt	1 tsp. lemon juice
Pepper	2 tbsp. Madeira wine

Prepare the chicken for roasting. Sauté the liver in the butter for 7 minutes, then chop and put through meat grinder. Remove the crusts and soak the bread in a little milk. Squeeze the bread fairly dry and add it to the ground liver. Season with salt, pepper, a dash of Cayenne if you like, and a small pinch of ground mace. If you have no mace, ½ teaspoon nutmeg or allspice will do.

Scald the walnuts. Remove the skins. Chop and pound the walnuts to a paste, or grind them in a nut grinder. Mix them with the liver and bread. Add the eggs whole. Stir together thoroughly. Stuff the chicken with this and roast, basting well with butter. When you make the pan gravy, thicken slightly, then add the sugar, lemon juice, and Madeira wine.

In the Russian cuisine this is a standard recipe either for chicken or for turkey. If you use it for turkey, double the quan-

170

tities of the ingredients in the stuffing. Turkey or chicken, the flavor is delicious in any case.

Braised Chicken with Chestnut Stuffing

1 lb. chestnuts	2 tbsp. chopped salt pork
1 tbsp. butter (or substitute)	Carrots, sliced
3 slices stale bread	Celery, sliced
2 tbsp. dried currants or raisins, chopped	Bay leaf
	6 peppercorns
Pepper	½ tsp. lemon juice
Salt	2 tbsp. Madeira or port wine
3- to 4-lb roasting chicken	½ tsp. ground cinnamon

Scald the chestnuts or fry them in oil for 5 minutes. Remove the shells and inner skin. Cook in water and milk till soft. The liquid should just cover the chestnuts. Rub them through a sieve. Soften the butter and add it to the chestnuts. You should have a medium thick purée. Remove the crusts, crumble the bread, and add it to the chestnut purée. Let stand 15 minutes. Add a little milk if the purée seems too stiff. Now add chopped currants or raisins, and pepper and salt to taste. Stuff the chicken with this mixture.

Sprinkle the chicken lightly with flour and lay it in a deep heavy pot. Surround the bird with chopped salt pork, sliced carrots and celery, a bay leaf and the peppercorns. Add ¼ cup water. Cover the pot and set over brisk heat for 20 minutes. Turn the bird once during this time, then diminish the heat and cook very slowly from 1-1½ hours. The chicken should be cooked *very* slowly, and should be turned at least 4 times during cooking. You may need to add a little water to the pot. When the chicken is tender, remove the cover and place the pot in a hot oven for 20-30 minutes for the chicken to brown.

Remove the chicken to a hot platter. Skim the gravy well, then strain. Thicken with a small amount of flour and add a little water. Add the lemon juice, some pepper, and the wine. If you like the flavor of cinnamon, as many Russians do, add ½ teaspoon to the gravy just before serving.

Roast Chicken with Liver-and-Apple Stuffing

1 lb. calves' or pork liver, sliced	Salt
	Pepper
3 tbsp. butter or substitute	1 roasting chicken
3 slices bread, 1 day old	2 onions, chopped
3 large apples	Dry bread crumbs
3 tbsp. raisins	¼ cup sherry or Madeira wine
2 eggs	(optional)
½ tsp. nutmeg	1 tbsp. flour

Sauté the sliced liver and onions 5 minutes in 1½ tablespoons of hot butter, then put through a meat grinder. Cut off the crusts and soak the bread in a little water. Squeeze the bread dry and add it to the ground liver. Peel the apples, core them, and slice them in eighths. Simmer them 5 minutes in water. Strain. To the liver mixture add the raisins, eggs, nutmeg, and salt and pepper to taste. Mix well, then add the apples. The slices of apple should remain whole.

Stuff the bird with the liver-apple mixture. Rub the outside with salt, pepper, and butter. Roast in an open pan. When nearly done, sprinkle with flour and bread crumbs. Brown 15 minutes in very hot oven. Skim the gravy and strain it before thickening with flour. The wine is optional. If you use it, add it to the gravy just before serving.

The same stuffing is used for turkey, but the proportions should be doubled. For turkey gravy, use Madeira wine instead of sherry.

Steamed Chicken Pudding

4 cups ground cold cooked chicken
4 cups stale bread crumbs
1 cup rich milk
½ tsp. nutmeg
3 eggs, separated

3 tbsp. butter
12 cooked shrimp, chopped
Pepper
Salt
Fine dry bread crumbs

The chicken should be ground very fine. Mix the bread crumbs with the milk, add the nutmeg, then simmer gently till the crumbs are entirely smooth. Add the yolks of the eggs. Do not cook after these are added. Cut the butter in very small pieces and stir it into the bread and egg mixture. Mix this with the chicken, taking care to stir well. Chop the shrimp fine and add them to the mixture. Season with a fair amount of freshly ground pepper and a little salt to taste. Let cool, then add the well-whipped whites of the eggs. Pour into a buttered mold which has been sprinkled with fine dry bread crumbs. Cover with buttered greaseproof paper. Steam 45 minutes, till the center of the pudding is firm to touch. Turn out onto a hot platter. Serve with cream sauce, tomato sauce, or shrimp sauce.

Chicken Fricassee with Prunes and Puff Pastry

1 chicken cut up for frying	Salt
4 tbsp. butter	1 slice lemon, seeded
1 carrot, sliced	1 tbsp. flour
1 onion, sliced	1½ cups cooked stoned prunes,
2 sprigs parsley	chopped
1 bay leaf	1 tsp. sugar
Pepper	Puff pastry

Fry the pieces of chicken lightly in 3 tablespoons of the butter. Add carrot and onion, parsley, bay leaf, lemon, pepper, and salt. Add 1 cup of water. Cover and simmer gently for 45 minutes. If the chicken is tender it should now be done. If not tender, continue cooking till ready

Take up the pieces of chicken, then strain and skim the broth. Brown the flour in the rest of the butter. Mix with the broth and boil up.

Add the chopped prunes to the gravy together with the sugar. Boil up once. Put the pieces of chicken in and reheat. Serve on a large platter, making a border of crescents of puff pastry. Or make a ring of pastry on a fireproof dish and bake it, then fill the ring with the chicken and prune fricassee.

The gravy must be tasted before serving. It may need a little more sugar or lemon juice, depending on the flavor of the prunes. This is an excellent way to use an old chicken that isn't very tender.

THE POJARSKI TAVERN AT TORJOK

Torjok was a small but prosperous town on the old post road between Moscow and St. Petersburg. Riders and travelers making the journey by carriage used to change horses at Torjok. They were always glad of the chance to dine at the tavern there. The tavernkeeper's name was Pojarski, and his cooking was famous all over Russia.

The culinary masterpiece of his invention was a dish called Pojarskiya Kotleti—meat cakes made originally of game, or of game and beef combined. Today they are usually made with chicken, or beef and veal.

In my schooldays, when I first visited Torjok, the town had already ceased to be a stopping-off place for travelers. The Nicolaevski Railway from St. Petersburg to Moscow had long since canceled the importance of the post road—a change that can be attributed in part to American enterprise, for the engineer who built the Nicolaevski Railway was the father of James McNeill Whistler, the American artist.

Torjok was something of a ghost town, as I knew it, yet the old clapboard tavern was still standing, still serving its celebrated kotleti. The day I first went to Torjok, before starting a thirty-mile drive to a cousin's estate, a crowd of my relatives took me to the Pojarski Tavern to dine and stay overnight.

The little town fascinated me as we drove through it to reach the tavern. Torjok is built upon a cluster of hills, and on the top of each and every hill there was a neat little church with a melon-shaped dome of glittering gold or azure blue, with an Orthodox Cross flashing its golden symbol above every dome. There were 37 churches in Torjok for a population of 15,000.

The great Volga River flows through Torjok, and when I went there I had never before seen the Volga, so dear to the heart of every Russian. All along the banks of the river, opposite the town, stretched a range of fantastic palaces built by the millionaire merchants of Torjok's earlier times. Florentine

175

villas and Byzantine castles mingled with French châteaux and English Tudor towers beside the Volga in an architectural extravaganza such as Hollywood might dream up.

Torjok was indeed a fitting birthplace for Pojarski's superlative kotleti—the delight of all who ever tasted them.

Pojarskiya Kotleti with Chicken

3½- to 4-lb. roasting chicken
2 cups crumbled bread from a French loaf 1 day old
½ cup sweet cream
½ tsp. salt

1 tbsp. vodka or gin
7 tbsp. butter
1 egg yolk
1 scant tbsp. flour

Remove the skin from the uncooked chicken. Cut off all the meat and discard all gristle. Put the chicken meat twice through a meat grinder. Crumble the soft inside part from a long French loaf. Soak 2 cups of the crumbs in the cream, then squeeze dry. Combine the bread with the ground chicken, the salt, the vodka or gin, and 2 tablespoons of the butter, creamed. Mix thoroughly, then add the egg yolk. It is best to do the mixing with your hands.

Turn the mixture out onto a wet wooden board. Divide into 12 parts. Form each part into a small, thick oval cake. Sprinkle these with flour and fry them immediately in very hot butter till golden brown.

A perfect Pojarski kotlet ought to be so buttery you'll have to watch out it doesn't spray you when you stick your fork in it.

At Pojarski's tavern the original recipe for these kotleti says they should be made with the meat of hazel hens or young

176

partridges, supplemented by a small amount of finely chopped fillet of beef.

Pojarskiya Kotleti with Veal

2 lb. shoulder of veal	2 egg yolks
2 cups crumbled bread from a French loaf 1 day old	1 tsp. salt
½ cup sweet cream	6 tbsp. butter
½ lb. ground top-round beef	1 tbsp. vodka or gin

Have the veal put twice through a meat grinder. Soak the soft inside bread from the loaf in the cream. Mix together the ground veal, ground beef, the bread soaked in cream, the egg yolks, salt, the vodka or gin, and 2 tablespoons of the butter, creamed. Stir well or knead with your hands till thoroughly smooth. Turn the mixture out onto a wet wooden board. Divide in 12 portions. Form small thick meat cakes as in the preceding recipe. Fry golden brown in hot butter, about 12 minutes.

These kotleti are usually served with mushrooms sliced and simmered in butter then thickened with a little flour and 1 or 2 tablespoons of sour cream.

Breast of Chicken, Kiev Style

3 large breasts of chicken	Fine bread crumbs
½ lb. sweet butter	Salt
1 egg	Pepper

Remove the breasts from the bone. Cut away all gristle. Separate the 2 halves of each breast, making 6 half-breasts, 1 half-breast for each portion.

Pound the breasts very flat and thin. Form 6 small rolls of butter about 2 inches long and ½ inch thick. Chill these rolls of butter in water with ice until they are hard. Take them up quickly, wipe dry, and place 1 roll of butter on each flattened breast of chicken. Roll the chicken around the butter, folding in at the ends so the butter is completely enclosed. Try to give each little rolled-up parcel a neat oval shape. Skewer firmly with wooden toothpicks.

Dilute the egg with a little water. Roll the rolled-up chicken breasts in bread crumbs. Dip in egg. Roll again in bread crumbs. Fry golden brown in plenty of hot butter. Drain and place in a hot oven for 5 minutes. Serve at once.

The same mushroom sauce which is served with the Pojarskiya Kotleti in the preceding recipe is the usual sauce for this dish.

Roast Chicken with Anchovy Butter

Roast a chicken according to your usual American recipe, but do not have the chicken stuffed. When it is nearly done, sprinkle with dry bread crumbs, pour on some melted butter, and let the chicken brown. Then take it out of the oven and fill the inside with softened anchovy butter, prepared as follows:

Mash 6 finely chopped anchovy fillets with 3 tablespoons of unsalted butter.

Put a few tablespoons of pan gravy around the chicken when you serve it. The anchovy butter will melt and run into the gravy, and the combination of the two is the distinguishing feature of this dish. As you carve and serve each portion, spoon a little of the combined butter and pan gravy on the plate with the chicken.

Russians consider this an extra-gourmet treat. A simple green salad should accompany it.

Partridge or pheasant can be prepared the same way.

Spring Chicken with Gooseberry Sauce

3 spring chickens	1 scant tbsp. butter
1 carrot, sliced	1 tbsp. flour
1 onion, sliced	2 cups water or consommé
4 sprigs parsley	¼ cup white wine
1 cup green gooseberries	Pepper
1 or 2 tbsp. sugar	Salt

Cut the chickens in halves if they are the right size so that a half chicken won't be too much for an individual portion. If they are larger, cut them in quarters.

Cook the sliced onion for 20 minutes in a pan with the 2 cups of water, or consommé, the sliced carrot, and the parsley. Have the water boiling. Put the chickens in and let the water boil up again, then cover and simmer very gently for 30 minutes. Take the chickens out and keep them warm. Strain the broth. To ¾ cup of broth add the gooseberries, which must not be overripe, and the sugar. Cover and simmer for 10 minutes. The berries should remain whole. Now melt the butter and blend in the flour; thicken the remaining broth; add the wine, the chicken, and the gooseberries. Boil up once and serve. The gooseberries may need a little more sugar or a little less. But the dish is supposed to be definitely sharp, not sweet.

Spring chickens fried in egg and bread crumbs are also served with a gooseberry sauce, the gooseberries being cooked in very little water and thickened slightly with flour and butter.

179

Broilers Braised with Tarragon

2 broilers	Salt
3 tbsp. olive oil or salad oil	Pepper
2 small cloves garlic	2 bouillon cubes
3 tbsp. fresh tarragon	¼ cup hot water

Have the broilers cut in quarters if they are large, in halves if small. Heat the oil in a pan; add the garlic and the tarragon leaves. Rub the pieces of chicken with salt and pepper, and brown them slightly in the pan. Dissolve the bouillon cubes in the hot water and add to the pan. Cover and cook 30 minutes over medium heat. Turn the pieces of chicken several times. If necessary, add 1 more tablespoon of hot water.

A good vegetable dish to serve with this is buttered green peas mixed with asparagus tips.

Braised Capon with Truffle Sauce

8 thin slices salt pork	Salt
2 carrots, sliced	Pepper
2 onions, sliced	Flour
3 sprigs parsley	1½ cups consommé
4 cloves	3 truffles
2 bay leaves	1 cup burgundy or claret wine
1 capon	½ cup rum

Line the bottom of a heavy pot with slices of salt pork. Lay the carrots and onions on the pork, also the parsley, cloves, and bay leaves. Rub the capon with salt and pepper inside and out. Sprinkle the outside of the bird with flour and put it in the pot on top of the pork and vegetables. Cover the pot. Cook

25 minutes over strong heat. Turn the bird over once during this time. Now add ½ cup of the consommé, re-cover, and cook slowly for 1½ hours. Turn the bird several times. At the end of 1½ hours it should be tender and nicely browned, but you can continue cooking for 30 minutes more if necessary. Add 2 more tablespoons of consommé if the pot gets too dry.

Cut the truffles in long thin slivers. Mix the wine and rum and soak the truffles in this for 30 minutes.

When the capon is ready, take it up and place it on a serving platter.

Now prepare the sauce. Skim off the fat and strain the liquid from the pot. Thicken with a little flour, then add the truffles, wine, and the rest of the consommé. Boil up and serve. There should be about 2 cups of sauce.

If truffles are unobtainable, you can substitute sliced mushrooms simmered beforehand in butter—but the result won't be as good. Truffles are not only more elegant, they taste better, too, in this dish.

Turkey Pashtet (Pie)

1 small turkey
Butter
1 cup white wine
2 tbsp. vinegar
3 onions
Rind of ½ lemon
1 bay leaf
1 stalk celery
4 sprigs parsley
6 peppercorns
Salt

1½ lb. veal without bones
½ lb. bacon
1½ cups crumbled stale bread
6 anchovy fillets, finely chopped
2 tbsp. minced olives or capers
3 egg yolks
½ tsp. nutmeg
Pepper
Short pastry (p. 101)
½ cup Madeira wine

Cut the turkey in joints and brown them in butter. Cover with the white wine, the vinegar, and a small amount of water. Add 2 tablespoons of butter, 2 onions, the lemon rind, bay leaf, celery, parsley, peppercorns, and a pinch of salt. Simmer gently till tender—about 45 minutes to 1 hour, depending on the turkey. Take the turkey out when done. Strain the broth and set it aside.

Put the veal and bacon through a meat grinder. Chop the remaining onion and cook it in 1 tablespoon of butter. Mix together the ground veal and bacon, the sautéed onion, bread, anchovies, minced olives or capers, egg yolks, nutmeg, and pepper. Stir till smooth and well blended. In Russia the mixture is forced through a fine sieve.

Now take a round metal spring-form and build up the sides with 2 layers of well-greased white paper, as is done for any raised pie. Roll out the pastry and line the dish with it. Put in a layer of the veal forcemeat, then a layer of turkey. Repeat till the dish is full. Cover with pastry and decorate. Cut 2 small slits in the top crust. Bake the pie 1 hour in a moderate oven (350°).

Make a sauce with the broth in which the turkey was cooked. Thicken the broth with a little flour, add the Madeira wine, and season with salt and pepper.

Remove the spring-form and paper from the pie and transfer the pie to a serving platter. Pour some of the sauce in through the slits in the top crust. Serve the rest of the sauce in a gravy boat. A few slivers of truffles can be added to the sauce.

This turkey pashtet is one of Russia's full-dress recipes, very popular for gala occasions. I suggest using it as the show dish at a wedding breakfast.

But in my opinion it can be simplified and improved. In

the first place, it will be much easier to serve if the bones are removed from the turkey joints after they are cooked. Also I find it more convenient to bake the pie in an extra large ovenproof glass casserole, without building up the sides with paper. The pie can then be served straight from the casserole, and you needn't transfer it to a platter, which is always a nerve-racking operation, performed at a risk of the whole pie's collapse, followed naturally by the emotional collapse of the cook.

Roast Goose with Apple Stuffing and Kasha

1 goose	2 large onions, chopped
1½ tbsp. salt	1 cup consommé
1 tbsp. thyme	1 tbsp. flour
8 large apples	Baked kasha
1 tbsp. marjoram	

Trim off some of the large pieces of fat near the neck and the tail end of the goose. Keep these for other cooking. Rub the goose inside and out with salt and thyme mixed. Let stand 30 minutes. Peel, core, and chop the apples. Sprinkle with salt and marjoram and stuff the goose with them. If you like applesauce, don't skimp the stuffing, because this is our Russian way of making applesauce—inside the goose.

Place the goose on a rack in a roasting pan. Put the chopped onion in the pan and set it in a hot oven (450°) for 30 minutes. Then lower the heat to 350° and add half the consommé to the pan. Continue roasting for 3 hours. From now on, baste the bird every 15 minutes till done, adding the rest of the consommé during this time. Prick the skin of the goose with a fork from time to time to let the fat run out. Thicken the pan

183

gravy with flour after skimming off nearly all fat. Add water. Boil up. Serve in a gravy boat.

In Russia we always bake a large pot of kasha—buckwheat groats—to serve with goose. You will find the kasha recipe in Chapter 4. We also bake 6 or 8 lightly sugared apples, basting them once or twice with fat from the roasting goose. The apples are served with the goose and kasha.

Duck can also be done this way.

Duck Stuffed with Macaroni

1 duck	½ tsp. nutmeg
Salt	1 egg yolk, slightly beaten
Pepper	1 onion
1 tsp. thyme	1 carrot
½ lb. macaroni	1 tbsp. flour
1 tbsp. melted butter	4 tbsp. chopped capers or olives
2 tbsp. cream	

Rub the duck inside and out with salt, pepper, and thyme. Cook the macaroni in salted water till just soft. Drain. Rinse with cold water. Drain again.

Place the macaroni in a pot. Add the melted butter, cream, nutmeg, and egg yolk. Stir for 3 minutes over medium heat, then stuff the duck with this mixture.

Set the duck on a rack in a roasting pan. Pour ¼ cup water in the pan. Add the onion and carrot cut in quarters. Roast for 15 minutes in a hot oven (450°), then diminish the heat to 350°. Baste every 10 minutes. For the cooking time, allow 20 minutes to the pound. When the duck is done, skim the fat from the pan gravy, thicken the gravy with the flour, add a little water, and boil up; then add the chopped capers or olives. Boil up again.

With roast duck Russians serve baked apples in preference to applesauce.

Duck with Mushroom Sauce

1 duck	Pepper
2 onions	Salt
1 carrot	1 lb. mushrooms
2 stalks celery	2 tbsp. butter
2 bay leaves	2 tbsp. flour
3 sprigs parsley	1 cup sour cream
1 clove garlic	

Place the duck in a large pan with just enough water to cover. Bring twice to a boil. Remove any scum that rises, and continue cooking for 20 minutes. Take the duck out and rinse it with warm water. Strain the water in which the duck was cooked. Cut the duck into joints and put the pieces back in the strained cooking water. Add the vegetables, coarsely cut. Add the bay leaves, garlic, pepper, and 1 teaspoon of salt. Simmer slowly till the duck is tender—about 1 hour.

Cook the unpeeled mushrooms 20 minutes in boiling salted water. Drain and slice. Melt the butter and blend in the flour. Stir in 3 cups of the water in which the duck is cooking. To this add the mushrooms and sour cream. Bring to a boil. Add the pieces of duck. Cook for another 10 minutes. Serve in a deep dish. Boiled potatoes are the usual accompaniment.

This is a very good way to make an appetizing presentation of a not-so-young duck

Braised Duck, Moscow Style

1 young duck	3 sprigs parsley
Pepper	6 anchovy fillets, finely chopped
1 onion	1 tbsp. flour
1 carrot	Juice of ½ lemon
1 stalk celery	1 cup consommé
3 tbsp. butter	1 cup Madeira or port wine
1 bay leaf	

Rub the duck with pepper. Cut the onion, carrot, and celery in large pieces. Brown the duck and vegetables in hot butter, add the bay leaf and parsley, then cover the pot and cook slowly for 1 hour, turning the duck several times. The bird should be tender at the end of an hour. If not, continue cooking from 15 to 30 minutes more. Be very careful not to overcook it.

Take the duck out. Pour off the excess fat. Remove the vegetables and bay leaf. Brown the flour in the pot; add the chopped anchovies, the consommé, and the lemon juice. Boil up. Simmer for a few minutes, then add the wine. Serve this sauce in a sauce boat.

Pheasant or Woodcock with Oriental Sauce

1 pair pheasants or woodcock	3 oranges
Butter	1 tbsp. butter
½ cup cold China tea	1 cup port wine
1 cup shelled hazelnuts	1 tsp. nutmeg
1 lb. sweet grapes	½ tsp. pepper

Rub the birds with butter. Roast them and cut them in portions for serving. Make the tea very strong, using 2 teaspoons of tea leaves, preferably green tea. Blanch the hazel-nuts, grind them fine, then pound them to a paste. The sweet grapes may be black or green. Crush them with a wooden spoon and add sections of peeled and seeded oranges. Press the grapes and oranges through a sieve. To this fruit purée add 1 tablespoon of softened butter, the wine, tea, nutmeg, and pepper. Boil up once. Serve with the roasted birds.

CHAPTER 9

VEGETABLES

Fresh vegetables are very scarce in most parts of Russia during the cold months of the year. The choice is limited chiefly to cabbage, carrots, turnips, and beets. Potatoes are plentiful as a rule. Green peas, green beans, asparagus, etc., all come out of cans, and there is nothing particularly Russian about the way we prepare them.

Summer is another story. Because of the short time during which we have an abundance of green vegetables and salads, we welcome them with great enthusiasm.

All Russians get out of town in summer if they possibly can do so. They either go to visit country relatives, or they rent a *datcha* at some outdoor resort. *Datcha* is our Russian word for a summer cottage.

Before the Revolution, when Russians had country estates, everyone who owned such a place, large or small, went there sometime in May and stayed until August. The fresh vegetables grown in quantity on these estates were varied and delicious. For a part of the summer many people took the healthy measure of living on a diet of vegetables, fortified by pitchers of cream, huge bowls of pot cheese, and dozens of new-laid eggs.

But in those days few Russians dared call themselves out-and-out vegetarians, for under the stupid and backward regime of the Romanoff tsars, *vegetarianism* was linked with the sub-

188

versive teachings of the radicals! It was a new idea, and was therefore considered dangerous. A number of Tolstoy's followers—all politically suspect in the eyes of the reactionary authorities—were acknowledged vegetarians.

I spent one heavenly summer as the guest of a friend of mine who had a small estate on the Moscow River. Never have I tasted such fine-flavored vegetables as were grown there. An hour or so before dinner the gnarled old gardener brought them in fresh from the garden, lovingly arranged in big flat baskets. My hostess was a vegetarian, and I wanted nothing more than those superb vegetables—yet the cook kept tempting me with broiled spring chickens and other handsome meat dishes which I didn't want. There was nobody else to eat them, since my hostess and I were alone, so the chicken and meat always went back to the kitchen untouched.

Then one morning the gardener came to us with a solemn, worried face. He spoke of my vegetable diet. He asked if I wouldn't please just pretend to eat a little meat.

To my hostess he said, "You see, Your Excellency, it's bad enough with you being a vegetarian. But now there's two of you, and the village is beginning to talk. Folks are whispering. They're saying this is a house of revolutionists!"

To hush the scandal I ate chicken once a week thereafter. The cook and the gardener were natural-born propagandists. They told the village gossips that I ate a whole chicken every day.

POTATOES

At dinner in many a Russian home the main dish often consists of boiled potatoes served with a sauce. We have a number of different sauces or garnishes that we use effectively

189

to dress up a potato dinner. Sometimes a meat soup or a vegetable soup may precede the potatoes, and in hot weather the potato dish may be followed by a salad. I believe our Russian potato recipes can be very useful to American families, particularly during a meat shortage.

Boiled Potatoes with Mushroom Sauce

3 lb. potatoes	1 cup sweet or sour cream
1 lb. mushrooms	½ cup consommé or water
1 onion, sliced	Salt
1½ tbsp. butter	Pepper
1 tbsp. flour	2 tbsp. minced parsley

Cook the potatoes in their skins. While the potatoes cook, prepare the mushroom sauce as follows:

Simmer the sliced mushrooms and onion for 20 minutes in hot butter. Add the flour and cook for 5 minutes, then add the cream, the consommé or water, salt, pepper, and the parsley. Boil up. Have the sauce in a large pan.

When the potatoes are done—do not overcook them—dry them out over low heat for 5 minutes. Peel them and cut them in thick slices. Add them to the sauce. Stir very gently with a fork. Heat for 10 minutes but do not boil. Serve piping hot.

Boiled Potatoes with Dill-Pickle Sauce

3 lb. potatoes	1½ cups strong consommé
1 onion, minced	4 small dill pickles
1 tbsp. butter	2 tbsp. minced parsley
1 tbsp. flour	

Have the potatoes cooked, peeled, and sliced. Small new potatoes can be used whole. Sauté the minced onion in the

190

butter. Add the flour and cook for 5 minutes. Now add the consommé and the dill pickles, peeled and sliced. Boil up. Cook for 10 minutes, then put in the potatoes and the parsley. Cook for 5 minutes more, and serve very hot.

Potato Soufflé with Shredded Ham

5 cups riced potatoes	½ lb. lean ham, shredded
3 whole eggs	Salt
2 egg yolks	Pepper
¼ lb. butter	

Mash the riced potatoes with a wooden spoon till entirely smooth. Beat the whole eggs and the 2 egg yolks together thoroughly. Save out 1 tablespoon of the butter, and cream all the rest of the butter with the beaten eggs. Add this to the potatoes. Now add the shredded ham, salt, and pepper. Pour the mixture into a buttered fireproof mold or casserole. Bake 25 minutes in medium oven (350°). The soufflé should be well browned on the outside. Turn it out onto a hot platter and serve at once.

This soufflé is sometimes sprinkled with a little grated cheese and melted butter after it is turned out on the platter.

With this Russian potato soufflé I like an American salad of plain lettuce, French dressing, a few sections of orange, and ½ teaspoon of grated orange rind.

Baked Potatoes Stuffed with Mushrooms

6 large baking potatoes	1 egg yolk, slightly beaten
1 leek or onion, chopped	Salt
3 tbsp. butter	Pepper
¼ lb. mushrooms, minced	Nutmeg

191

Scrub the potatoes. Rub them on the outside with a small piece of pork fat, and place them in the oven to bake.

Cook the leek or onion—leek tastes a little better if you can get one—in 2 tablespoons of hot butter for 10 minutes, without browning. Add the minced mushrooms to the pan with the leek or onion and cook slowly for 10 minutes. Season with salt, pepper, and a small pinch of nutmeg. Add the egg yolk. Remove the pan from the fire. When the potatoes are baked, cut off a lengthwise slice and scoop out a little more than half of the inside. Mix the scooped-out potato with the mushrooms, adding 1 tablespoon of cream or milk if the mixture seems too thick—this will depend on whether or not the mushrooms were watery. Stuff the potato shells, rounding off the top to a neat mound shape. Sprinkle over with the remaining tablespoon of butter, which should be melted. Place in very hot oven for 15 minutes.

Scalloped Potatoes with Anchovies

2 onions, chopped	1½ cups sour cream
3 tbsp. butter	Bread crumbs
8 anchovy fillets, minced	Pepper
6 cups cooked potatoes, sliced	

Sauté the onions in the butter. Have the anchovy fillets very finely minced and drained of all oil. Add them to the onions and cook for 2 minutes.

Butter a fireproof dish. Put in a layer of potatoes, moisten with a little of the sour cream, then put in a layer of the anchovies and onions. Sprinkle with pepper. Repeat till the dish is full. Top with bread crumbs and 1 tablespoon of melted butter. Brown 30 minutes in a medium oven (350°). Serve with a bland green salad.

Scalloped Potatoes with Hard-Cooked Eggs

Follow the preceding recipe, but instead of the anchovies use 5 chopped hard-cooked eggs. Minced parsley can be added when you sauté the chopped eggs and onions. When the dish goes in the oven it should be baked only 20 minutes.

Artichokes Cooked in Malaga Wine

6 globe artichokes	2 tbsp. lemon juice
2 tbsp. sweet butter	2 egg yolks, slightly beaten
1 cup Malaga wine	Salt
2 cups consommé	Pepper
1½ tbsp. flour	

Snip the hard tips off the leaves of the artichokes. Soak the artichokes 1 hour in cold water. Place on the stove in a large pot of salted cold water. Bring to boil. Cook 5 minutes. Take up and drain for at least 30 minutes. Now heat 1 tablespoon of the butter in a pan; put in the artichokes with ½ cup of the wine and 1½ cups of the consommé. Simmer till tender, about 40 minutes. Take the artichokes out, drain them, and keep them hot. Melt the remaining tablespoon of butter and blend in the flour. Add the remaining ½ cup consommé and ½ cup Malaga; bring to a boil; then add the lemon juice and the egg yolks and season to taste. Serve with the artichokes.

193

Asparagus Baked with Bread Crumbs and Cream

2 lb. asparagus	1 tbsp. lemon juice
1 cup bread crumbs	1 cup sweet cream
3 tbsp. butter	

Add a little sugar as well as the salt to the water in which you cook the asparagus. Cook till just soft. Drain for 1 hour. Cut off the stalks, leaving only the really soft parts. Lay these in a buttered fireproof dish. Use a dish you can serve at table. Fry the bread crumbs in butter. Sprinkle the lemon juice on the asparagus; dust with pepper, cover with half the bread crumbs; pour the cream on; cover with rest of bread crumbs. Bake 15 minutes in a hot oven.

Braised Cucumbers

6 or 8 small cucumbers	2 tbsp. flour
Salt	4 tbsp. sour cream
2 tbsp. butter	Pepper
1 small onion, chopped	Nutmeg

The cucumbers should be young, firm, with small seeds. Peel them and cut them lengthwise, each in 4 slices. Sprinkle with salt and let stand 20 minutes. Dry well with a towel. Heat 1 tablespoon of the butter; add the cucumbers and sauté them for 15 or 20 minutes. Sauté the chopped onion with remaining butter till golden brown. Add the flour to the onion, cook for 5 minutes, then add the cucumbers. Stir in the sour cream. Boil up once. Season with freshly ground pepper and a dash of nutmeg. Simmer for 5 minutes. Serve with roast lamb.

Young Carrots, Potatoes, or Turnips Browned in Cream

Cook the vegetable in salted water. Drain well and let stand 30 minutes. Then sauté in hot butter, and when the vegetable begins to brown, add 3 tablespoons of thick sour cream to every 2 cups of vegetable. Continue cooking over brisk heat. Just before serving add minced parsley, pepper, and salt.

Small carrots and turnips are usually cut in halves. Larger ones are sliced fairly thick. Small potatoes are left whole.

Russians like to add a pinch of ground ginger to the carrots before frying them.

Macédoine of Vegetables in Béchamel Sauce

2 egg yolks	1 cup cooked cauliflower
2½ cups thick cream sauce	flowerets
1 tbsp. sherry	6 cooked new potatoes
1 cup cooked young carrots	1 cup cooked green
½ cup cooked young turnips	peas
1 cup cooked young lima beans	

Make a rich cream sauce. Add the yolks of eggs and the sherry. Keep hot but do not boil.

Have all the vegetables warm. Add them to the sauce. Let stand 5 minutes, then serve.

The carrots, turnips, and potatoes are usually cubed. All vegetables must be well drained before adding them to the sauce. If you don't care for sherry, flavor the sauce instead with a pinch of ground nutmeg and a squeeze of lemon juice.

195

Cooked kohlrabi and cooked asparagus tips are sometimes added to the other vegetables.

Try serving this dish with cold sliced tongue. It's delicious.

Turnips Baked in Cream-and-Egg Sauce

4 cups sliced cooked turnips	1 egg
1 cup bread crumbs	Salt
2 tbsp. butter	Pepper
¾ cup sweet cream	

Cook the turnips in salt water till soft but not overcooked. Slice them thin in pieces about ½ inch wide and 3 inches long. Mix the turnip slices with the bread crumbs and the butter cut in small pieces, and place them in a fireproof dish. Mix the cream and the egg together, add salt and pepper to taste, and pour over the turnips. Bake in moderate oven (350°) till lightly browned on top—about 25 minutes.

Stuffed Baked White Turnips

6 small white turnips	Pepper
1 cup cooked farina (cooked in milk)	1 tbsp. grated cheese
1 egg, slightly beaten	2 tbsp. butter
Salt	Dry bread crumbs

Peel the turnips. Bring them to a boil twice in salted water. Cook them 10 minutes longer, then take them up and drain them. Scoop the middle out of each turnip, leaving a thick wall. The farina should be cool and quite thick. Mince the scooped-out part from the turnip very fine and mix it with the farina, together with the egg, salt and pepper, cheese, and 1 tablespoon of the butter. Fill the turnip shells with this mixture, piling it dome-shaped on top. Place the turnips in a baking dish; sprinkle with bread crumbs and the remaining butter, melted. Bake 40 minutes in slow oven. The turnips should be nicely browned.

This is a favorite luncheon dish in Russia. A cream sauce is sometimes served with it.

Winter Jardinière of Mixed Vegetables

4 cups sliced cabbage, scalded	1 cup cubed turnip
4 cups cubed potatoes	1½ cups cubed carrots
1 cup Jerusalem artichokes, cubed	2 tbsp. sour cream
½ cup chopped celery	¼ cup water
8 small onions, scalded	

Wash the vegetables, cut them up, and dry them thoroughly. Mix them together well and pack them in a fireproof pot with a lid that fits closely. Add the sour cream and the water. Do not add salt. Cook for 2 hours in a slow oven (325°). Serve in the pot in which they were cooked, with melted butter or a thin cream sauce. This dish should be salted at table to suit individual tastes. When you salt the vegetables before you cook them, the salt slows the cooking and impairs the flavor.

Here in America where we have green produce even in winter, a few fresh peas can be added to this jardinière after the other vegetables are half cooked. In Russia we often use dried celery leaves, fresh celery being hard to get.

197

Baked Cabbage

1 cabbage, 2 to 3 lb.
1 onion, chopped
3 tbsp. butter (or substitute)
½ cup dry bread crumbs
3 tbsp. minced parsley
½ cup consommé or thinned gravy
Pepper
Salt

Cut the cabbage in eighths. Cook 5 minutes in boiling salted water. Take up, drain, then dry on a towel. Arrange the 8 pieces of cabbage neatly in a flat fireproof dish. Sauté the chopped onion in the butter; add the bread crumbs and brown lightly, then add the parsley, pepper, and salt. Pour the consommé or thinned gravy over the cabbage. On top sprinkle the browned bread crumbs and onion. Bake 30 minutes in a medium oven.

Cabbage-and-Mushroom Cutlets with Tomato Sauce

2½ lb. cabbage
½ lb. mushrooms, chopped
1 onion, chopped
Butter (or substitute)
5 slices stale bread
Salt
Pepper
4 egg yolks, well beaten
2 egg whites, slightly beaten
Dry bread crumbs
Tomato sauce
Sherry

Chop the cabbage very fine. Scald it with boiling water for 10 minutes. When the cabbage is soft, drain it for 30 minutes. Sauté the chopped mushrooms and onion in butter. Soak the bread in a little milk, then squeeze dry. Mix the cabbage with the mushrooms and onion and the bread. Salt and pepper to taste. Add the egg yolks. Shape the mixture into round cakes. Dip the cakes in the slightly beaten whites of eggs; dust them with bread crumbs; fry in hot butter. Drain on paper. Pile on a platter and serve very hot.

Russians surround the cabbage cakes with French-fried potatoes or sautéed potatoes. The tomato sauce, which is served in a gravy boat, should be spiked with 1 tablespoon sherry.

Oven-Baked Cabbage and Potatoes

1 head cabbage, about 2½ lb.	Salt
1 egg	Pepper
Dry bread crumbs	1 tbsp. flour
4 tbsp. butter	½ cup sour cream
6 medium-sized potatoes, cooked	½ cup water

Cut the cabbage in half after trimming off the outside leaves. Drop it in boiling water and cook for 20 minutes. Take up and drain thoroughly. Cut in slices, lengthwise. Dip in egg diluted with a little water; coat with bread crumbs; sauté in hot butter.

Slice the cooked potatoes in rounds and sauté them in butter. Arrange cabbage and potatoes in layers in a greased casserole. Dust generously with salt and pepper. Brown the flour slightly in the pan in which the potatoes were cooked, adding a little butter if necessary, then add the sour cream and the water. Boil up. Pour over cabbage and potatoes. Sprinkle with bread crumbs and bake 20 minutes in hot oven.

This is an excellent dish to serve with cold ham or any cold meat. It goes well at a buffet supper.

Sauerkraut with Mushrooms

4 cups sauerkraut	1 tbsp. butter
½ lb. fresh mushrooms or 4 dried mushrooms	1 cup sour cream
1 tbsp. flour	Pepper
	Salt

199

Scald the sauerkraut in boiling water. Drain and place in a pot. If you are using dried mushrooms, these must be soaked overnight in a little water. Fresh mushrooms should be cooked 15 minutes in boiling salted water. In either case, slice the mushrooms very thin, add to the cabbage, and simmer for 20 minutes. Brown the flour in the butter, add the sour cream, pepper, and a little salt, and boil up. Now add this to the cabbage and mushrooms. Continue simmering for 25 minutes, stirring from time to time.

Russians eat this dish with boiled beef.

Cauliflower with Fried Bread Crumbs

In Russia this very simple way of serving cauliflower is preferred to the fancier recipes. Fry 1 cup of sifted dry bread crumbs in 1 tablespoon of butter. Pour the hot butter and bread crumbs over a whole cooked cauliflower just before serving.

Cauliflower with Sauce of Hard-Cooked Eggs

Chop 2 hard-cooked eggs coarsely. Mix them with ½ cup of melted butter and pour over a cooked cauliflower.

Celery or Leeks in Parsley Sauce

This recipe is the same for hearts of celery or for whole leeks. Cook the leeks or celery slowly in meat consommé. When they are ready—they should be soft but not mushy—take them up carefully and drain them. Place them in a heated deep dish. Make a cream sauce, using butter, flour, the consommé from the vegetables, a little cream, a dash of Worcestershire, and 2 tablespoons of minced parsley to each cup of sauce. Pour this over the deep dish of vegetables. Place the dish in a warm oven—not hot—for 5 minutes before serving.

A few quarters of cooked potatoes may be added to the leeks or celery to make this a substantial luncheon dish.

Russian Applesauce

6 or 8 medium-sized apples	3 or 4 tbsp. water
1 tbsp. chicken fat	1 tbsp. sugar

Peel the apples, core them, and cut them in quarters. Place them in a pan. Add the chicken fat and the water. Sprinkle with sugar. Cover the pan and simmer till the apples are soft but not mushy. The quarters of apples should retain their shape. Slow cooking is essential for this dish. Serve it warm with meat or chicken, duck or goose.

Baked Onion Dumplings

6 large onions	Salt
1 tbsp. butter	Pepper
2 cups consommé	Puff pastry

With a thin skewer pierce the onions carefully in 3 or 4 places. Put them in cold salted water and bring to a boil. Throw off the water. Drain the onions. Put them in a pot with the butter and consommé. Bring to a boil, then simmer till tender. The onions must remain whole. When they are done, drain them for 1 hour. Dry them in a towel. Dust them with salt and pepper, then wrap them in puff pastry as you would wrap an apple for apple dumplings. Set them in the refrigerator for 30 minutes. Bake 20 minutes in a hot oven. Serve very hot.

Personally I consider this one of our finest Russian contributions to vegetable cookery. Try these onion dumplings with roast lamb.

Grated Beets, Russian Style

4 cups grated raw beets
2 tbsp. butter
Juice of 1 lemon
1½ tsp. salt

Pepper
1 tbsp. flour
½ cup water

Grate the beets on a coarse grater. Heat the butter in a pan. Add the beets, the lemon juice, salt, and a little pepper. Cover the pan and cook 25 minutes over very low heat, stirring from time to time. Now sift the flour on top of the beets. Do not stir. Cover and continue cooking for 15 minutes, then stir and add the water. Bring to a boil and serve.

This recipe is of Polish origin, but most Russians think of it as one of their own national ways of serving beets.

Turkish Eggplant

2 medium-sized eggplants
4 tbsp. salad oil
3 carrots, finely chopped
4 tomatoes, chopped

4 tbsp. tomato purée
Pepper
Salt

Cut the eggplants in slices lengthwise. Make the slices about ½ inch thick. Simmer in hot oil till nearly tender—about 15 minutes. Take out of pan. Combine the chopped carrots and tomatoes, season with pepper and salt, and simmer in hot oil till the mixture is fairly thick.

Spread each slice of eggplant with the tomato-and-carrot sauce. Lay the slices on top of each other, building them up to look like an uncut eggplant. Tie together with fine string. Place in a baking dish.

Add ½ cup water to the tomato purée and pour over the eggplant. Bake 40 minutes in a moderate oven (350°). Baste the eggplant from time to time, and if the pan becomes too dry, add a little water. Serve hot or cold, as an accompaniment to any roast meat.

This is one of the oriental dishes that have become incorporated into Russian cooking. It is served throughout Russia wherever eggplants are obtainable.

CHAPTER 10

SALADS AND SALAD DRESSINGS

When Russians speak of a salad, what they have in mind isn't necessarily a fresh green salad, or even a vegetable salad. It may be nothing more than a dish of sauerkraut mixed with grated carrots. It may be spiced cherries, perhaps spiced cranberries. Actually any fresh-tasting preparation of vegetables or fruit, served cold with meat or fish or game, is what we call *salat* in Russia. We make the most of anything along that line, because of the fact that genuine green salads are unobtainable throughout a large part of Russia during many months in the year.

But to keep this book practical, for the use of readers outside of Russia, I have limited my salad recipes to those which really are salads in the American sense of the word.

As to salad dressings, we have several in our Russian cuisine which are specially characteristic, and I have found that my American friends like them very much.

In Russia we always serve salad in a large bowl, as you serve a tossed salad here.

Russian Mayonnaise

2 yolks hard-cooked eggs	1½ cups sour cream
1 tsp. salt	3 tbsp. olive oil
½ tsp. pepper	1 tsp. lemon juice
1 tsp. dry mustard	1 tbsp. vinegar
1 tsp. sugar	

Rub the yolks of the eggs through a fine sieve. Mix till smooth with the salt, pepper, mustard, and sugar. Add a little of the sour cream. Stir well, then add the rest of the cream. Now begin stirring in the oil drop by drop, as for mayonnaise. The mixture must be quite thick by the time all the oil has been added. Put the vinegar and the lemon juice in last of all.

Russian Mayonnaise with Herbs

Follow the preceding recipe for Russian Mayonnaise, and when it is ready, add:

1 tbsp. minced chives	1 tbsp. minced sour gherkins
1 tsp. minced tarragon	1 tsp. minced parsley
1 tsp. minced chervil	1 tbsp. minced dill pickle

This mayonnaise is usually served with cold steamed fish or cold boiled fish. It is really a version of Sauce Tartare. It is also excellent as a dressing for potato salad, with the whites of hard-cooked eggs chopped and sprinkled on top.

Plain Sour-Cream Dressing

1 tsp. salt	1 tbsp. salad oil or olive oil
¼ tsp. pepper	1 tbsp. vinegar
1 tsp. sugar	1 cup sour cream

Mix together all the ingredients except the sour cream. Let stand 5 minutes, then add 2 tablespoons of the cream and stir hard till well mixed. Add the remainder of the cream and stir till smooth. If the cream is very thick, use 1 tablespoon of water with it, or you can add a little more of the vinegar if it isn't too sharp.

Spicy Sour-Cream Dressing

1 tsp. salt	1½ cups sour cream
¼ tsp. pepper	2 tbsp. oil
1 tsp. prepared mustard	1 tbsp. tarragon or cider vinegar
2 tsp. sugar	

Mix the salt, pepper, mustard, and sugar together. Add the cream and stir well, then add the oil drop by drop as for mayonnaise, stirring always in the same direction. The mixture must be smooth, with the oil thoroughly incorporated. Last of all add the vinegar.

If the sour cream is very thick, add 1 scant tablespoon of water or diluted vinegar, but be careful not to thin this dressing too much.

Romaine Lettuce Salad with Spicy Cream Dressing

Break up the leaves of the romaine lettuce after cutting out the ends of the hard ribs in the leaves. Dry your leaves thoroughly and crisp them on ice. Mix them with the Spicy Sour-Cream Dressing just before serving, then after you have mixed them with the dressing, add 1 tablespoon of oil. Mix again and sprinkle with coarsely chopped whites of hard-cooked eggs.

Boston Lettuce with Sour-Cream Dressing

Have the lettuce chilled and crisped on ice. Just before serving mix it with Plain Sour-Cream Dressing. For flavor you can add 2 very thin slices of onion or 1 thick slice of cucumber. Remove the cucumber before serving, as it is used for flavor only with this salad.

Potato and Water-Cress Salad

Slice cold cooked potatoes and mix with finely minced onion or scallions. Dress with French dressing. Let stand 1 hour. Have an equal quantity of water-cress sprigs crisped on ice. There should be as much water cress as potatoes. Mix together thoroughly just before serving.

Beet and Cauliflower Salad with Russian Mayonnaise

1 head cooked cauliflower	1 cup Russian mayonnaise
1 cup finely minced cooked beets	1 tbsp. minced parsley

Arrange the flowerets of cooked cauliflower in a dish. Or you can cut down the bottom of a whole cooked cauliflower so it will stand firm in the dish. Mix the finely minced beets with the Russian mayonnaise and spread over the cauliflower. Sprinkle with minced parsley. Chill 30 minutes before serving.

This salad looks very pretty. It is excellent for buffet suppers or luncheons, served with a platter of cold cuts. It is also very much liked as an accompaniment to cold boiled lobster. If you serve it with lobster, surround the cauliflower with wedges of lemon.

Turnip and Cucumber Salad

3 cups sliced cooked white turnips	Lemon juice
2 cups sliced cucumbers	1 cup sour cream dressing

The younger the turnips, the better this salad will be. The best cucumbers to use for this and for other Russian salads are the small sweet cucumbers usually sold here for pickling.

207

Have the turnips chilled. Peel the cucumbers and slice them about ½ inch thick. Squeeze a little lemon juice over the turnips. Mix the turnips, cucumbers, and dressing together. You can use either the Plain Sour-Cream Dressing or the Spicy Sour-Cream Dressing.

Russians like to eat this salad with baked fish or boiled fish.

Radishes, Cucumbers, and Scallions with Sour Cream

2 cups sliced radishes	2 tsp. salt
2 cups sliced cucumbers	1 tsp. sugar
½ cup minced scallions	1 cup sour cream

Make the radish slices very thin, the cucumber a little thicker. Mix the 3 vegetables together. Add the salt and sugar to the sour cream, pour over the vegetables, and mix thoroughly just before serving. Both cream and vegetables must be well chilled before you mix them.

Sliced Tomatoes with Sour-Cream Dressing

Peel good ripe tomatoes and slice them rather thick. Sprinkle with 1 scant teaspoon of sugar and 1 teaspoon of salt. Chill well. Drain. Cover with Plain Sour-Cream Dressing. On top sprinkle chopped whites of hard-cooked eggs and 1 tablespoon of minced parsley or scallions.

Salad of Cooked Green Peas, Celery, and Potatoes

1½ cups cooked green peas	1 tbsp. minced celery leaves
3 cups diced cold potatoes	1½ cups Spicy Sour-Cream
½ cup minced celery	Dressing

Mix all ingredients together carefully. Serve on lettuce leaves.

This salad becomes a main dish by the easy addition of cooked shrimps or any cold cooked fish that is fairly firm. Surround the salad with quarters of hard-cooked eggs.

Marinate the shrimps or fish in a little lemon juice before adding to the salad.

Carrot and Sauerkraut Salad

Drain 2 cups of sauerkraut thoroughly and chill. Shred raw carrots fine or grate them on a coarse grater until you have 1 cup. Mix the carrots with sauerkraut and 2 tablespoons of olive oil or salad oil. In Russia this is a favorite winter salad to serve with meat or fish.

Russian Cole Slaw

5 cups finely shredded cabbage	1 tsp. minced dill or parsley
2 medium-sized apples	2 tbsp. mayonnaise
1 small carrot	1 tsp. sugar
1 tsp. minced onion	¼ cup sour cream

Sprinkle the shredded cabbage with salt and let stand 15 minutes, then scald for 3 minutes. Drain well and dry in a towel. Chop the apples very fine or grate them on a coarse grater. Grate the carrot. Mix all the ingredients together and let stand 30 minutes on ice before serving.

CHAPTER 11

SAUCES

For the most part the sauces used in Russian cooking are the classic sauces of France. They were imported 200 years ago during the reign of Catherine the Great, who introduced the French cuisine at the Russian court. It is interesting to note that Catherine, herself a German, embraced all French culture with enthusiasm. Her correspondence with the French encyclopedists of the eighteenth century opens a remarkable page in Russian history. Many of these priceless letters, inherited by Russian friends of mine, were lost in the revolutionary looting of estates and libraries. At a village near Moscow I myself discovered Voltaire letters being used as paper with which to roll cigarettes.

But if the Revolution destroyed irretrievable relics of the past, as every cataclysm must, it also revealed many hidden treasures.

Catherine II, Empress of Russia, has been remembered more universally for her love life than for her skill as a ruler. One of the long-lost documents unearthed during the Revolution consists of memoirs written in Catherine's time by the obscure governor of a distant province, and these memoirs present a striking picture of her as an administrator.

Always early to rise, Catherine made coffee for herself at a hearth fire. In a quilted dressing gown of voluminous folds, she took her first cup of coffee at 6 o'clock in the morning, at the same time receiving visits from provincial persons of importance. Her *Hausfrau* hospitality enchanted them, and with shrewd queries she encouraged them to tell her their problems as informally as though they had been at home. This was the hour when Catherine learned the latest prices of grain, of horses, of calico cloth. Like any farmer, she asked questions about crop prospects or cattle conditions. In exchange she passed along the gossip and the information she had gleaned from her busy correspondence with foreign notables. To her morning callers from the rural districts she imparted the facts of life as it was lived in other countries, describing refinements unknown in Russia. Much of the information she gave out was no doubt cleverly selected for political purposes. Even in her casual words on foreign cooking, she knew very well how to enlist home loyalties. Many a small functionary, returning to some distant part of Catherine's empire, carried in his pocket a recipe for a French sauce—a recipe dictated by the Empress herself.

This brief chapter deals only with sauces that are truly Russian. In other chapters of this book I give the complete recipes for all the special sauces that accompany the dishes described. Any standard cookbook will provide the recipes for the classic French sauces used in Russia. Therefore I have thought it unnecessary to deal with French sauces here.

First I'll acquaint you with our three Russian horse-radish sauces. We like them particularly with boiled beef, roast beef, or roast lamb, and with all kinds of fish.

Hot Horse-radish Sauce

2 egg yolks	1 tsp. lemon juice
1 cup sour cream	1 tsp. salt
½ cup freshy grated horse-radish	1 tsp. sugar

211

Beat the yolks and add them to the sour cream, stirring well. Add the horse-radish. Place over very gentle heat for 5 minutes. Stir constantly. The sauce will thicken slightly. Add lemon juice, salt, and sugar. Serve hot.

Cold Horse-radish Sauce

½ cup fresh bread crumbs   ½ cup freshly grated horse-radish
1 tbsp. vinegar   1 tsp. salt
1½ cups sour cream   1 tsp. sugar

Soak the bread crumbs in the vinegar. Add them to the sour cream. Beat well. Then add the horse-radish, salt, and sugar. Serve cold.

Frozen Horse-radish Sauce

1 tbsp. mayonnaise   1 tsp. salt
1½ cups sour cream   2 tsp. sugar
½ cup freshly grated horse-radish   1 tbsp. vinegar

Combine the mayonnaise with the sour cream. Add the horse-radish, salt, sugar, and vinegar. Freeze 6 hours in an ice tray in your refrigerator. Or you can chill it close to the ice for 12 hours.

Russian Tomato Cream Sauce

1½ tbsp. flour   3 tbsp. sour cream
1 tbsp. butter   ½ tsp. salt
3 tbsp. tomato purée   1 egg yolk, well beaten
2 cups consommé   Cayenne pepper

Brown the flour in the butter. Cook it really brown. Add the tomato purée, cook for 12 minutes, then add the consommé. Boil up and add the sour cream very gradually, stirring briskly. Boil up again. Add salt, egg yolk, and a pinch of Cayenne pepper. If the tomato purée isn't sharp enough, add a few drops of lemon juice to the sauce.

This is excellent with meat, chicken, or fish.

Anchovy Sauce

8 anchovy fillets	3 tbsp. olive oil or salad oil
Yolks of 2 hard-cooked eggs	1 tsp. sugar
Pepper	2 tbsp. tarragon vinegar

Chop the anchovies very fine, then pound them to a paste with the egg yolks, which should first be rubbed through a sieve. Add pepper, then oil drop by drop till you have a thick paste. Mix the sugar in and let stand 15 minutes. Dilute with the vinegar.

Russians use this sauce on potato salad or with cold boiled fish.

Hot Anchovy Sauce

8 anchovy fillets, finely chopped	½ cup consommé
1 onion, finely chopped	Pepper
1 tbsp. butter	2 egg yolks, well beaten
½ cup cream	½ tsp. Worcestershire sauce

Simmer the chopped anchovies and onions in hot butter but do not brown. Add the cream, consommé, and pepper to taste. Boil up once. Let it cool a little, then add the egg

213

yolks. Cook over very slow heat till the sauce thickens slightly. Add the Worcestershire sauce. Serve hot.

This goes with baked fish or boiled fish.

Walnut Sauce

½ lb. shelled walnuts	1 tsp. sugar
3 tbsp. water	1 tbsp. fine bread crumbs
1 tsp. salt	1 tsp. hot prepared mustard
Yolks of 2 hard-cooked eggs	½ cup vinegar
2 tbsp. salad oil	

Grind the walnuts very fine or pound them in a mortar. Gradually add the water and salt. Stir well. Rub the yolks of egg through a sieve, then add the oil to them drop by drop, stirring as for mayonnaise. When you have all the oil in, add the sugar, bread crumbs, and mustard, and combine this yolk mixture with the walnuts. Stir and add the vinegar.

Usually this sauce is spread on baked fish or fried fish. Walnut sauce is seldom served separately.

CHAPTER 12

DESSERTS

A pudding called *guriev kasha* is considered by Russians to be the supreme magnifico of all our national desserts. Rich with cream and an assortment of sugared fruits, it commands a position of high esteem at feasts, much as the Great Plum Pudding used to be honored in Elizabethan England.

For celebrations of a less formal nature, the party dessert in Russia is usually some kind of custard, baked or boiled, or prepared in the same way that you make Bavarian cream. Russians are also very partial to layer cakes and *torten,* which you will find described, with recipes, in Chapter 13.

Eating their everyday meal at home, the Russian family is more than likely to have a very simple dessert known as *kissel.* This is a purée of fresh fruit thickened with cornstarch. Along with various combinations of plain stewed fruit, it is the sweet most frequently served in all parts of Russia.

Russians love ice cream, and they have it as often as they can get it. They like the richest French-type ice cream. They buy it usually at a fancy bakery, for nearly all Russian ice cream is made by bakeries, though exceptionally energetic Russians sometimes make it at home. Buying or making it in Russia has always been expensive. I predict that a fortune will be scooped up by the enterprising person who first starts a chain of moderate-priced ice-cream parlors in Russia on the American basis—eat it there, take it home, or have it delivered.

Guriev Kasha

½ lb. shelled walnuts or pecans
3 cups milk
3 cups cream
¾ cup semolina or farina
½ cup sugar
½ cup chopped raisins

½ tsp. almond extract
Puff pastry
1 cup mixed candied fruits
Fine bread crumbs
Sugar

Most Russian cooks serve their Guriev Kasha on a platter with a surrounding border of puff pastry. But the puff pastry may be omitted.

Blanch the walnuts or pecans in boiling water. Remove the skins. Chop the nuts very fine and pound them in a mortar, or put them through a nut grinder.

For the milk choose a low flat pan, preferably enameled. Pour the milk and the cream in this pan. Heat on the mildest possible flame, with 1 or 2 asbestos mats under the pan. The next operation requires a lot of patience. As soon as a golden-brown skin forms on the milk, carefully skim it off and put it aside on a large plate. Repeat the process 6 times. Go right on warming the milk and skimming off the top until you have 6 brown milk skins on your plate.

Now bring the milk to a boil. Sprinkle in the semolina or farina and cook for 7 minutes, stirring continuously. Take the pan off the stove. Add the sugar, ground nuts, raisins, and almond extract.

On a fireproof dish make a border of puff pastry. In the center spread a layer of the cooked semolina or farina. On this layer of *kasha*, spread one of the 6 browned milk skins. And on this arrange a layer of the candied fruit in thin slices.

216

Excellent candied fruits such as apricots, cherries, peaches, pears, etc., come to the market now both from California and Florida.

On the sliced candied fruit put another layer of kasha and a brown milk skin, then another layer of fruit, and so on. The top layer should be kasha. A little apricot jam can be spread on each layer of fruit if you like.

When the center of the dish is filled, sprinkle the top with fine bread crumbs and sugar. Place in hot oven (450°) just long enough to bake the pastry and brown the top layer of kasha—about 20 minutes. If you don't use the pastry border, it is easier to brown the kasha under a hot broiler. Serve in the baking dish. Serve warm, but not hot.

Russian Apple Pie

8 large apples
½ cup raisins
½ cup sugar
3 tbsp. dry wine, white or red
1½ tsp. grated orange rind

4 tbsp. finely chopped almonds
3 bitter almonds, chopped fine
2 tbsp. cherry jam or currant jelly
Pastry for a 2-crust pie

Peel and core the apples. Slice fairly thin. Mix the sliced apples with the raisins, sugar, orange rind, wine, and almonds. Cook over low heat for 15 minutes, taking care not to let the apples burn. Stir in the jam or jelly while the apples are still warm, then let the mixture cool. It should be quite thick. Roll out the pastry and line a pie plate with a bottom crust; fill with the apple mixture and cover with a top crust. Bake 45 minutes in a hot oven (350°).

Russian Brown Betty

8 large apples
½ cup water
1 cup sugar
½ cup raisins
1 tsp. orange rind
1 tsp. ground cinnamon
¼ cup finely chopped nuts

4 cups crumbled dark rye bread
3 tbsp. salad oil
1 tsp. lemon rind
½ tsp. ground cloves
Dry bread crumbs
4 tbsp. tart jelly or jam

Peel and core the apples. Cut them in eighths. Add to the water ½ cup of the sugar, the raisins, orange rind, and cinnamon. Simmer the apples with this mixture until just tender. Add the nuts when the apples are tender.

The bread should be at least 1 day old. Crumble and fry it for 5 minutes in 2 tablespoons of the oil. Add the lemon rind, cloves, and the rest of the sugar.

Brush the inside of a fireproof casserole with the remaining oil. Dust with fine bread crumbs. Put in 2 cups of the fried bread. Cover with the apples and 1 cup of bread. Spread with jelly or jam. Top with the remaining bread. Bake 1 hour in a medium oven (350°). Serve hot or cold with a pitcher of sweet cream.

Russian Rice with Orange Compote

4 cups milk
1 cup rice
½ tsp. salt
¾ cup sugar
2 tsp. unsalted butter
1 tsp. vanilla extract

½ tsp. almond extract
2 tbsp. gelatine
½ cup hot water
2 cups whipping cream
4 or 5 oranges

Bring the milk to a boil in a saucepan. Shower in the rice. Add the salt and sugar. Cook in the top of a double boiler till rice is soft and nearly smooth—about 1½ hours. Add the butter when the rice is half cooked. Let cool when done, then add vanilla and lemon extracts. Soften the gelatine in a little cold water; add ½ cup boiling water to it; cool a little, then add to the rice. Whip the cream fairly stiff and stir it into the rice. Pour the rice mixture into a well-chilled bowl. Place in the refrigerator for at least 4 hours.

Cut 4 or 5 oranges into sections and remove the seeds. Make a thick syrup of 1 cup sugar and 1 cup water, with a little orange juice and 1 tablespoon of grated orange rind. Drop the sections of orange into this while the syrup is still hot. Chill well and serve poured round the rice mold.

For parties this is a dessert that tastes delicious and looks very handsome. It can be made to look extra gala by using a ring mold for the rice, then decorating the top of the rice with chopped candied cherries, candied angelica, and candied orange peel. If you have any curaçoa cordial, add 1 teaspoon of it to the orange compote.

Chilled Cream of Apples

7 tart apples for baking	1 tsp. grated lemon rind
2 egg whites	½ cup sugar
1½ tbsp. gelatine	½ tsp. vanilla extract
3 tbsp. cold water	2 tbsp. rum or whisky
½ cup boiling water	¾ cup whipping cream

Bake the apples, then rub the pulp from them through a sieve. Let cool. Whip the egg whites nearly stiff; fold in the apple pulp and whip again till quite stiff. Soften the gelatine

219

in the cold water, then add the boiling water and lemon rind, and let cool until it begins to set. Combine this with the whipped apple, adding the sugar, vanilla, and rum or whisky. Add the cream, whipped fairly stiff. Now whip the entire mixture for 3 minutes. Pour into a chilled mold previously rinsed with ice water. Chill for at least 4 hours. Unmold and serve plain, or with a chilled custard sauce made with the yolks of 2 eggs, 1½ cups milk, 1 teaspoon flour, and rum or vanilla flavoring.

This dessert can be made with peaches instead of apples. The peaches should be simmered in very little water and rubbed through a sieve, and with peaches the flavoring should be almond instead of vanilla.

Kissel

Kissel is the simplest of all our Russian desserts, and the one most often served. We pronounce the word *Key-sell.*

It is nothing more than fresh fruit cooked to a sweetened purée and thickened with cornstarch. However, there is a special technique involved in cooking it exactly long enough and no longer. Properly done, it has a delicious taste when served ice cold with thick cream, or with rich milk well chilled. Cranberries or ripe red currants are used most frequently, but any other tart fruit is suitable—strawberries, raspberries, or a combination of the two. A really superlative kissel is made with black currants, which seem for some reason to have disappeared completely from American markets. Raspberry syrup added to a cranberry kissel gives it a more interesting flavor.

Pick over 3 cups of fruit. Put the fruit in a pan with just enough water to cover. Bring quickly to a boil, reduce the heat, and simmer for 10 minutes. Rub through a sieve. Add sugar according to the acidity of the fruit, about 1 cup to 3 cups of cranberries or red currants, less for sweeter fruits. Bring once more to a quick boil.

For every 2 cups of the fruit purée, allow 1 level tablespoon of cornstarch. Moisten the cornstarch with water, rub it smooth, and add it to the hot fruit purée. Cook for 3 minutes, stirring constantly. Chill for several hours. Serve in deep saucers with cream or milk.

Ukrainian Pelmeny

1½ cups white flour	3 cups blueberries or pitted
1 cup buckwheat flour	cherries or plums
1 tsp. salt	Sugar
3 egg yolks	Syrup from the fruit
¾ cup water (approximately)	Cinnamon

This might be termed a "frontier" dessert, for in the Russian language the word Ukraine means "frontier," or "borderland." Sprinkled with sugar and dunked in plenty of fruit syrup, these Ukrainian pelmeny often make a whole meal in the south of Russia. They are something like ravioli filled with fruit. The mixture of wheat and buckwheat flour gives them a different taste from that of the Siberian pelmeny. With them you can serve a bowl of thick sour cream as an extra accompaniment, though it isn't always included in Russia.

Sift the 2 flours together with the salt. Mix the egg yolks in whole, with sufficient water to make a stiff dough. Set aside for 1 hour. Roll out as thin as you can. Cut in squares or rounds about 4 inches across.

Plums should be cut in half after pitting them. Pitted cherries should be left whole. Whatever fruit you use, mix it with sugar to suit your taste. Let stand 1 hour, then drain and boil up the syrup. To plums or cherries add a few kernels from cracked pits.

On each piece of rolled-out dough place 1 spoonful of the drained fruit. Brush the edges of the dough with white of egg and pinch together firmly.

Throw a few of the fruit-filled pelmeny into a large pot of rapidly boiling water. They will rise to the top in about 10 or 15 minutes. Continue cooking them for 15 minutes after they come to the top, then take them out with a strainer. Keep them on a hot platter till all are done. They taste better when served on a large roomy platter, not piled up in a small dish.

With them serve a bowl of granulated sugar mixed with cinnamon. The syrup from the fruit should be served hot in a pitcher. If you serve sour cream also, sweeten it and flavor it with a little cinnamon or nutmeg.

Cherry Vareniki

3 cups flour	2 lbs. cherries
1 tsp. salt	Kernels from 6 cherry stones
3 egg yolks	1 cup sugar
½ cup water (approximately)	¾ cup water

Sift the flour and salt together. Add the egg yolks and sufficient water to make a stiff paste. Let stand 1 hour. Roll out as thin as possible and stamp into rounds about 4 inches across.

Stone the cherries; mix them with sugar and let stand about

3 hours in the sun. Crack some cherry stones. Crush the kernels and add to the cherries. Put the cherries and water into a pan and bring to a boil. Simmer for 10 minutes. Strain and cool. The juice should be kept warm.

Place 1 spoonful of cherries on each round of dough. Brush the edges with white of egg; fold over to form a crescent and pinch the edges together. Throw the vareniki into a large pot of boiling water, a few at a time. Keep the water boiling. In about 15 minutes the vareniki will rise to the surface. Take them out. They are done. Drain them and place them on a hot platter. Serve very hot with a bowl of warm cherry juice, a bowl of sugar, and a pitcher of well-chilled cream.

Pot-Cheese Vareniki

3 cups sifted flour	1 cup sour cream
½ tsp. salt	2 eggs
2 egg yolks	1 tbsp. sugar or 1 tsp. salt
½ cup water (approximately)	2 tbsp. thick sour cream
1½ lbs. pot cheese	Melted butter

Sift the flour and salt together. Add the yolks of eggs and enough water to make a stiff dough. Let stand 1 hour. Have the pot cheese thoroughly drained of all water. The best way is to hang the cheese in a piece of gauze and let it drip for 3 or 4 hours, then wrap it in a towel and squeeze it dry.

Mix the pot cheese with the whole eggs and the sour cream. Add the sugar if you want to eat the vareniki as a dessert. The salt is used instead of sugar when you are making vareniki the main dish of the meal.

223

Roll the dough out thin. Stamp or cut it in rounds about 4 inches across. Place a heaping teaspoonful of the cheese mixture on half of the round of dough. Brush the edges with water or white of egg; fold over and pinch together firmly. Drop the vareniki in boiling salted water, a few at a time. Cook for 15 minutes, or until they rise to the surface. Drain and serve very hot with a bowl of sour cream and a bowl of melted butter.

Other Fillings for Vareniki are:

1. Thick purée of dried apricots, well sweetened
2. Thick purée of prunes, sweetened and flavored with lemon rind
3. Blueberry jam spiced with cinnamon.

Khvorost ("Twigs")

3 eggs
3 cups sifted flour
½ cup water (approximately)
1 jigger of gin, rye whisky, or rum
¼ cup sugar

½ tsp. salt
Sugar
Ground cinnamon
Fat for deep-frying

Mix the eggs into the flour one at a time. Add the water, the gin or rum or whisky, the ¼ cup of sugar, and the salt. Knead the dough well and let it stand for 15 minutes. Roll out very thin on a floured board. Cut in strips about 7 inches long and 1½ inches wide. About an inch from one end of each strip cut a small lengthwise slit. Twist the other end of the strip through this slit, so that you have a sort of loop. Prepare a large pan of deep fat as for doughnuts. Throw in 8 or 10 of

224

the strips at a time. Cook till slightly brown—about 10 minutes. Drain on paper. Serve piled up on a hot platter. Sprinkle with sugar mixed with a little cinnamon.

Waffle or Pancake Pudding with Custard and Jelly

12 waffles or pancakes	1 cup whipping cream
1½ cups thick boiled custard	Sugar
1 cup tart jelly	

Made either with waffles or pancakes, this dessert is a nationwide favorite in Russia. A ready-prepared pancake mix does excellently for this dish. I use the waffle recipe that is printed on the package, but sometimes I fry the waffle batter in pancake form.

Make a thick boiled custard flavored with vanilla. Have the custard lukewarm. The jelly should be slightly warmed and whipped with a fork. Spread each waffle or pancake with a little jelly, then with custard. Pile them up one on top of another. On the top one spread sweetened whipped cream, letting it run down the sides. Cut in wedges to serve.

Smettanick (Jam and Cream Pie)

Puff pastry	¼ tsp. almond extract
1½ cups cherry or raspberry jam	3 tbsp. sour cream
1½ cups ground blanched almonds	1 egg yolk
or pecans	½ tsp. ground cinnamon
¼ sweet cream	

Line a pie plate with the pastry. Spread the jam over the pastry in an even layer. Mix the ground nuts with the sweet cream, adding the almond extract. Mix the sour cream with the egg yolk and cinnamon, and combine this with the nut and cream mixture. Spread this over the jam. Cover with a top crust. Sprinkle with sugar and bake in a hot oven (400°) till slightly brown—about 25 minutes.

Compote of Cherries and Pears

Pit 1 pound of cherries. Save 6 of the cherry stones; crack them, blanch the kernels, then peel off the skin and mash the kernels to a paste. Make a syrup with 1 cup of water, I cup of sugar, and the mashed cherry kernels. Bring to a boil; cook for 10 minutes; then throw in the cherries and simmer for 5 minutes. Take the cherries out and drain them. Cook the syrup 10 or 15 minutes more till it is fairly thick. Pour it over the cherries and allow to cool.

Peel and core 6 fresh pears and cut them in halves. (You may use canned pears instead.) Make a syrup of 1½ cups of water and ¼ cup of sugar. When the syrup has cooked for 10 minutes, put the pears in and simmer till they are soft. Remove the pears and drain them. Cook the syrup 20 minutes longer, adding vanilla extract. Pour over the pears and chill.

Canned pears should be drained, the syrup cooked down, the vanilla added when the syrup is ready.

Arrange the cherries in the center of a glass bowl. Surround with the halves of pears. Pour the 2 syrups into the bowl. Serve thoroughly chilled.

All this may sound like too much fuss for a simple dessert, but the taste and effect are really worth while when the fruit is prepared with such care.

Compote of Oranges and Prunes

6 large oranges

1 cup sugar

2 tbsp. rum

6 cloves

3 cups water

1 tbsp. grated orange rind

12 large prunes

Grate the rind from 1 of the oranges. Peel the oranges with a sharp knife; cut them into sections and remove the seeds. Put the orange sections in a dish. Sprinkle them with 2 tablespoons of sugar and pour the rum over them. Chill for 2 hours. The syrup that forms during this process should be spooned up and poured over the orange sections 2 or 3 times.

Now make a syrup with the rest of the sugar, 1½ cups water, and the grated orange rind. Bring to a boil, then cook for 30 minutes. Strain, chill, and pour over the orange sections.

Soak the prunes 30 minutes in the remaining 1½ cups of water. Take the prunes out and drain them. Bring the water in which they soaked to a boil, drop the prunes back in, and simmer till soft—about 15 minutes. Take out the prunes and drain. Chill the prunes, then arrange them in a circle around the orange sections. Serve very cold. Don't use the water in which the prunes were cooked.

Melon Compote

5 cups melon cubes

1½ cups water

¾ cup sugar

Small piece preserved ginger root

Peel a ripe cantaloupe, honeydew, or other melon. Remove the seeds and cut the melon in cubes about 1 inch square. Make a syrup of the water and sugar, adding the ginger cut

227

in thin slices. Cook for 30 minutes. Pour hot over the melon cubes. Chill for several hours. This compote is best when kept in the refrigerator overnight.

This is a good way to utilize a melon that didn't turn out to be as flavorsome as you hoped.

Russian Pistachio Ice Cream

¼ lb. shelled pistachio nuts
1 tbsp. orange-flower water
3 cups cream
3 egg yolks

½ cup sugar
1 tbsp. vanilla extract
Few drops green coloring

We used to make this with an old-fashioned ice-cream freezer in Russia, and turning the crank by hand was a labor of love. Pistachio ice cream was a complicated undertaking in all respects, but Russians went at it with holiday gusto. It was one of their favorite treats when company was coming for dinner. Here is how we made it:

The pistachio nuts should not be blanched. Pound them to a smooth paste in a mortar with the orange-flower water. Add the cream, stirring till well mixed. Work the egg yolks and sugar together till lemon-colored, then mix with the cream and the pistachio paste. Heat very carefully over a low flame. Stir constantly till slightly thickened. Don't let the mixture get too hot or it will curdle. Strain through a fine sieve. Add the vanilla and the green coloring. Let cool, then chill overnight.

Freeze according to standard instructions for whatever kind of freezer you use.

This is a delightfully delicate ice cream, particularly if you refrain from using almond flavoring instead of vanilla. Outside of Russia most pistachio ice cream is almond-flavored. It isn't nearly as good that way.

Tvorojniki (Cottage-Cheese Cakes)

1 lb. cottage cheese or pot cheese	1 tbsp. sugar
4 tbsp. sifted flour	2 tbsp. sour cream
½ tsp. baking powder	2 eggs, slightly beaten
1 tsp. grated lemon rind	Butter (or substitute)
½ tsp. vanilla extract	

Here is one of Russia's popular national desserts. Many a day it constitutes the main dinner dish, after the family bowl of soup.

The cheese must be cold and thoroughly dry. The best to use is the kind that is generally sold as pot cheese. That kind has less liquid, but even so, it must be wrapped in several layers of gauze and hung up to drip for 2 or 3 hours, then placed in a colander with a plate on top of it, and a weight on the plate to squeeze it completely dry. Then chill for 2 hours.

Press the cheese through a sieve. Rub it very smooth. Add the sifted flour and baking powder, lemon rind, vanilla, sugar, sour cream, and lastly the beaten eggs. The mixture should be thick and smooth. Chill for 30 minutes. Shape into flat round cakes about 2 inches across and ½ inch thick. Fry golden brown in hot butter. Serve with granulated sugar and chilled sour cream.

Drachena (Russian Cottage Pudding)

3 tbsp. butter	½ tsp. salt
3 egg yolks	2 cups sifted flour
⅓ cup confectioners' sugar	2 cups milk

229

Cream 2 tablespoons of the butter until white. In another bowl mix the egg yolks and confectioners' sugar. Do not use granulated sugar. Stir until the sugar and eggs are white. Now combine the butter with the sugar-and-egg mixture. Add the salt. Sift the flour in gradually, adding milk as you go. Beat thoroughly. The batter should be medium thick, depending on the type of flour. You may need a little less than 2 cups of milk.

In a heavy pan heat the remaining tablespoon of butter, but don't let it bubble. Pour in the batter. Bake 10 minutes in hot oven (400°). Diminish the heat to 350° and continue baking for 20 minutes more.

In Russia this is served with vanilla sugar—granulated sugar which has been kept a few days in a closed jar with a piece of vanilla-bean pod buried in the sugar.

Paskha (Russian Easter Dessert)

3 lb. fresh pot cheese	½ lb. unsalted butter
Salt	1 cup sugar
½ cup raisins	3 egg yolks
1 tbsp. chopped citron	1 whole egg, well beaten
¼ lb. blanched almonds, ground or finely chopped	1 cup whipping cream
	1 tsp. vanilla extract

Pot cheese can be bought loose, by the pound, at delicatessen stores. The lumps are the size of hazelnuts, and the cheese has the advantage of being much drier than the cottage cheese sold in containers.

Wrap the cheese in several layers of gauze and hang it up to drip. When it is dry, place it in a colander with a plate and a weight on top. Let all the liquid drain off, then rub the cheese through a very fine sieve. Add a pinch of salt. Add the raisins, citron, and almonds. Soften the butter and stir with the sugar till very smooth. Add the egg yolks and continue stirring. Combine with the cheese. Add the whole egg beaten frothy. Whip the cream and stir it in. Now place the mixture in a pan over very low heat. Stir and stir till bubbles form at the edges of the pan. Remove from fire, but continue stirring while the mixture cools. If you stop stirring the paskha won't be smooth. Add the vanilla extract.

The real Russian mold for paskha is made of 4 wooden boards that notch together and turn the paskha out in a pyramid shape. But an ordinary flowerpot will serve the purpose, provided you line it with a double layer of gauze dampened with cold water. The hole at the bottom of the flowerpot allows excess liquid to drain off.

Pour the mixture into the mold. Cover the top with a dampened cloth. Put a weight on top and chill for at least 1 day, better for a day and a night. Unmold. If possible decorate with flowers and green leaves at the base. Cut in slices to serve.

CHAPTER 13

CAKES

Any plain cake, such as a poundcake or a raisin cake, is known in Russia as an "English" cake. Sometimes these appear on the table in the evening at the hour when family and friends gather around the samovar, and are liked most by elderly folk. In bygone days they were also favored by Russian Anglophiles who affected the practice of serving a British 5-o'clock tea.

But to the average Russian, *cake* means a fancy layer cake, and the fancier the better. Cakes of this type are called "tortes," a Russianized form of the German *torten*, which came originally from the French *tarte*.

Actually the only real native Russian cake is a tall, cylindrical yeast-raised cake rich with eggs and shortening. This is called a *baba*, and I suppose its name derives from its shape. *Baba* is the colloquial Russian word for woman. The equivalent here might be "jane" or "skirt." The plump tower of cake suggests a statuesque matron in peasant dress.

The *kulitch*, a glorified *baba* baked for Easter, holds the highest rank of importance among Russian cakes. Finer than the ordinary *baba*, taller and richer, it is still a yeast-raised cylinder, made the same way. Looks very decorative for supper parties at any time of the year. Best pan for baking it is a tin container in which the delicatessen stores receive their pot cheese. About 12 inches high, this tin is ideal for a *kulitch* or *baba.* Most delicatessen stores will sell you one with a little coaxing.

Kulitch (Russian Easter Cake)

10 cups sifted flour	7 eggs
1 cup white raisins	1 cup sugar
1 tbsp. rum	¾ lb. butter
1 tsp. saffron	4 tbsp. chopped almonds
1½ yeast cakes	4 crushed bitter almonds
½ cup warm water	1 tsp. lemon extract
2½ cups milk, scalded and cooled	1 tsp. salt
to lukewarm	Fine bread crumbs

Be sure the flour is dry. Soak the raisins in the rum. Dry the saffron for 30 minutes, then crush it to powder.

Crumble the yeast and stir with the warm water till smooth. Mix 5 cups of the flour with the milk. Combine the yeast with the flour and milk and beat thoroughly. Set aside to rise for 2 or 3 hours in a warm place, not hot. When the batter is light, it is ready for the next mixing.

Beat the yolks of 5 eggs with the sugar. Beat 1 whole egg and add to the yolks. Mix the eggs with the batter. Melt the butter and let it cool slightly, then mix it with the almonds, raisins, lemon extract, and salt. Add these to the batter. Combine the dry powdered saffron with the rest of the flour. Sift this into the batter and knead well. The dough should be rather stiff, but you can add a little water if it seems too stiff to handle. Do the kneading on a large board. Knead for at least 15 minutes, till the dough is springy and smooth and does not stick to your hands or to the board.

Take the dough up. Fold the edges under so it is rounded

on top. Place in a buttered and floured cake pan or pans. If you use an ordinary round pan, build up the sides to greater height with a double thickness of greased brown paper. If possible, use one of those delicatessen-store tins I described at the beginning of this chapter.

Brush the top of the kulitch with a little butter. Cover with a cloth and set in a warm place to rise. To start with, the pan should be not more than half filled with dough, since it must double in bulk through rising.

When the kulitch has risen, brush the top with a little yolk of egg diluted in water. Sprinkle with fine bread crumbs—this keeps the top even. Place in a hot oven (400°) for 15 minutes. Reduce the heat to moderate (350°) and continue baking from 45 to 55 minutes. Let it cool in the pan for 15 minutes before tipping it gently onto a cake rack.

Kulitch is always sliced in rounds, across the cake, the top being first taken off to be saved and put back, like a lid, on the part which remains.

Kulitch with Cardamom

1 oz. compressed yeast	1 cup raisins
2 cups scalded milk, cooled to lukewarm	2 tbsp. crushed cardamom seeds
8 cups sifted flour	2 tbsp. shredded candied orange peel
1 cup sugar	2 tsp. grated lemon rind
1 tsp. salt	
1 cup softened butter	
4 eggs, well beaten	

Crumble the yeast into a large bowl. Add the lukewarm milk and stir till smooth. Sift in 1 cup of flour and 1 tablespoon

234

of sugar and the salt. Cover the bowl with a cloth and set aside in a warm place to rise.

Cream the butter. Add the remaining sugar and the eggs, the rest of the flour, the raisins, cardamom seeds, orange peel, and lemon rind. Combine this with the yeast mixture and knead till the dough is smooth and elastic. Set aside to rise again, till the dough has doubled in bulk. Shape into 1 large cake or 2 smaller cakes. Brush over very sparingly with melted butter and let the cakes rise in their pans for about 30 minutes. Bake 15 minutes in hot oven (400°). Reduce the heat to moderate (350°) and bake from 50 minutes to 1 hour. The kulitch should be evenly browned all over.

Hazelnut Torte

½ lb. shelled hazelnuts
8 eggs, separated
1½ cups sugar
½ cup bread crumbs
Grated rind of 1 lemon

Juice of ½ lemon
1 tsp. vanilla extract
½ cup whipped cream
1 cup tart jelly

Grind the unblanched hazelnuts very fine. Put 2 tablespoons of the ground nuts aside for the outside of the cake.

Beat the egg yolks with the sugar till very light. Add the bread crumbs, lemon rind, lemon juice, vanilla, ground nuts, and lastly the egg whites whipped very stiff but not dry. Bake in 2 layers, 30 minutes in slow oven (325°). Cool in the pans. Take out and put together with whipped cream and a little jelly spread between the layers. Whip the rest of the jelly with a fork and spread it over the top and sides of the cake. Powder with the unused 2 tablespoons of ground nuts. Decorate the top of the cake with a swirl of whipped cream. Chill before serving.

Chocolate Torte with Mocha Frosting

1 cup butter	1 tsp. ground cinnamon
2 cups sugar	2 tsp. rum
4 eggs, separated	1½ cups pastry flour
½ cup cream	2 tsp. baking powder
1 cup freshly riced cooked potatoes	1 tsp. vanilla extract
1 cup ground almonds	Apricot jam
4 squares chocolate, melted	

Cream the butter and sugar together. Add the egg yolks one at a time. Then add the cream, potatoes, ground nuts, melted chocolate (melt it over hot water), cinnamon, rum, flour, baking powder, vanilla, and lastly the whites of eggs well beaten. Transfer the mixture carefully to a spring form very lightly greased and floured. Bake 1½ hours in a slow oven (325°). When the cake has cooled, cut it into 2 layers. Put the layers together with apricot jam spread between. Cover the cake with mocha-rum frosting made as follows:

Mocha-Rum Frosting

3 tbsp. unsalted butter	1 oz. chocolate, melted
1½ cups confectioners' sugar	1 tbsp. dark strong rum
2 tbsp. very strong coffee, warm	½ tsp. vanilla extract

Cream butter and sugar together till white. Add the coffee, melted chocolate, rum, and vanilla. The frosting should be thin enough to spread. Cover the sides of the torte with it,

236

then make a thick border around the edge of the top. Fill the center on top with apricot jam. Decorate with a center whirl of the frosting. A sprinkle of chopped almonds on the jam adds to the gala effect.

Russian Layer Cake with Coffee Cream

5 eggs, separated
1 cup granulated sugar
Juice ½ large lemon
Grated rind of ½ lemon
4 tbsp. sifted potato flour
3 tbsp. sifted white flour
Fine dry bread crumbs

½ cup tart jelly
¼ lb. unsalted butter
1¼ cups confectioners' sugar
4 tbsp. very strong coffee
½ tsp. vanilla extract
Butter

Stir the egg yolks with the granulated sugar till quite white. Add the strained lemon juice and the grated lemon rind. Now add the potato flour and white flour. Whip the whites of the eggs till stiff and shiny, and stir them in very slowly. Butter a cake pan, or 2 layer pans, and sprinkle lightly with fine dry sifted bread crumbs. Fill with the cake mixture and bake 40 minutes in a slow oven (325°). Let cool 20 minutes in the pans after taking from oven, before transferring to a cake rack.

When the cake is thoroughly cool, in about 3 hours, spread jelly between the layers and cover with coffee cream made as follows:

Cream the ¼ pound of butter. Add the confectioners' sugar. Continue stirring for 10 minutes. Add the coffee very gradually, a small amount at a time, stirring all the while. Add the vanilla. Spread on the cake. Decorate with candied violets if you can get any, or pieces of candied angelica.

Layer Cake with Preserves and Custard Cream

1 Russian layer cake
½ cup cherry preserves
1 cup apricot preserves
½ cup peach preserves
1 cup milk
1 whole egg, lightly beaten

2 egg yolks, lightly beaten
3 tbsp. sugar
1 tsp. cornstarch
1 tbsp. rum or sherry or Marsala
    wine

Mix the Russian layer cake according to the preceding recipe, but bake it in 1 pan, not in 2 layer pans.

Cut a thick slice from the top of the cake. Hollow out the bottom part of the cake and fill it with pieces of fruit taken out of the preserves. Mix these pieces of fruit with some of the cake crumbs and some of the liquid portion of the jam to make the filling. Put the top slice on the cake and cover it with chilled custard made as follows:

Scald the milk. Beat lightly the egg and egg yolks and add the sugar. Add to the scalded milk. Add the cornstarch mixed to a smooth paste with a little water. Cook over a low flame till the custard coats the spoon. Cool. Add the rum, sherry, or Marsala. Chill before pouring over the cake. The custard should be quite thick. Decorate with whole cherries from the preserves.

A Russian Version of Washington Pie

1 Russian layer cake, 2 days old
½ cup Marsala wine
½ cup water
½ cup sugar
1 tbsp. butter

1 tbsp. flour
1 cup rich milk
Vanilla extract
2 eggs, separated

After the cake is baked, let it cool, then wrap it in wax paper and keep it for 2 days.

Mix the wine with the water and 2 tablespoons of the sugar. Pour this on both layers of the cake.

Make a cream sauce with the butter, flour, and milk, and add the rest of the sugar. Flavor to taste with vanilla or any flavoring you prefer. Cool for 5 minutes, then add the egg yolks, slightly beaten. Stir well. Cook for 5 minutes, being very careful not to boil or even simmer.

When the custard is cool, spread it on the bottom layer of the cake. Cover with the top layer. Whip the whites of eggs stiff. Add the sugar as you would for any meringue. Spread it on the top of the cake and place the cake in a slow oven (325°) for 15 minutes to brown the meringue. Serve warm or cold.

Medoviya Prianiki (Honey Cookies)

2 cups dark honey	½ tsp. ground cloves
1 cup sifted rye meal	1 tsp. ground ginger
1 cup sifted flour	1 tbsp. gin or whisky
½ tsp. baking powder	2 drops anise flavoring (optional)

Heat the honey in a pan until it is thin. Dark buckwheat honey gives the best flavor for these cookies. Let the honey come once to a boil. Keep it very hot.

Sift together the rye meal and flour and heat it in a skillet, stirring constantly. Keep the heat low. Be sure the flour doesn't brown. Add the baking powder, cloves, and ginger to the flour. Mix quickly and add part of the flour to the hot honey. Remember, the honey must be very hot. Stir up. Quickly add the gin or whisky, the anise flavoring, and the rest of the flour.

Beat the mixture as hard as you can with a wooden spoon. Go on beating till the dough comes off the spoon easily. Shape the dough into a long roll. Flatten the roll slightly and cut in slices about ½ inch thick. Put these on a cookie sheet, lightly greased and floured. Bake in slow oven (325°) till light brown —about 30 minutes. The cookies should come out quite dry.

In Russia when village people visit friends or relatives in the city, they always bring along a batch of these honey cookies as a gift.

CHAPTER 14

PRESERVES AND PICKLES

To appeal to a Russian, any preserve or jam must be made so the fruit remains whole in it. This becomes reasonable when you understand that Russians seldom spread their jam on bread. Jams and preserves go on the table most often with the evening tea, and are eaten with a teaspoon from a small saucer. The whole berries or pieces of fruit in very sweet syrup are appreciated as fruit confections, rather than as an inducement to make the bread taste nice.

Spiced grapes, spiced plums, spiced cherries, etc., are prepared in Russia much the same as in America. They are served with meat and game all through the winter months when salads are unobtainable.

Prepared with vinegar, the spiced fruits are regarded as pickles, and I have included them here as such. I have left out the recipes for cucumber pickles, for sauerkraut, and for many pickles of great popularity in Russia, since they are practically identical wth those you have in this country.

Russians usually put up their own preserves while spending the summer out of town. At any railway station, even if you are blindfolded, you can tell when the vacationists have returned to the cities. You don't need to see it—you can feel it. At that time of year every station platform is sticky and strewn with broken glass from the jars of preserves and pickles that have slipped and fallen from hastily

241

packed impedimenta—the rope-tied bundles and bags and boxes of the Russian traveler.

Raspberry Preserves

Select 1 pound of raspberries, perfectly ripe, whole, and freshly gathered. Put a layer of berries in a flat enameled pan. Cover with 1½ cups of sugar. Now another layer of berries and another 1½ cups of sugar. Leave the pan in your refrigerator overnight. Next day place it on the stove as is, without adding any water. The heat should be brisk. Watch the berries carefully. Don't let them boil more than once. Take off any scum that rises. Cook the berries from 20 to 25 minutes. Let them cool, then pour them into hot sterilized jars and seal. Do not attempt to make raspberry preserves by this method in any larger quantity than this recipe calls for. There must not be more than 2 layers of berries in the pan. Cooling them before pouring them into the jars prevents the berries from floating to the top.

Gooseberry Preserves

1 lb. green gooseberries   5 cups water (approximately)
1 cup grain alcohol or gin   4 cups sugar
Cherry leaves

The gooseberries must be unripe or this recipe won't turn out right. Snip off the stalks and blossom ends with scissors. Discard all imperfect berries. With a very sharp small knife cut a slit across the top of each berry, and take the seeds out with a quill toothpick. Rinse the berries in cold water. Drain well. Place them in a shallow bowl. Pour the alcohol or gin

242

over them. The spirits should cover the berries. Let stand 1 hour, then drain the berries in a colander.

Meanwhile line an enameled pan with cherry leaves. Add about 5 cups water and boil up 3 times. Pour this over the gooseberries in the colander, which should be placed over a bowl. Have another bowl ready. Pour the cherry-leaf water 3 times over the berries, changing bowls each time to save the water. Then rinse the berries with cold water and let drain.

Dissolve the sugar in 1 cup of fresh water. Boil up several times, removing the scum each time. Add the berries when the syrup runs off a silver spoon like water, easily, without sheeting. Boil up 3 times, removing the pan from the fire after each boiling. Remove all scum during this part of the cooking. Reduce heat and simmer gently for 20 or 30 minutes. Do not stir. Just shake the pan from time to time. The berries will remain whole. Cool before putting into jars and sealing.

Strawberry Preserves

1 lb. strawberries	4 cups sugar
½ cup grain alcohol or gin	1 cup water

The berries should be gathered in dry weather. Discard all imperfect berries. Snip off the leaves at the top without pulling out the attached stem which is inside the berry. Spread the berries out in a flat dish. Sprinkle with the alcohol or gin, then with 1 cup of the sugar. Let the dish stand in your refrigerator overnight.

Make a syrup next day of the remaining sugar and the water. Boil up several times. Skim and cook till the syrup runs easily off a silver spoon. Drop the berries in the syrup. Quickly boil

243

up 3 times, taking the pan off the fire after each boiling. Then cook slowly over gentle heat until a skin begins to form on the syrup. Cool. Put in jars and seal.

Greengage or Yellow Plum Preserves

1 lb. greengage or yellow plums	2 cups water
4 cups sugar	½ tsp. vanilla extract

The plums should be not quite ripe. Pierce each plum in several places with a wooden toothpick. Place the plums in a bowl and cover them with boiling water. Let stand till water is cool. Drain the plums in a colander. Make a syrup of the sugar and 2 cups of water. Boil up several times, then let cool. Put the plums back in the bowl and pour the cooled syrup over them. Let stand overnight at room temperature. Next day drain the plums again. Boil up the syrup, cool it, and again pour it over the plums. Repeat this process for 3 days. On the fourth day, when the syrup is boiling, add the plums and cook gently for 30 minutes, removing all skum. Add the vanilla. When cool, put in jars and seal.

Melon Preserves

1 lb. cubes from melon	Small piece dried ginger root
½ cup grain alcohol or gin	1 cup water
4 cups sugar	

Use cantaloupe, honeydew, or similar melon. It should be slightly unripe. Peel it and remove the seeds, then cut the melon in cubes about 1 inch square. Drop these into boiling water; boil up once and drain. Then pour plenty of ice water over the melon cubes. Drain again for 20 minutes. Spread the cubes on a platter, Sprinkle them with the alcohol or gin, and let stand 15 minutes. Make a syrup of 2 cups of the sugar and the 1 cup water. Add the ginger. Boil up several times. Skim, then add the melon to the syrup. Cook gently, gradually adding the rest of the sugar. Continue cooking till the melon cubes become transparent. Remove the ginger. Let cool, place in jars, and seal.

Pastilla Iz Yablok (Candied Apple Foam)

This must be made in early summer when the apples are still unripe but not too acid.

Use green apples, the kind with the flesh that comes out white when baked. Put about 8 whole apples in an earthenware pot that can be tightly closed. Bake in a hot oven for 2 or 3 hours, until the apples are soft. The time will depend on the apples. Leave the pot in the oven, taking out a few apples at a time. Rub them through a sieve. You get more apple purée by doing it like this, while the apples are hot. Beat the apple purée until it is quite white. Measure it, and to every 2 cups of purée add 1 cup of sugar and the well-beaten whites of 2 eggs flavored with ¼ teaspoon of vanilla extract. Whip again for at least 10 minutes.

Have ready small paper cases such as are used for baking cupcakes. In Russia the cook used to make these paper cases herself, and they were oblong in shape. Fill the cups with the apple mixture. Place the cups on a cookie sheet and leave them from 6 to 8 hours in a barely hot oven. They are done when dry enough so you can carefully remove the apple foam from the paper cups. Powder them lightly with confectioners' sugar if you like.

245

Pastilla may also be made with raspberries, cranberries, or strawberries. The method is the same—a thick fruit purée mixed with sugar and white of egg. Berries require more sugar. Berry pastilla is much more difficult to make.

Spiced Plums

6 lb. firm ripe plums
4 cups vinegar
1 stick cinnamon

10 whole cloves
1 cup red wine
2 cups sugar

Wipe the plums, discarding any bruised fruit. Prick each plum in several places with a wooden toothpick. Add the spices to the vinegar and simmer for 30 minutes. Strain through a sieve. Add the wine. Boil up once. Let cool till lukewarm, then pour over plums. Let stand overnight.

Pour off the vinegar, boil it up twice, and pour it back over the plums boiling hot. Set the plums aside in a cool place for 3 days.

Again pour off the vinegar, boil it up, cool it, and pour it again over plums. Put the plums in sterilized jars. Fill jars to brim with vinegar and seal. Keep in a cool dry place.

After 3 weeks open the jars and strain off the vinegar. Add the sugar to the vinegar, boil it up, let it cool, then once more pour it over the plums. Return the plums and vinegar to the jars. Seal and store for at least 1 month before using.

Spiced Cherries

4 lb. cherries
1 cup water
2 cups vinegar
3 cups sugar

½ tsp. ground nutmeg
½ stick cinnamon
1 tsp. ground cloves
1 tsp. ground allspice

Pit the cherries. Cook any bruised or imperfect fruit 30 minutes with the water, mash with a spoon, strain through a sieve, and keep. This is your cherry syrup.

Mix the cherry syrup, vinegar, sugar, and spices. Cook 30 minutes and let cool. Put the cherries in a large bowl and pour the cooled vinegar over them. Let stand 3 days, stirring from time to time.

On the third day pour off the vinegar, boil it up, and let it cool. Put the cherries in sterilized jars. Fill the jars with the vinegar. Seal and keep in a cool, dry place. Allow to mature for 2 months before using.

CHAPTER 15

AROUND THE SAMOVAR

Among Russians who have gone away to dwell in other countries, it is easy enough to arouse mild attacks of homesick longing for Russian life and Russian flavors. But to launch the expatriate Russian soul on a really unbridled jag of nostalgia, try mentioning our *vechernyi t'chai,* our evening tea.

There is the magic phrase that reawakens all our dearest memories of home!

When the samovar goes on the dining-room table, usually about 10 o'clock in the evening, the entire family gathers for the most intimate kind of get-together. This is the hour of comfortable relaxation, with old and young meeting as equals in talk, drinking innumerable glasses and cups of tea while wandering conversationally into all fields of anecdote and gossip, of thought and speculation.

The babies and younger children are in bed. The adolescents feel grown up. The oldsters are sure of an audience. And guests always drop in. It is perfectly correct for friends to drop in, uninvited, for evening tea at any time between 10 P.M. and midnight. The lady of the house is not expected to set out anything special for company. There is no fuss or formality. The scene is cozy and homelike. When you come for evening tea, you take potluck with the family.

The dining-room table is covered with an embroidered tablecloth. Beside the lady of the house, at her right hand,

248

the steaming samovar stands on a little table of its own. Or if there is no side table, the samovar will be standing directly on the dining-room table, with the hostess peeking around it to see and take part in whatever is going on.

A small china teapot fits into a metal fixture on top of the samovar. The hostess herself has measured tea leaves into the china teapot, has brewed the tea with boiling water from the samovar, and has set the pot of tea on top of the samovar to keep on brewing.

The tea is made as strong as household supplies permit. A few drops of this strong tea from the small china pot will be poured into each cup or glass, which will then be filled with hot water from the samovar.

Tea glasses in metal or silver holders that have handles, like American ice-cream-soda glasses, are set out for the men. In Russia the men drink tea from glasses, and the women drink tea from cups.

The cups rarely match, not because of any lack of complete tea sets, but for a much more sentimental reason. Every woman in a Russian family likes to have her own individual teacup. It is nearly always a birthday or Christmas gift, specially chosen to please the taste of the recipient. A psychologist would take delight in tracing the different qualities of feminine character revealed by the family teacups. The girl of romantic dreams has a cup decorated with old-fashioned flowers, charmingly innocent and naïve. Ladies of social ambition sip proudly from expensive cups of magnificent workmanship, gold tracery on solid dark cobalt-blue or rose-red china from fine factories such as Gardner's—a Russian firm originally established by an Englishman. In the old days, if someone in the family had "connections," one of the lovely unique cups from the imperial factory might find its way into a private home. Otherwise you never could buy any imperial china during the days of the Tsar, for the entire output went to the royal family, excepting a surplus of slightly flawed pieces which could be purchased only by privileged court officials.

On our evening tea table are plates of cold cuts and plates of sliced cheese. We don't serve fish at evening tea unless the season is Lent, or when times are particularly hard. The bread basket offers slices of black bread and slices of white. Unsalted butter is on the table in a pretty dish. The number of things we have to eat at evening tea will depend upon how long ago the family had dinner. If we had an early dinner, between 5 and 6 P.M., then this 10 o'clock tea will be a substantial supper. But if we ate dinner later than 6 o'clock, we won't have many cheese or meat snacks now.

Plenty of sweet things will be arrayed in front of us in any case. There will be homemade preserves, crystallized fruits, fruit confections known as *pastilla,* and the semi-jellied fruit candies that Russians call *marmelade*—all these will be arranged attractively in glass dishes. And you can be sure of several cakes to choose from, Russian layer cakes of the *torte* type, richly made with preserves and nuts and cream and sugar icings.

Apart from the ordinary family tea hour, more elaborate samovar parties used to be popular, and they were a considerable undertaking in the old days. When I kept house in Petrograd—before it was renamed Leningrad—I conformed to that very social city's tradition of crowding the table with 6 kinds of cake for any evening party. You could get by with a mere 5 kinds of cake, plus a plate of *petits fours,* but it was not *quite* the right thing to do. The difficulty lay in the fact that certain bakeries specialized in certain cakes, cakes that

250

were absolutely necessary, and those bakeries were scattered all over Petrograd.

True, any hostess could reckon that most of her guests would arrive bearing some gift for the party table—candy perhaps, or a cake, or a bottle of liqueur. This involved a campaign of discreet telephoning in advance, to make sure all the guests didn't bring the same thing. At any rate the hostess had to ride all over town collecting her specialty cakes at the bakeries.

From one bakery came the Zemlyianichnyi torte, a celestial strawberry layer cake that perfumed your whole apartment with the piny aroma of fresh strawberries, even though it was made of berries in a preserved state. From a distant baker on the islands, the part of Petrograd that reaches out into the mouth of the Neva River, came the best of all chocolate cakes with a creamy filling and a deliciously sticky top coat of preserves. The finest of hazelnut cakes from another bakery at the opposite end of the town. Your housemaids eagerly volunteered to go and get the cakes, but you knew from experience they would be gone half the day, so you did your own cake-collecting if you were wise. You hired an *izvoschick,* an open hack, and you took the driver into your confidence. All Petrograd hack drivers knew the location of every bakery, and they knew all about the cakes in which each bakery specialized. When you came out of a bakery carrying a box with an exceptionally fragile cream cake in it, your hack driver would know what was in the box, and he would help you and your cake into his carriage with the gentlest care.

At *vechernyi t'chai* it seemed that the tea was consumed endlessly, most Russians taking it with thin slices of lemon. The hostess always sliced the lemon herself with a special silver knife. After cutting the lemon she always held the knife for a moment in the steam from the samovar to prevent the knife from tarnishing.

Everyone at the tea table had a plate and a small saucer, usually of cut glass. The saucer was for preserves, which you either ate with a spoon or put into your tea. Many Russians like preserves better than sugar as a sweetening for their tea. After years in America it still irks me not to be able to find saucers of the right size for preserves to go with Russian tea. We call these saucers *blewdichki dlia vareniya*. They are about 3 inches across. Very few Russians take milk or cream in their evening tea. They take it that way only for breakfast.

In the center of the table at evening tea there is nearly always a crystal bowl or an epergne of fruit, with the handles of fruit knives sticking out, porcupine fashion. Usually there will be small carafes of vodka and liqueur cordials, with a tray of very small liqueur glasses.

I have described the manner in which our evening tea was served when it was served with some elegance. In much humbler surroundings, when it was served without pretty tableware or luxurious things to eat and drink, there was nevertheless the same atmosphere of cozy relaxation, and, though quality might differ, the tea-table fare was very much the same in kind.

Above all, there was the same kind of talk. And there still is.

Perhaps because Russians have never at any time enjoyed the freedom of airing their opinions openly in public, *vechernyi t'chai*, the evening tea hour, plays the part actually of a national forum. Politics are discussed there, and religion and business, and science and art, and war and peace and love. Arguments can be heated, yet somehow the way we are placed around the table, the friendly ceremony of tea sipping, the mixed ages of those present—somehow all this seems to hold us within a frame of fairly reasonable compromise.

That, I suppose, is the reason why Russians all over the world, in whatever country they may be, like best to be entertained with an evening around the samovar.

Russian Cuisine and Menu Terms

Ivan says to Masha:
"Our national food is shchi and kasha."
Says Klava to Vlas:
"Our national drink is vodka. And kvas."

A Brief Talk about Russian Cuisine

The traditional Russian cooking has come to us through the depths of history. Since the dimensions of the country are huge indeed, in various areas and districts, nooks and corners there developed different styles of cuisine. Still, despite all shades and tones, the major hors d'oeuvres and snacks, dishes and beverages are basically the same.

Hors d'oeuvres

The main purpose of serving snacks is to arouse appetite. And Russian cuisine has always been rich and abundant in cold and hot hors d'oeuvres. They may be fresh and pickled vegetables and mushrooms; numerous jellies (meat, fish, mushroom, etc.); dried, smoked and salted fish; meat and pork sausage, suckling pigs and stuffed poultry; and a whole gamut of mixed salads (meat, fish, egg) and vinaigrettes.

It should be pointed out that many snacks contain onion and garlic (as well as some soups and main course dishes). An old Russian saying goes: "Garlic and onion will cure all pains and maladies for sure." Also of interest might be the following fact: in the United States and elsewhere in the West only one type of mushrooms is used for cooking—champignons. In Russia dozens of various kinds of mushrooms are fried and boiled, pickled and salted, wrapped in flour and soaked with sour cream. Mushroom hunting is a favorite pastime for the young and the old alike.

To top it all, caviar, the Czarina of all the hors d'oeuvres, will be a pride of any table, be it in the Kremlin palace or in a modest home somewhere in the depths of the country. The best black caviar comes from beluga sturgeon, the best red — from fresh-water salmon.

Soups

The common ancestor of all Russian soups is *ukha* — a fish soup. Originally the root of the word comes from ancient Sanskrit and means broth (liquid). Up to the 19th century any soup was called ukha, but then the word got its today's meaning. There might be a single, double or treble ukha — consecutively one, two or more kinds of fish are boiled, the broth is kept and the fish itself thrown away, and only the last which is always the best is used for eating.

Today *shchi* is the most popular soup in Russia (though not so much in the restaurants as in the family cooking). It is a cabbage soup and it may be sour or sweet, depending on whether the major ingredient is sauerkraut or fresh cabbage. There is an old folk tale how a travelling soldier staying overnight at a village house and being hungry told the greedy hostess that he could cook shchi out of an axe. To begin with, he put up fire in the stove and threw the axe into the pot filled with water. When it started boiling he took his spoon, sipped a few drops and said to the greedy woman: "Delicious! I need just a tiny little bit of something." "What is it?" — asked the intrigued woman. "Salt." So she gave him salt. In a minute he said he needed a slice of garlic. So within an hour he got from her about 25 spices, meats and vegetables which are usually used in cooking Russian shchi.

Equally popular, but mostly in the southern regions of Russia, in the Ukraine and Byelorussia and, perhaps, Lithuania is *borshch*. Its basic substance is beet. Otherwise shchi and borshch are more or less alike in all their one hundred odd varieties. Last but not least — they should be thick, so thick that the spoon is to stand in your plate upright as if at the command "Shun!"

Among others, *rassolnik* with salted cucumbers and kidneys as its base *solianka*, also with salted cucumbers and up to twelve different sorts of either meat or fish, *okroshka*, chilled chopped vegetable and sausage soup, *botvinia*, chilled vegetable and fish soup, and *svekolnik*, chilled beetroot soup, should be mentioned. The last three are summer soups and have *kvas* as their stock. Kvas is a fermented beverage made from grain. It is number one nonalcoholic drink of the country. The first mention of it in the ancient chronicles dates as far back as 988. It was then that after the baptism of Rus in Kiev Duke Vladimir "ordered to give to the newly baptized citizens of the city kvas and honey".

Naturally, there is a whole host of foreign soups which came to Russia from abroad. The "invaders" broadly represent two groups — French and Oriental. A bright representative of the first is consomme, and of the second — *harcho*, a Georgian beef, tomato and onion soup-stew.

Main Course

Depending on the place, season and taste non-vegetarian as well as vegetarian dishes can be enjoyed. They may be cooked from meat or pork, chicken or duckling, crawfish or stellate sturgeon, flour or eggs, cottage cheese or vegetables.

Among the meat dishes one will find braised veal with caviar sauce, marinated skewered beef, roast suckling pig, stuffed cabbage rolls, skewered lamb, sauteed beef with mushrooms and onions in sour-cream sauce.

Poultry may be represented by braised chicken with prune

sauce, chicken a la mode de Kiev (deep-fried chicken rissoles), roast chicken with walnut sauce, pressed fried chicken (chicken *tabaka*) and chicken and rice pies.

If you are a fish connoisseur, you will be glad to order sturgeon on a spit or sturgeon (or halibut) in tomato and mushroom sauce, carp in sour cream or pike in tomato marinade, fish cakes with mustard sauce or fish baked monastery style, fish balls or pies, trout with pomegranates and grapes or pike-perch fillet in Russian sauce.

Pelmeni, meat-filled dumplings, are a pride of Russian cuisine. They are small balls and to make them well one should have a special talent. Meat is of two kinds, properly ground and mixed (usually pork and beef). The noodle dough must be rolled flat and thin and the best balls are not to exceed a quarter in diameter. Garlic and onion, pepper and salt, milk or broth are added, as well as butter and eggs. Pelmeni bear a distant resemblance to ravioli. But only a distant one. In Siberia they prepare in winter hundreds and thousands of pelmeni and put them in big sacks which are hung in cold sheds or barns. Whenever the guests are coming the hosts are ready to welcome them with pelmeni, a masterpiece of Russian cuisine. Ten minutes of boiling and the delicious meal is ready. And as the saying goes, they jump into your mouth themselves.

Sweet Dishes

Thin jelly (*kisel*) and stewed fruit (*kompot*), tarts and pastry, pies and curd cakes (*vatrushki*), sweet pan-cakes and apples baked with honey, patties and sugared porridges are just a few examples of traditional Russian sweet dishes.

Some very old Russian sweet dishes are not yet forgotten. Cucumbers with honey, sweet omelette (*drachona*), baked turnip stuffed with honey and jam, home-made cake of fruit jelly (*pastila*), and candied watermelon peels are on the menu of experienced and hospitable housewives.

* * *

To conclude these random notes a few words must be said about Russian vodka. First it appeared in Russia in 15th century. Before that they used to drink various brands of honey. Those were raspberry and strawberry, blackberry and apple and many other brands prepared with hops. Initially vodka was called "grain wine". In 17-19th centuries, landlords had their own breweries. Some of the richer nobles would brew up to two hundred brands of vodka. Also it should be remembered that vodka was distilled three times and was almost as strong as pure spirits. Herbs, berries and fruits would build dozens and dozens of colors and flavors and tastes—bitter, sour or sweet. Now at best one will find 10-12 sorts of vodka — and that too with great difficulty. The only consolation however is that *Stolichnaya* is available at many of the good restaurants. The Russian way to drink vodka is during the meals (with snacks, first and main courses).

* * *

To round off this brief talk about Russian cuisine, we reproduce here the menu of the Golden Hall, a restaurant at the Intourist Hotel in Moscow. We had dinner there with some of our American friends and enjoyed jointly a charming variety show presented by Teatr na Tverskoi — the theater on Tverskaya Street. The unforgettable event took place on February 21, 1992. Below follows the menu.

ФИРМЕННЫЕ БЛЮДА
/fírmennye bliúda/

SPECIALITIES
/спе́шиэ́литиз/

Рыбная закуска
"Русский букет"
/rýbnaia zakúska
rússkii bukét/

"Russian Bouquet"
fish hors d'oeuvre
/рашн буке́й
фиш оде́ёвр/

Ассорти мясное
"Изобилие"
/assortí miasnóe
izobílie/

"Cornucopia"
assorted meat
/ко́рньюко́упиэ
эсо́ртыд миит/

Салат "Интурист"
/salát inturíst/

"Intourist" salad
/инту́эрист сэ́лэд/

Солянка любительская
с грибами
/soliánka liubítel'skaia
s gribámi/

"Lyubitelskaya" solyanka
with mushrooms
/люби́тельская
соля́нка виз ма́шрумз/

Судак "Селигер"
/sudák seligér/

"Seliger" pike-perch
/селиге́р па́йкпёрч/

Шницель из кур
"Интурист"
/shnítsel iz kur inturíst/

"Intourist"
chicken schnitzel
/инту́эрист чикин шни́тцел/

Мороженое "Лада"
/morózhenoe láda/

"Lada" ice-cream
/ла́да а́йскри́им/

Торт "Интурист"
/tort inturíst/

"Intourist" cake
/инту́эрист кейк/

ХОЛОДНЫЕ ЗАКУСКИ
/kholódnye zakúski/

COLD HORS D'OEUVRES
/ко́улд оде́ёврз/

Икра зернистая

Granular caviar

/ikrá zernístaia/

/грэ́ньюлэ кэ́виар/

Шпроты с лимоном
/shpróty s limónom/

Sprats in oil and lemon
/спрэтс ин ойл энд лéмэн/

Осетрина отварная
с хреном
/osetrína otvarnáia
s khrénom/

Boiled sturgeon
with horse-radish
/бойлд стёёджн
виз хóосрэ́диш/

Колбаса с/к
/kolbasá syrokopchónaia/

Uncooked smoked sausage
/анкýкт смóукт сóсидж/

Бок осетра х/к
/bok osetrá/
kholódnovo kopchéniia/

Cold-smoked sturgeon side
/кóулд смоýкт стёёджн сайд/

Сельдь с картофелем
и маслом
/sel'd' s kartófelem
i máslom/

Herring with
potatoes and butter
/хéринг виз пэтэ́йтоуз
энд бáтэ/

Крабы п/м
/kráby pod marinádom/

Crab meat pickled in marinade
/крэб миит пиклд ин
мэ́ринэйд/

Сельдь в сметане
с яблоками
/sel'd' v smetáne
s iáblokami/

Herring in sour
cream and apples
/хéринг ин сáуэ
криим энд эплз/

Ветчина с гарниром
/vetchiná s garnírom/

Ham with side-dish
/хэм виз сáйдиш/

Индейка с солениями
/indéika s soléniiami/

Turkey with pickles
/тёрки виз пиклз/

Масло сливочное
/máslo slívochnoe/

Butter
/báтэ/

САЛАТЫ И СОЛЕНИЯ
/saláty i soléniia/

SALADS AND PICKLES
/сэ́лэдз энд пиклз/

Салат из осетрины
/salát iz osetríny/

Sturgeon salad
/стёёджн сэ́лэд/

Салат с крабами
/salát s krábami/

Crab meat salad
/крэб миит сэ́лэд/

Салат с крабами
по-итальянски
/salát s krábami
po ital'iánski/

Crab meat salad
a l'italienne
/крэб миит сэ́лэд
а литалья́н/

Салат по-чешски
/salát po chéshski/

Salad a la tcheque
/сэ́лэд а ля чек/

Салат из свежих
огурцов
/salát iz svézhikh ogurtsóv/

Cucumber salad
/кьюю́кэмбэ сэ́лэд/

Салат из свежих помидоров
/salát iz svézhikh pomidórov/

Tomato salad
/тэмэ́атоу сэ́лэд/

Маслины
/maslíny/

Olives
/о́ливз/

ГОРЯЧИЕ ЗАКУСКИ
/goriáchie zakúski/

HOT HORS D'OEUVRES
/хот одёёврз/

Кнели из судака
с грибами
/knéli iz sudaká s gribámi/

Pike-perch kneli
with mushrooms
/па́йкпёрч кнéли виз
мáшрумз/

Жульен мясной
/zhul'én miasnói/

Meat Julienne
/миит джу́улие́н/

СУПЫ
/supý/

SOUPS
/суупс/

Бульон с пирожком
/bul'ón s pirozhkóm/

Broth and patty
/брос энд пэ́ти/

Бульон с яйцом
/bul'ón s iaitsóm/

Broth with egg
/брос виз эг/

Борщ московский

/borshch moskóvskii/

Moscow borsh (beetroot
and cabbage soup)
/мо́скоу борщ
(би́итрут энд кэ́бидж сууп)/

Солянка рыбная
/soliánka rýbnaia/

Fish solyanka
/фиш соля́нка/

Солянка мясная сборная
/soliánka miasnáia sbórnaia/

Assorted-meat solyanka
/эсо́ртыд миит соля́нка/

Суп-пюре из кур
/sup piuré iz kur/

Chicken cream soup
/чи́кин криим сууп/

РЫБНЫЕ ГОРЯЧИЕ БЛЮДА
/rýbnye goriáchie bliúda/

HOT FISH DISHES
/хот фиш ди́шиз/

Судак отварной —
соус польский
/sudák otvarnói sóus pól'skii/

Boiled sturgeon,
polonaise sauce
/бойлд стёёджн полоннэ́з
соос/

Судак "фри"
/sudák fri/

Fried sturgeon
/фрайд стёёджн/

Осетрина припущенная —
соус паровой
/osetrína pripúshchennaia
sóus parovói/

Lightly-stewed sturgeon,
fish sauce
/лáйтли стьююд стёёджн
фиш соос/

Осетрина, запеченная
по-московски
/osetrína zapechónnaia
po moskóvski/

Sturgeon baked a la
mode de Moscou
/стёёджн бэйкт а ля
мод дэ москý/

Осетрина на вертеле —
соус "Тартар"
/osetrína na vertelé
sóus tartár/

Sturgeon on a spit,
tartare sauce
/стёёджн он э спит
тартáр соос/

МЯСНЫЕ ГОРЯЧИЕ БЛЮДА
/miasnýe goriáchie bliúda/

HOT MEAT DISHES
/хот миит дишиз/

Антрекот
/antrekót/

Rib roast
/риб рóуст/

Бифштекс по-деревенски
/bifshtéks po derevénski/

Beefsteak a la paysanne
/бийфстэ́йк а ля пэйзáн/

Бифштекс с яйцом
/bifshtéks s iaitsóm/

Beefsteak with egg
/бийфстэ́йк виз эг/

Лангет в соусе
/langét v sóuse/

Long flank steak in sauce
/лонг флэнк стейк ин соос/

Филе на вертеле
/filé na vertelé/

Fillet on a spit
/фи́лит он э спит/

Жаркое по-берлински
/zharkóe po berlínski/

Roast meat a la mode de Berlin
/рóуст миит а ля мод дэ
берли́н/

Бефстроганов	Beef a la Stroganoff
/befstróganov/	/бииф а ля строганóф/
Бастурма	Basturma
Шашлык по-кавказски	Shashlik (mutton grilled on a spit) a la caucasienne
/shashlýk po kavkázski/	/шашлúк (матн грилд он э спит) а ля коказьян/
Люля-кебаб	Lyulya kebab
/liuliá kebáb/	/люля кебáб/
БЛЮДА ИЗ ПТИЦЫ И ДИЧИ	POULTRY AND GAME
/bliúda iz ptítsy i díchi/	/пóултри энд гейм/
Филе куриное паровое	Steamed chicken fillet
/filé kurínoe parovóe/	/стиимд чúкин фúлит/
Котлеты по-киевски	Rissoles a la mode de Kiev
/kotléty po kíevski/	/рúсоулз а ля мод дэ кúев/
Котлеты пожарские	Rissoles a la Pozharsky
/kotléty pozhárskie/	/рúсоулз а ля пожáрски/
Цыплята "Табака"	"Tabaka" chickens
/tsypliáta tabaká/	/табакá чúкинз/
Утка с яблоками	Duck with apples
/útka s iáblokami/	/дак виз эплз/
Индейка жареная с вареньем	Roast turkey and jam
/indéika zhárenaia s varén'em/	/рóуст тёрки энд джем/

Рябчик жареный в
сметанном соусе
/riábchik zhárenyi
v smetánnom sóuse/

Roast hazel grouse in sour
cream sauce
/póуст хэйзл гráус ин
сáуэ криим соос/

ЯИЧНЫЕ, ОВОЩНЫЕ,
МУЧНЫЕ БЛЮДА
/iaíchnye ovoshchnýe
muchnýe bliúda/

EGG, VEGETABLE AND
FARINACEOUS DISHES
/эг вéджитэбл энд
фэ́ринэ́йшес ди́шиз/

Яичница-глазунья
натуральная
/iaíchnitsa glazún'ia
naturál'naia/

Fried eggs

/фрайд эгз/

Омлет с ветчиной
/omlét s vetchinói/

Ham omelette
/хэм óмлит/

Капуста цветная запеченная —
соус голландский
/kapústa tsvetnáia
zapechónnaia sóus
gollándskii/

Baked cauliflower,
hollandaise sauce
/бэ́йкт кóлифлауэ
холандэ́з соос/

Морковь, тушенная
с яблоками
/morkóv' tushónnaia
s iáblokami/

Stewed carrots with apples

/стьююд кэ́рэтс виз эплз/

Блинчики с мясом
/blínchiki s miásom/

Small meat pancakes
/смоол миит пэ́нкейкс/

Сырники со сметаной
/sýrniki so smetánoi/

Curd fritters with sour cream
/кёрд фри́тэз виз сáуэ криим/

СЫРЫ
/syrý/

CHEESE
/чииз/

Ассорти из русских сыров
/assortí iz rússkikh syróv/

Assorted Russian cheese
/эсо́ртыд рашн чииз/

СЛАДКИЕ БЛЮДА
/sládkie bliúda/

SWEET DISHES
/свиит ди́шиз/

Мороженое с наполнителем
/morózhenoe c napolní telem/

Ice-cream with filler
/а́йскри́им виз фи́лэ/

Компот консервированный —
ассорти
/kompót konserví rovannyi
assortí/

Assorted canned fruits

/эсо́ртыд кэнд фруутс/

Суфле ванильное
/suflé vaníl'noe/

Vanilla soufflé
/вани́лэ су́уфлей/

Фрукты со взбитыми
сливками
/frúkty so vzbítymi slívkami/

Fruits with whipped cream
/фруутс виз випт криим/

Кофе гляссе
/kófe gliassé/

Ice coffee
/айс ко́фи/

Кофе гляссе со взбитыми
сливками
/kófe gliassé so vzbítymi
slívkami/

Ice coffee with
with whipped cream

/айс ко́фи виз випт криим/

Какао гляссе
/kakáo gliassé/

Ice cocoa
/айс ко́укоу/

ГОРЯЧИЕ НАПИТКИ
/goriáchie napítki/

HOT DRINKS
/хот дринкс/

Чай с лимоном
/chái s limónom/

Tea and lemon
/тии энд лéмэн/

Чай с молоком
/chái s molokóm/

Tea and milk
/тии энд милк/

Чай с вареньем
/chái s varén'em/

Tea and jam
/тии энд джем/

Кофе черный
/kófe chórnyi/

Black coffee
/блэк кóфи/

Кофе по-восточному
/kófe po vostóchnomu/

Oriental coffee
/óориéнтл кóфи/

Кофе с молоком
/kófe s molokóm/

Coffee and milk
/кóфи энд милк/

Кофе со сливками
/kófe so slívkami/

Coffee and cream
/кóфи энд криим/

Какао
/kakáo/

Cocoa
/кóукоу/

Шоколад
/shokolád/

Hot chocolate
/хот чóкэлит/

ФРУКТЫ
/frúkty/

FRUITS
/фруутс/

Апельсины
/apel'síny/

Oranges
/óринджиз/

Виноград
/vinográd/

Grapes
/грэйпс/

Груши
/grúshi/

Яблоки
/iábloki/

КОНДИТЕРСКИЕ
ИЗДЕЛИЯ
/kondíterskie izdéliia/

Пирожное ассорти
/pirózhnoe assortí/

Торт "Снежинка"
/tort snezhínka/

Пай яблочный
/pái iáblochnyi/

Рулет шоколадный
/rulét shokoládnyi/

Кекс лимонный
/keks limónnyi/

Печенье берлинское
/pechén'e berlínskoe/

Конфеты трюфели
/konféty triúfeli/

Шоколад
/shokolád/

ВОДКА
/vódka/

"Пшеничная"

Pears
/пе́эз/

Apples
/эплз/

CONFECTIONERY
/кэнфе́кшнэри/

Assorted pastries
/эсо́ртыд пэ́йстриз/

"Snezhinka" cake
/снежи́нка кейк/

Apple pie
/эпл пай/

Chocolate Swiss roll
/чо́кэлит свис ро́ул/

Lemon cake
/ле́мэн кейк/

Berliner biscuits
/бёли́нэ би́скитс/

Truffle chocolates
/трафл чо́кэлитс/

Chocolate
/чо́кэлит/

VODKAS
/во́дкэз/

"Pshenichnaya"

"Столичная"	"Stolichnaya"
"Юбилейная"	"Yubileinaya"
КОНЬЯКИ /kon'iakí/	**BRANDIES** /брэ́ндиз/
"Юбилейный"	"Yubileiny"
"Отборный"	"Otborny"
"Двин"	"Dvin"
"ОС"	"OS"
ЛИКЕРЫ /likióry/	**LIQUEURS** /ли́кэз/
"Шартрез"	"Chartreuse"
"Бенедиктин"	"Bénédictine"
"Южный"	"Juzhny"
ВИНА СТОЛОВЫЕ—БЕЛЫЕ /ví na stolóvye bélye/	**WHITE TABLE WINES** /вайт тэйбл вайнз/
"Цинандали" — сухое грузинское /tsinandáli — sukhóe gruzínskoe/	"Tsinandali", dry wine from Georgia /цинанда́ли драй вайн фром джо́оджье/
"Гурджаани" — сухое грузинское /gurdzhaáni — sukhóe gruzínskoe/	"Gourdgaani", dry wine from Georgia /гурджаа́ни драй вайн фром джо́оджье/
"Фетяска" — сухое	"Fetyaska", dry

молдавское	wine from Moldavia
/fetiáska — sukhóe	/фетя́ска драй
moldávskoe/	вайн фром молдэ́йвье/

"Твиши" — полусладкое	"Tvishi", semisweet
грузинское	wine from Georgia
/tvishí — polusládkoe	/твиши́ сэ́мисвит
gruzínskoe/	вайн фром джо́оджье/

| "Рислинг" | "Riesling" |

| ВИНА СТОЛОВЫЕ—КРАСНЫЕ | RED TABLE WINES |
| /vína stolóvye krásnye/ | /рэд тэйбл вайнз/ |

"Мукузани" — сухое	"Mukuzani", dry
грузинское	wine from Georgia
/mukuzáni sukhóe	/мукуза́ни драй
gruzínskoe/	вайн фром джо́оджье/

"Напареули" — сухое	"Napareuli", dry
грузинское	wine from Georgia
/napareúli sukhóe	/напареу́ли драй
gruzínskoe/	вайн фром джо́оджье/

"Хванчкара" — полусладкое	"Khvanchkara", semisweet
грузинское	wine from Georgia
/khvanchkára polusládkoe	/хванчка́ра сэ́мисвит
gruzínskoe/	вайн фром джо́оджье/

"Киндзмараули" —	"Kindzmarauli", semisweet
полусладкое грузинское	wine from Georgia
/kindzmaraúli polusládkoe	/киндзмарау́ли сэ́мисвит
gruzínskoe/	вайн фром джо́оджье/

ВИНА ВИНОГРАДНЫЕ—	FORTIFIED TABLE
КРЕПЛЕНЫЕ	WINES
/vína vinográdnye krepliónye/	/фо́ртифайд тэйбл вайнз/

"Мадера"   "Madeira"

"Портвейн 777"   "Port 777"
/portvéin sem'sót   /порт сэвн хáндрэд
sém'desiat sem'/   сэ́внти сэвн/

Портвейн "Сурож"   "Sourozh" port
/portvéin súrozh/   /сýрож порт/

Портвейн "Крымский"   "Krymsky" port
/portvéin krýmskii/   /крымский порт/

"Мускат"   Muscat
/muskáт/   /мáскет/

"Фрага"   "Fraga"

СОВЕТСКОЕ ШАМПАНСКОЕ   SOVIET SPARKLING
                                  WINES
/sovétskoe shampánskoe/   /сóувьет спáрклинг вайнз/

Шампанское сухое   Sec
/shampánskoe sukhóe/   /сэк/

Шампанское полусухое   Demi-sec
/shampánskoe polusukhóe/   /дéмисэк/

Шампанское сладкое   Doux
/shampánskoe sládkoe/   /дуу/

Шампанское полусладкое   Semisweet
/shampánskoe polusládkoe/   /сэ́мисвит/

ПИВО   BEERS
/pívo/   /бúэз/

"Московское"   "Moskovskoe" (Moscow Beer)
/moskóvskoe/   /мóскоу бúэ/

"Двойное золотое"

/dvoinóe zolotóe/

"Dvoinoe Zolotoe"
(The Golden Double)
/зэ гóулдн дабл/

ХОЛОДНЫЕ НАПИТКИ,
СОКИ
/kholódnye napítki sóki/

COLD DRINKS
AND JUICES
/кóулд дринкс энд джýусыз/

Квас "Петровский" с хреном

/kvas petróvskii s khrénom/

"Petrovsky" kvass with
horse-radish
/петрóвский квас виз
хóосрэ́диш/

Напиток фруктовый
/napítok fruktóvyi/

Fruit drink
/фрууут дринк/

Вода минеральная
/vodá minerál'naia/

Mineral water
/мѝнерал вóотэ/

Соки фруктовые
/sóki fruktóvye/

Fruit juices
/фрууут джýусыз/

ТАБАЧНЫЕ ИЗДЕЛИЯ
/tabáchnye izdélia/

TOBACCO
/тэбэ́коу/

Сигареты
/sigaréty/

Cigarettes
/сѝгэрэ́тс/

Папиросы
/papirósy/

Russian cigarettes
/рашн сѝгэрэ́тс/

Продажа указанных блюд и напитков производится на
свободно конвертируемую и советскую валюту.
The aforementioned dishes and beverages are on sale for hard
currency and roubles.

272

INDEX

American Museum of Natural History, 120, 121
Anchovies:
kilki on egg slices, 55
scalloped potatoes with, 192-3
Anchovy butter, 138, 178
—— piroshki, cooked meat and, 104
—— sauce, 213
—— ——, hot, 213-4
Anton apples, 35-6
Apple foam, candied, 245-6
—— pie, Russian, 217
Applesauce, Russian, 201
Apples, chilled cream of, 219-20
——, Russian, 35-6
——, "soaked," 32-3
Apple stuffing (goose), 183-4
Apricot vareniki, 224
Artichokes cooked in Malaga wine, 193
Aquavit, Swedish, 46
Asparagus baked with cream, 194

Baba, 232-3
Baked buckwheat kasha, 113
—— cabbage, 198
—— —— and potatoes, 199
—— kotleti with cream sauce, 150
—— liver loaf, 58-9

—— milk, 28
—— millet kasha, 113
—— onion dumplings, 201-2
—— porgies in saffron cream, 131-2
—— potatoes stuffed with mushrooms, 191-2
—— sturgeon steaks, 123
—— turnips in cream-and-egg sauce, 196
—— white turnips, stuffed, 196-7
—— yellow pike with rice-and-egg stuffing, 126-7
Baking powder, 21-2
Banquets, Russian, 2
Bass stuffed with buckwheat kasha, 134-5
Bear meat, 33
Béchamel sauce, macedoine of vegetables in, 194-5
Beef, 22, 143-8:
jellied corned, 147-8
kidneys with dill pickles and potato slices, 146-7
pot roast cooked with wine, 144-5
—— —— with mushroom gravy, 146
—— —— —— special gravy, 145-6
Siberian pelmeny, 162-3

273

284

White consommé, 73
  garnishes for, 75
—— -flour blini, 117, 118
Winter jardinière of mixed
  vegetables, 197
Woodcock with oriental sauce,
  186-7

Yellow consommé, 73-4
  garnishes for, 75
—— plum preserves, 244
Yeshte na zdorovie, 11

Zakooskas, 6, 26, 40-65
  calves' brains in mayonnaise,
    59
  caviar, 48-50
  chicken livers in Madeira
    wine, 62
  chopped chicken livers, 56-7
  dragomir forshmak, 61
  eggplant caviar, 56
  frankfurters in tomato sauce,
    60
  herring, 50-3
  ——, chopped, with eggs, 53

—— salad with beets, 53
—— with mustard sauce, 52
—— —— oil and vinegar,
  51-2
—— —— roe sauce, 52
—— —— vegetable garnish,
  52-3
  hot, 60-2
  how to serve, 40-1
  kilki on egg slices, 55
  list of, 42-4
  menus, 64-5
  mushrooms in sour cream,
    60-1
  pashtet of liver, 58-9
  party, 60-3
  pickled mackerel, 57
  ——mushrooms, 54
  salad Olivier, 54-5
  salads, 44
  salmon vinaigrette, 58
  specialties, 53-9
  vodka, 37, 45-8
Zavtrak, 5
Zubrovka, 46